THE HISTORY

OF THE

GREAT INDIAN WAR OF 1675 AND 1676,

COMMONLY CALLED PHILIP'S WAR.

ALSO,

THE OLD FRENCH AND INDIAN WARS, FROM 1689 TO 1704.

BY THOMAS CHURCH, ESQ.

WITH NUMEROUS NOTES AND AN APPENDIX.

BY SAMUEL G. DRAKE.

REVISED EDITION.

The unexampled achievements of our fathers should not be forgotten.
WASHINGTON.

CLEARFIELD

Revised Edition
Originally published
Hartford, 1851

Reprinted for
Clearfield Company, Inc. by
Genealogical Publishing Co., Inc.
Baltimore, Maryland
2003

International Standard Book Number: 0-8063-5164-0

Made in the United States of America

NOTICE
This work was reproduced from the original edition. A characteristic of this copy, from which the printer worked, was that the image was uneven. Every effort has been made by the printer to produce as fine a reprint of the original edition as possible.

THE EDITOR'S PREFACE.

Church's History of "King Philip's War," &c. was first published at Boston, in 1716, in quarto. It was reprinted in Newport, in 1772, in octavo. I have never met with a copy of the first edition, therefore I copy from the second. This is now very scarce and rarely to be met with. It is however preserved in some private libraries in the old colony, in the Atheneum at Boston, and other literary institutions there and elsewhere.

The lamentable manner in which Hutchinson in his History of Massachusetts passed over the Indian wars, causes us much regret, and a desire to catch at every thing that can give any light upon them. He is particular in relating the witch affairs of the colony, but when we have followed him into Philip's war, being led at first with interesting particulars, he stops short and says, "It is not my design to enter into every minute circumstance of the war." But does not tell us why. This is the more to be lamented, as his means were more ample for such history than can now be had.

In 1825 I published a small edition of this history, containing however but few additions to the old, which being immediately taken up, occasioned the early appearance of this. In an early period it was designed to publish the work as it now appears. Accordingly many valuable papers and rare works had been collected, but not used in the first edition, on account of the magnitude and early promise of the work.

The papers had been much forwarded previous to the Courtstreet fire, of 10 November, 1825, in the time of which a trunk was stolen, containing many of the manuscript notes, relating particularly to the biography of the principal persons that figured in the Indian wars. These in many instances I could not restore, which is very much regretted; though not more than my want of information on subjects in general. But a consciousness is felt, that something though small, is redeemed from oblivion, which will be thought valuable by posterity.

Of such gentlemen as have had the opportunities of many years to examine the history of our country, together with every advantage from access to all publick and private documents, I have every indulgence to ask.

In regard to the accurate performance of the work, I can only observe, that a scrupulous regard to accuracy has been paid; yet, errours may have been committed, but in no case inadvertently. And as our most authentick historians have failed in many of these points, perfection will not be expected in me.

The same indulgence for the commission of literal errours, as for others, is solicited, though the excuse for such cannot be so good; but if every thing be found simple, and easy to be understood, my chief aim is answered. For so " all historical memoirs (says Dr. Colman) should be written." In a number of particulars I have deviated from common usage; but in none without good reasons, and to me satisfactory. As one instance it is observed, that compound names of places, in general, are written like simple names. For this deviation from general custom, no apology will be expected of me, as it has been proved to be preferable by a writer of great eminence.*

---

* Joel Barlow, Esq. See his Columbiad, printed 1807, Philadelphia, 4to.

THE EDITOR'S PREFACE.

In correcting the text, superfluous words are sometimes left out; but this [—] sign is substituted, and the word or words omitted are given in the margin included by the same marks. When a word is altered, it is also included in brackets, and the word given in the margin as it stood in the original, and included in the same way. All words, presumed to be wanting, are inserted between brackets without reference to the margin, and are by the present editor. All notes included by the parenthesis were by the former editor, and attached to the old edition.

I should take it as a great kindness, should any person communicate to me any information where it is presumed to be wanting in the notes to this work; or point out any errours in what is already done, that future editions may be more perfect.

It being the particular design of this edition to render it uniform and consistent with respect to arrangement and "originality" of expression, few liberties have been taken with the composition; few indeed, unless pointed out as above expressed. In some instances however, some connective particles have been dropped and the signs omitted. But in such cases what is omitted was superfluous tautology. Therefore the reader may be assured that the text is correctly copied. From the present appearance of the work, its former erroneous composition is too easily discovered; yet it is some consolation, that innumerable errours have been detected, and generally, inasmuch as the design of the subject would admit.

It was thought advisable to accompany the work with an Appendix, wherein something new, or of later date might be given, as young persons generally prefer new things to old. It was rather difficult to make the selection for this part, not for want of materials, but because they were so numerous; and so many seem to deserve the same attention. But the articles are authentick, and as interesting, it is presumed, as can be found.

THE EDITOR'S PREFACE.

As there are different editions of many of the authors cited in this work, for the convenience of reference, a table, containing the chief of them, is here given.

Title	Author	Where printed	When	No. of vols.	Form
American Annals	A. Holmes	Cambridge	1805	2	8 vo
American Biography	J. Belknap	Boston	1794, 1798	2	8
American Biography	W. Allen	Cambridge	1809	1	8
Annals of Newengland	T. Prince	Boston	1826	1	8
Antiquarian Researches	E. Hoyt	Greenfield	1824	1	8
Annals of the Revolution	J Morse	Hartford	1824	1	8
History of America	W. Robertson	Philadelphia	1821	2	8
History of Connecticut	B. Trumbull	Newhaven	1818	2	8
History of Massachusetts	T. Hutchinson	Salem	1795	2	8
History of Maine	J. Sullivan	Boston	1795	1	8
History of Massachusetts	G. R. Minot	Boston	1798, 1803	2	8
History of Maryland	J. L. Bozman	Baltimore	1811	1	8
History of Newengland	J. Winthrop	Boston	1825, 1826	2	8
History of Newengland	H. Adams	Boston	1799	1	8
History of Newengland	Morse & Parish	Charlestown	1804	1	12 mo
History of Newhampshire	J. Belknap	Phil. & Boston	1812, 1813	3	8 vo
History of Newyork	W. Smith	Albany	1814	1	8
History of Pennsylvania	R. Proud	Philadelphia	1797, 1798	2	8
History of Northcarolina	H. Williamson	Philadelphia	1812	2	8
History of U. States	B. Trumbull	Boston	1810	1	8
History of Vermont	S. Williams	Burlington	1809	2	8
Hist. Coll. Mass. Hist. Soc.		Boston	from 1792	20	8
Hist. Col. N. Y. Hist. Soc.		Newyork	1811 to 14	4	8
Hist. Col. Newhampshire	Farmer & Moore	Concord	1822, 3, 4	3	8
Hist. Col. N. H. Hist. Soc.		Concord	1st in 1824	1	8
Humphreys' Works	D. Humphreys	Newyork	1804	1	8
Magnalia C. A.	C. Mather	Hartford	1820	2	8
Nar. of Indian Wars	W. Hubbard	Brattleboro.	1814	1	12 mo
Newengland Biography	J. Eliot	Boston	1809	1	8 vo
Newengland's Memorial	N. Morton	Newport	1772	1	8
Newhampshire Gazetteer	Farmer & Moore	Concord	1823	1	12 mo
Sum. Hist. Mass. bay	W. Douglass	Boston	1749	2	8 vo
Travels throughout N. A.	J. Carver	London	1781	1	8
Wonders Invisible World.	R. Calef	Salem	1796	1	12 mo
Wars of Newengland.	S. Penhallow	Boston	1726	1	12

In addition to the above list, many works have been consulted, but the assistance from them has been smaller. Some of the most important are Hubbard's History of Newengland, Stiles' History of the Judges, Whitney's History of Worcester, and the Histories of several of the southern states. The free use I have made of every author's works is amply acknowledged in the notes. Reference is made to some late editions of works in preference to the first, not only as they are more uniform, but because they will now be oftener met with. But in most cases such have been compared with the originals. To two works in particular, it was thought most advisable; namely, Penhallow's "Wars of N. England," and Prince's Annals. The first of these is now reprinted in the I Vol. of the N. H. Hist. Soc. Col., which, though not so perfect as it might have been, is, on the whole, a work to be prized. A handsome edition in octavo of the valuable Annals was published last year, by Messrs. Cummings, Hilliard, and Company, Boston. Though this is not *exactly* reprinted, yet, nothing is altered, that I have met with, but for the better; and, excepting a few typographical errours, is splendidly executed.

Having already drawn out my preface to too great a length, the whole is submitted without any apology. And the publisher takes this opportunity of giving his grateful respects to all his patrons, and with pleasure subscribes himself, their much obliged and sincere friend.

SAMUEL G. DRAKE.

Boston, 2 January, 1827.

ADVERTISEMENT TO EDITION OF 1845.

The present edition of this work has been revised and corrected in several places, by comparison with more recent publications of high authority; some obsolete and objectionable words and phrases have been changed, and typographical and other errors of the earlier editions corrected. It is hoped that so authentic and valuable a contribution to the Indian History of our country, will find a place in every Library, and the interesting personal narrative of Col. Church will doubtless engage the attention of the reader in the careful perusal of the whole work.

[The following is an exact copy of the title page of the old edition.]

THE

ENTERTAINING

HISTORY

OF

KING PHILIP'S WAR,

WHICH BEGAN IN THE MONTH OF JUNE, 1675.

AS ALSO OF

EXPEDITIONS

MORE LATELY MADE

AGAINST THE COMMON ENEMY, AND INDIAN REBELS, IN THE EASTERN PARTS OF NEW-ENGLAND:

WITH SOME ACCOUNT OF THE DIVINE PROVIDENCE TOWARDS

COL. BENJAMIN CHURCH:

BY THOMAS CHURCH, ESQ. HIS SON.

SECOND EDITION.

BOSTON : PRINTED, 1716.
NEWPORT, RHODE-ISLAND : REPRINTED AND SOLD BY SOLOMON SOUTHWICK, IN QUEEN-STREET, 1772.

TO THE READER.

THE subject of this following narrative, offering itself to your friendly perusal, relates to the former and later wars of Newengland, which I myself was not a little concerned in: For in the year 1675, that unhappy and bloody Indian war broke out in Plymouth colony, where I was then building, and beginning a plantation, at a place called by the Indians, Sogkonate, and since, by the English, Little Compton. I was the first Englishman that built upon that neck, which was full of Indians. My head and hands were full about settling a new plantation, where nothing was brought to; no preparation of dwelling house, or outhouses, or fencing made; horses and cattle were to be provided, ground to be cleared and broken up; and the utmost caution to be used, to keep myself free from offending my Indian neighbours all round about me. While I was thus busily employed, and all my time and strength laid out in this laborious undertaking, I received a commission from the government to engage in their defence: And with my commission I received another heart, inclining me to put forth my strength in military service: And through the grace of God I was spirited for that work, and direction in it was renewed to me day by day. And although many of the actions that I was concerned in were very difficult and dangerous, yet, myself, and those who went with me voluntarily in the service, had our lives, for the most part, wonderfully preserved by the overruling hand of the Almighty from first to last; which doth aloud bespeak our praises: And to declare his wonderful works is our indispensable duty.

I was ever very sensible of my own littleness, and unfitness to be employed in such great services. But calling to mind that God is strong, I endeavoured to put all my confidence in him, and by his Almighty power, was carried through every difficult action; and my desire is, that his name may have the praise.

It was ever my intent, having laid myself under a solemn promise, that the many and repeated favours of God to myself and those with me in the service might be published for generations to come. And now my great age requiring my dismission from service in the militia, and to put off my armour, I am willing that the great and glorious works of Almighty God, to us, children of men, should appear to the world: And having my minutes by me, my son has taken the care and pains to collect from them the ensuing narrative of many passages relating to the former and latter wars; which I have had the perusal of, and find nothing amiss, as to the truth of it, and with as little reflection upon any particular person, as might be, either alive or dead.

And seeing every particle of historical truth is precious, I hope the reader will pass a favourable censure upon an old soldier, telling of the many rencounters he has had, and yet is come off alive.

It is a pleasure to remember what a great number of families, in this and the neighbouring provinces, in Newengland, did, during the war, enjoy a great measure of liberty and peace by the hazardous stations and marches of those engaged in military exercises; who were a wall unto them on this side and on that side.

I desire prayers, that I may be enabled well to accomplish my spiritual warfare, and that I may be more than conqueror through Jesus Christ's loving me.

BENJAMIN CHURCH.

THE LIFE OF COL. CHURCH.*

COLONEL BENJAMIN CHURCH was born in 1639, at Duxbury, near Plymouth, of reputable parents, who lived and died there. His father's name was Joseph, who, with two of his brethren, came early into Newengland, as refugees from the religious oppression of the parent state. Mr. Joseph Church, among other children, had three sons, Joseph, Caleb, and Benjamin. Caleb settled at Watertown, the other two at Seconet, or Little Compton. Benjamin, the hero of this history, was of a good stature, his body well proportioned, and built for hardiness and activity. Although he was very corpulent and heavy in the latter part of his life, yet, when he was a young man he was not so; being then active, sprightly and vigorous. He carried dignity in his countenance —thought and acted with a rational and manly judgment—which, joined with a naturally generous, obliging and hospitable disposition, procured him both authority and esteem. He married Mrs. Alice Southworth, by whom he had a daughter, Mrs. Rothbotham, and five sons, viz., Thomas Church, the author or publisher of this history, and father of the honourable Thomas Church, Esq., now living in Little Compton; Constant Church a Captain under his father in the eastern expedition, and in the militia; and of a mili-

---

* The life of Church was not added to the first edition.-- But to the second it was, and was the last article in the book; excepting a Latin ode of one page, which is now omitted. This life containing some prefatory remarks, it was thought proper to place it at the beginning of the work. It was judged best to omit the above mentioned Latin ode to give place to more interesting articles. What follows was placed at the head of the page. *Ode Heroica (a nepote Herois composita) Biographiæ pracedenti diffigenda sit.*

tary and enterprising spirit; Benjamin Church, who died a bachelor; Edward Church,* whose only son now living, is Deacon Benjamin Church† of Boston, who furnishes these memoirs of the family; and Charles Church, who had a numerous issue.

Colonel Church was a man of integrity, justice, and uprightness, of piety and serious religion.‡ He was a member of the church of Bristol at its foundation, in the Rev. Mr. Lee's§ day. He was constant and devout in family worship, wherein he read and often expounded the scriptures to his household. He was exemplary in observing the Sabbath, and in attending the worship and ordinances of God in the sanctuary. He lived regularly, and left an example worthy of

---

* He was also a Captain under his father in the last eastern expedition.

† Probably the same whose name is found associated with the venerable JAMES OTIS, SAMUEL ADAMS, JOSEPH WARREN, and others, as a "Committee of correspondence" in the memorable revolution, and to which he probably belonged when he wrote this account of the family. See American Annals, II, 300. Also the standing which he appears to have maintained among the fraternity of Masons, speaks his eminence.

‡ What is here said of the Colonel, is placed after his son Edward, by a writer in Farmer and Moore's Collections; where this account appears to be copied. It must be an errour in the copyist, and one, too, which it required some pains to commit; not but that the son (for aught I know) deserved as high encomiums, but we have no right to bestow such upon the son, at the father's expense. But thus much were it intentional.

§ Rev. Samuel Lee, the first minister of Bristol, R. I. He was born in London, 1625, came to this country in 1686; but in two or three years came to the conclusion to return to his native country. Before he sailed, he told his wife that he had discovered a star, which, according to the laws of Astrology, presaged captivity, which unfortunately came to pass. He sailed in 1691, and in his passage was taken by the French, and carried into France, where he died the same year. See Allen's Biog. 381. Dr. C. Mather represents him as possessing very extraordinary learning. See Magnalia Christi Americana, I, 548.

the imitation of his posterity. He was a friend to the civil and religious liberties of his country, and greatly rejoiced in the revolution.* He was Colonel of the militia in the county of Bristol. The several offices of civil and military trust, with which he was entrusted from time to time, through a long life, he discharged with fidelity and usefulness.

The war of 1675, was the most important Indian war, that Newengland ever saw. PHILIP or Metacomet† (a son of good old MASSASOIT,‡ and his second successor) had wrought up the Indians of all the tribes through Newengland, into a dangerous com-

---

* By William and Mary.

† Though the chiefs of savage nations are generally called Kings, yet says Smith, they "have no such dignity or office among them." Hist. N. Y. 197. Philip, at different periods of his life, was known by different names, as at first, he was called Metacomet or Metacom. See Morton, 171, 172. This celebrated chief has been called by some, though wrongly I contend, King of the Narragansets. He was King or chief of the Wampanoags, or Pokanokets, the situation of whose country will be described in my first note to "Philip's War." It is true that these Indians as well as the Narragansets themselves inhabited about the bay of that name, but they had their King as well as the Pokanokets, and were independent of each other.

Different opinions seem to have prevailed with regard to this chief's pedigree; that is, whether he were a son or grandson of Massassoit. Prince and Trumbull inform us that he was his grandson; Hutchinson and Belknap, that he was his son. Why these respectable authors saw cause to differ, and not inform us, is not easy to tell. These are not all the authors on each side, but most readers are apprised of this, no doubt, before I had taken this trouble to inform them.

‡ Prince, in his text, writes Masassoit ; but adds this note. "The printed accounts generally spell him Massasoit ; Governour Bradford writes him Massasoyt, and Massasoyet ; but I find the ancient people from their fathers in Plymouth colony, pronounce his name Ma-sas-so-it." N. E. Chron. 187. However, the most preferable way seems to be Massassoit. Some account of the life of this constant friend of the Pilgrims will be found in the course of this history.

bination to extirpate the English. It was one of the last works of the commissioners of the united colonies, (a council [in] which subsisted the great security of Newengland, from 1643 to 1678) to break up this confederacy. An army of one thousand English was on foot at once, under the command of Governour Winslow. Whoever desires further information concerning this war, may consult Mr. Hubbard's* history of it. The part Colonel Church acted in it is exhibited in this plain narrative, given by his son, two years before his father's death.

Colonel Church perfectly understood the manner of the Indians in fighting, and was thoroughly acquainted with their haunts, swamps, and places of refuge, on the territory between Narraganset and cape Cod. There he was particularly successful; on that field he gathered his laurels. The surprisal and seizure of ANNAWON was an act of true boldness and heroism. Had the eastern Indians been surrounded with English settlements, there is reason to think that he would have been more successful among them. But on a long and extended frontier, open to immense deserts, little more has ever been done by troops of undoubted courage, than to arouse and drive off the Indians into a wide howling wilderness,

---

* Mr. William Hubbard, minister of Ipswich, the best historian in Newengland, of the age, unless we except Mr. Prince. The truth of which his works abundantly prove. Although some labour has been done to detract from him some of his justly acquired fame, yet, it does and ever will remain unimpaired. This would be true had he never written any thing but his NARRATIVE. To his "History of Newengland," Mather is chiefly indebted for what is correct in his renowned book of jargons, the Magnalia Christi Americana. See president Allen's Biog. Dictionary. He died Sept. 1704, aged 83 years. Gov. Hutchinson remarks on the character of him, that "he was a man of learning, of a candid and benevolent mind, accompanied, as it generally is, with a good degree of catholicism; which, I think, was not accounted the most valuable part of his character in the age in which he lived." Hist. Mass. II, 136.

where it was as much in vain to seek them, as for Cæsar to seek the Gauls in the Hyrcanian forests.

The present edition* of this history is given without alteration in the body of it; being thought best to let it go down to posterity, (like the *Periplus of Hanno*†) with its own internal marks of originality. However the editor in the margin hath given the English names of places described by Indian names in the narrative; and also some few notes and illustrations.

After Philip's war Colonel Church settled; and at first at Bristol, then at Fallriver, (Troy) lastly at Seconet. At each of which places he acquired, and left a large estate. Having served his generation faithfully, by the will of God he fell asleep, and was gathered unto his fathers. He died and was buried at Little Compton.

The morning before his death, he went about two miles on horse back to visit his only sister, Mrs. Irish, to sympathise with her on the death of her only child. After a friendly and pious visit, in a moving and affecting manner, he took his leave of her, and said, it was a last farewell. Telling her, [that] he was persuaded he should never see her more; but hoped to meet her in heaven. Returning homeward, he had not rode above half a mile, before his horse stumbled, and threw him over his head. And the Colonel being exceeding fat and heavy, fell with

---

* The edition from which this is taken.

† Hanno was "the famous Carthaginian," who in a remote age of navigation, made a voyage into the Atlantick ocean, and "sailed seeking for thirty days the western parts," taking his departure from the pillars of Hercules (straits of Gibraltar.) Hence some infer that he must have discovered some parts of America, because Columbus did in about the same length of time. He wrote a book containing an account of his discoveries, which he entitled Periplum or Periplus. See a work lettered "America Known to the Ancients," Dr. Robertson's Hist. America, I, i. Belknap's Biog. I, 16.

such force, that a blood vessel was broken, and the blood gushed out of his mouth like a torrent. His wife was soon brought to him. He tried but was unable to speak to her, and died in about twelve hours. He was carried to the grave with great funeral pomp, and was buried under arms, and with military honours. On his tomb stone is this inscription.

HERE LIETH INTERRED THE BODY

OF THE HONOURABLE

COL. BENJAMIN CHURCH, Esq.;

WHO DEPARTED THIS LIFE,

JANUARY 17TH, 1717—18,

IN THE 78 YEAR OF HIS AGE.*

Newport April 8, 1772.

---

* " High in esteem among the great he stood;
His wisdom made him lovely, great and good.
Tho' he be said to die, he will survive;
Thro' future time his memory shall live."

See a poem called "A description of Pennsylvania, Anno 1729," by Thomas Makin, in Proud's Hist. II, 361. The above though applied to the founder of that province, as good, at least, is deserved by the venerated Church; who, through the foul intrigue, and low caprice of office seekers, and the blind zeal of ambitious bigots, suffered much, both as to fame and fortune, in his time. The truth of this remark will fully appear in the ensuing history

THE

ENTERTAINING HISTORY

OF

PHILIP'S WAR,

WHICH BEGAN IN THE YEAR 1675. WITH THE PROCEED-

INGS OF

BENJAMIN CHURCH, Esq.*

In the year 1674, Mr. Benjamin Church of Duxbury, being providentially at Plymouth† in the time of the

---

* As the author does not begin with the causes and first events of this war, it may be proper to introduce the most important here. His intention appears to have been to give an account of this war, so far, only, as his father was engaged in it, as himself observes in another place.

Although not a year had passed since the settlement of Plymouth without some difficulties with the Indians, I will go so far back, only, as immediately concerns Philip's War. After the close of the Pequot war, in 1637, it was conjectured by the English, that the Narragansets took some affront on account of the division of the captive Pequots, among themselves and the Mohegans; and that the English showed partiality. These tribes had assisted in the conquest of the Pequots, and were in a league with the English, and each other. For some time the Narragansets practiced secret abuses upon the Mohegans; but at length they were so open in their insults, that complaints were made to the English, whose interest it was to preserve peace between them. In 1642, it was thought that they were plotting to cut off the English. They so pressed upon the Mohegans,

in

---

† Some authors, both ancient and modern wrote this word Plimouth, but custom has adopted the manner as used in the text.

court, fell into acquaintance with Captain John Almy of Rhodeisland. Captain Almy with great impor-

in 1645, that the colonies were obliged to interfere with an armed force.

The Wampanoags, or Pokanokets, of which Philip was King, inhabited the tract of country where Bristol now is, then called Pokanoket, thence north around Mounthope bay, thence southerly, including the country of considerable width, to Seconct. At the head of this tribe was Massassoit, when the pilgrims arrived at Plymouth, who always lived in friendship with them. He had two sons, who were called Alexander and Philip, which names they received from Gov. Prince of Plymouth, while there renewing a treaty, probably from Philip and Alexander of Macedon. Alexander being the elder assumed the power on the death of his father, and it was soon found that he was plotting with the Narragansets against the English; but his reign was short. On being sent for to answer to the court at Plymouth, to certain allegations, he went, and after explaining his conduct, was taken sick on his return, and died soon after. This was about 1657. Philip succeeded, and his plottings were continual. But he frequently renewed treaties and affected friendships until 1671, when he made a loud complaint that some of the English injured his land, which in the end proved to be false. A meeting was held at Taunton, not long after in consequence of the hostile appearance of Philip's men, by Gov. Prince of Plymouth, and deputies from Massachusetts. Philip was sent for to give reasons for such warlike appearances. He discovered extreme shyness, and for some time would not come to the town, and then with a large band of his warriors with their arms. He would not consent to go into the meetinghouse, where the delegates were, until it was agreed that his men should be on one side of the house, and the English on the other. On being questioned, he denied having any ill designs upon the English, and said that he came with his men armed to prevent any attacks from the Narragansets; but this falsehood was at once detected, and it was evident that they were united in their operations. It was also proved before him, that he had meditated an attack on Taunton, which he confessed. These steps so confounded him that he consented to deliver all his arms into the hands of the English as an indemnity for past damages. All of the guns which he brought with him, about 70, were delivered, and the rest were to be sent in, but never were. What would have been the fate of Newengland had Philip's warriors possessed those arms in the war that ensued? This prevented immediate war, and it required several years to repair their loss. Philip

PHILIP'S WAR.

tunity invited him to ride with him and view that part of Plymouth colony that lay next to Rhodeisland, known then by their Indian names of Pocasset and Sogkonate.* Among other arguments to persuade him, he told him the soil was very rich, and the situation pleasant: Persuades him by all means to purchase of the company some of the court grant rights. He accepted his invitation, views the country and was pleased with it, makes a purchase, settled a farm, found the gentlemen of the island† very civil and obliging. And being himself a person of uncommon activity and industry, he soon erected two buildings upon his farm, and gained a good acquaintance with the natives; got much into their favour, and was in a little time in great esteem among them.‡

The next spring advancing, while Mr. Church was diligently settling his new farm, stocking, leasing and disposing of his affairs, and had a fine prospect of doing no small things; and hoping that his good success would be inviting unto other good men to become his neighbours: Behold! the rumour of a war between the English and the natives, gave check to

---

was industrious to do this, and, at the same time, used his endeavours to cause other tribes to engage in his cause. He was not ready when the war did begin, to which, in some measure, we may attribute his failure. Three of his men were tried and hanged for the alleged murder of John Sassamon, whom Philip had condemned as a traitor. It so exasperated Philip and his men that their friends should be punished by the English, that they could no longer restrain their violence. Thus are some of the most prominent events sketched which led to this bloody war. The history of John Sassamon or Sausaman, will be found in a succeeding note.

* Pocasset, now Tiverton, was the name of the main land against the north part of Rhodeisland. Sogkonate, afterwards Seconet, now Little Compton, extends from Fogland ferry to the sea; in length between 7 and 8 miles.

† Rhodeisland, which was now quite well inhabited. It was settled in 1638. Its Indian name was Aquetneck, and afterwards called the Isle of Rodes by the English.

‡ Mr. Church moved here in the autumn of 1674.

his projects. People began to be very jealous of the Indians, and indeed they had no small reason to suspect that they had formed a design of war upon the English.* Mr. Church had it daily suggested to him that the Indians were plotting a bloody design. That Philip the great Mounthope Sachem, was leader therein, and so it proved. He was sending his messengers to all the neighbouring Sachems, to engage them into a confederacy with him in the war.† Among the rest

---

* It may be diverting to some, to introduce here what Cotton Mather calls an omen of the war that followed. "Things," says he, "began by this time to have an ominous aspect. Yea, and now we speak of things *ominous*, we may add, some time before this, [before those were executed for the murder of Sassamon] in a clear, still, sunshiny morning, there were divers persons in Malden who heard in the air, on the southeast of them, a *great gun* go off, and presently thereupon the report of *small guns* like musket shot, very thick discharging, as if there had been a battle. This was at a time when there was nothing visible done in any part of the colony to occasion such noises; but that which most of all astonished them was the flying of *bullets*, which came singing over their heads, and seemed very near to them, after which the sound of *drums* passing along westward was very audible; and on the same day, in Plymouth colony in several places, invisible troops of horse were heard riding to and fro," &c. Magnalia, II, 486. This is quite as credible as many witch accounts in that marvellous work.

† The following is a statement of the probable numbers of the Indians in Newengland at the time of Philip's war, also of the English.

Dr. Trumbull in his Hist. U. States, I, 36, supposes there were in Newengland at the time of settlement about 36,000 Indian inhabitants; one third of which were warriours. Their numbers gradually diminished as the whites increased, so that we may conclude that there were not less than 10,000 warriours at the commencement of Philip's war. Hutchinson, I, 406, says that the Narragansets alone were considered to amount to 2000 fighting men, in 1675. Hubbard, Nar. 67, says they promised to rise with 4000 in the war. Governour Hinkley states the number of Indians in Plymouth county, in 1685, at 4000 or upwards. Hist. U. States, I, 35. Beside these there were in different towns about 2000 praying Indians, as those were called who adhered to the English religion; they took no part in the war.

PHILIP'S WAR.

he sent six men to Awashonks, squaw sachem of the Sogkonate Indians, to engage her in his interest;* Awashonks so far listened unto them, as to call her subjects together, to make a great dance, which is the custom of that nation† when they advise about momentous affairs. But what does Awashonks do, but sends away two of her men that well understood the English language, (Sassamon‡ and George§ by

---

In 1673, the inhabitants of Newengland amounted to about 120,000 souls, of whom, perhaps, 16,000 were able to bear arms. Holmes' American Annals, I, 416.

* Dr. Belknap, in his Hist. N. Hampshire, I, 108, says, on the autnority of Callender, that "The inhabitants of Bristol shew a particular spot where Philip received the news of the first Englishmen that were killed, with so much sorrow as to cause him to weep." This he observes was very different from the current opinion. No doubt the consternation of the people, caused by an approaching war, had great effect in establishing every thing unfavourable of Philip.

† It is the custom of most, if not all, the N. American Indians. See Capt. Carver's Travels in America, 269.

‡ John Sassamon, or as others spell it, Sausaman, was instructed in English by the celebrated Indian apostle, John Eliot, and pretended to believe in the christian religion. But for some reason he neglected its duties, and returned to a savage life. About this time, or perhaps before, he advised the English of some of Philip's plots, which so enraged him, that he sought Sassamon's death, whom he considered as a rebel and traitor. And this is the principle on which the English themselves acted; yet, they would not suffer it in another people, who, indeed, were as free as any other. The particulars were these: Sassamon was met on "a great pond," which I suppose to be Assawomset, by some of Philip's men, who killed him and put him under the ice, leaving his hat and gun on the ice, where they were found soon after; and also the dead body. See Hubbard's Narrative, 70, 71. This must have been late in the spring of 1675, but there was ice. Marks were found upon the body of Sassamon, that indicated murder, and an Indian soon appeared, who said that he saw some of Philip's Indians in the very execution of it. Three were immediately apprehended, and tried at the court in Plymouth,

---

§ An Indian, who from this time, was very friendly to Mr. Church. All I can find concerning him is in this history.

name) to invite Mr. Church to the dance.* Mr
Church, upon the invitation immediately takes with
him Charles Hazelton, his tenant's son, who well
understood the Indian language, and rode down to the
place appointed, where they found hundreds of
Indians gathered together from all parts of her
dominion. Awashonks herself in a foaming sweat,
was leading the dance; but she was no sooner sensible of Mr. Church's arrival, but she broke off, sat
down, calls her nobles around her, [and] orders Mr.
Church to be invited into her presence. Compliments being passed, and each one taking seat,
she told him [that] King Philip had sent six men
of his, with two of her people,† that had been over
at Mounthope,‡ to draw her into a confederacy with

Plymouth, in June, by a jury, says Mather, consisting of half
Indians, and half English, and brought in guilty of the murder.
Two of them persisting in their innocence to the end, and
the third denied that he had any hand in the murder, but
said that he saw the others commit it. Perhaps he made this
confession in hopes of pardon, but it did not save him. Magnalia, II, 486. Mather places the death of Sassamon in 1674,
this was old style, hence it was previous to the 25th of March
1675. Hubbard, 69, says that Sassamon had been Philip's
secretary, and chief counsellor. To what tribe he first belonged I have not ascertained, but from this history it appears
that he belonged to the Sogkonate Indians, in the spring of
1675.

* One might conclude this transaction to have been about
the middle of June, by its connexion with the commencement of the war, but by the death of Sassamon it must be
placed much earlier.

† These two I conclude, were those, or among those mentioned by Hubbard, 69, who discovered the plots of Philip,
one of whom might be Sassamon.

‡ (Or *Mont-haup*, a mountain in Bristol.)
Why the author writes this word so I do not know, unless it were so pronounced in his day. Its ancient name was
Pokanoket. It is quite an eminence about two miles east
from the village of Bristol, very steep on all sides and termi-
nates in a large rock, which at a distance has the appearance
of a large dome of an amphitheatre. It is apparently composed of pebbles and sand. On this now stands a small oc-
tagonal building. From many places on the east shore, par-

him, in a war with the English; [and] desired him
to give her his advice in the case; and to tell her the
truth, whether the *Umpame** men, (as Philip had told
her) were gathering a great army to invade Philip's
country. He assured her he would tell her the truth,
and give her his best advice. Then he told her it
was but a few days since he came from Plymouth,
and [that] the English were then making no preparations for war; that he was in company with the
principal gentlemen of the government, who had no
discourse at all about war, and he believed no thoughts
about it. He asked her whether she thought he
would have brought up his goods to settle in that
place, if he apprehended an entering into [a] war with
so near a neighbour. She seemed to be somewhat
convinced by his talk, and said she believed he spoke
the truth. Then she called for the Mounthope men,
who made a formidable appearance, with their faces
painted, and their hairs trimmed up in comb fashion,
with their powderhorns and shot bags† at their backs

---

ticularly at the little village of Fallriver, this mount forms
a beautiful acclivity in the landscape ; very nearly resem-
bling a view of the State house at Boston from a distance.
On an excursion there in the summer of 1824, many gratifying objects were discovered, relating to the times of which
we treat. A most beautiful prospect of Providence and the
surrounding country and bay appears from this mount.

* The Indian name for Plymouth.

† It has been a question among many, how the Indians became furnished, so soon, with our implements of war. It is
not probable that every source is known ; but they no doubt,
had a large supply from the French in the east of Newengland. A man by the name of Morton, who came to this country in 1622, is said to have been the first that supplied the
Indians with arms and ammunition, and taught them their
use, in the country adjacent to Cape Cod. This he done
that the Indians might hunt and procure furs for him. Secretary Morton, in his Newengland's Memorial, 76, says, " he
had been a petty-fogger at Furnival's Inn, having more craft
than honesty ;" but in justice to him it may be observed,
that the Memorialist has made every circumstance appear in
the darkest dress, and not only of him, but others, whom, in-

which among that nation is the posture and figure of preparedness for war. She told Mr. Church these were the persons that had brought her the report of the English preparations for war, and then told them what Mr. Church had said in answer to it. Upon this began a warm talk among the Indians, but it was soon quashed, and Awashonks proceeded to tell Mr.

---

deed, we had rather speak in praise. All historians, with whom I am conversant, agree that he was a disorderly person, of bad morals, and gave people much trouble. He resided first in Mr. Weston's Plantation at Wessagusset, now Weymouth; but that breaking up the next year, 1623, he next settled with Captain Wallaston at or near the same place in 1625, and the place being near the hill that separates Weymouth from Quincy, was called Mount Wallaston. Capt. Wallaston with most of his company abandoned the plantation, and Morton usurped the government. They soon found themselves involved in difficulties with the Indians and with one another. They erected a Maypole, and practiced their excesses about it. Selling arms to the natives being a breach of the laws among others, he was seized by order of the court, and soon after, 1628, sent to England. No notice of the complaints against him being taken, he returned the next year. He was afterwards imprisoned for his writings. He died at Agamenticus in 1644 or 5, according to Allen, American Biog. 441. He has been accused of giving currency to the story of "hanging the weaver instead of the cobbler." The author of Hudibras getting hold of the story, has, in that work, Part II, Canto II, line 403, &c., set it off to the no small expense of the zeal of the Pilgrims. See Belknap, Amer. Biog. II, 318, Prince Chron. 212, and Savage's edition of Winthrop, I, 34, 35, 36, where the passage may be seen. The latter author says it was not so, on the authority of Morton himself; but as the affair happened at Weston's plantation, where Morton was concerned, it is natural that he should say the right one was hanged. In a note to line 413, in the passage above referred to, is the following positive assertion: "The history of the Cobbler had been attested by persons of good credit, who were upon the place when it was done." Early authors hinted at the affair, and late ones have enlarged upon it. The truth no doubt is as follows: The people of that plantation were in a state of starvation, and by stealing from the Indians had incurred their vengeance, which to satisfy, they hanged one; who, Hudibras says, was a bedrid weaver, whereas the right one was a useful cobbler, whom they could not so well spare.

Church, that Philip's message to her was, that unless she would forthwith enter into a confederacy with him in a war against the English, he would send his men over privately, to kill the English cattle, and burn their houses on that side of the river, which would provoke the English to fall upon her, whom, they would without doubt, suppose the author of the mischief. Mr. Church told her he was sorry to see so threatening an aspect of affairs; and stepping to the Mounthopes, he felt of their bags, and finding them filled with bullets, asked them what those bullets were for. They scoffingly replied, " To shoot pigeons with." Then Mr. Church turned to Awashonks, and told her, [that] if Philip were resolved to make war, her best way would be to knock those six Mounthopes on the head, and shelter herself under the protection of the English. Upon which the Mounthopes were for the present dumb. But those two of Awashonks' men, who had been at Mounthope, expressed themselves in a furious manner against his advice. And Littleeyes,* one of the Queen's counsel joined with them, and urged Mr. Church to go aside with him among the bushes, that he might have some private discourse with him, which other Indians immediately forbid; being sensible of his ill design. But the Indians began to side, and grow very warm. Mr. Church, with undaunted courage, told the Mounthopes, [that] they were bloody wretches, and thirsted after the blood of their English neighbours, who had never injured them, but had always abounded in their kindness to them. That for his own part, though he desired nothing more than peace, yet, if nothing but war would satisfy them, he believed he should prove a sharp thorn in their sides: Bid the company observe those men that were of such bloody dispositions, whether providence would suffer them to live

---

* He was afterward taken in the war that followed, by Church, and treated very kindly, as will be seen in the progress of this history.

B

to see the event of the war, which others, more peaceably disposed, might do. Then he told Awashonks, [that] he thought it might be most advisable for her to send to the Governour of Plymouth,* and shelter herself and people under his protection. She liked his advice, and desired him to go on her behalf to the Plymouth government, which he consented to. And at parting advised her, [that] whatever she did, not to desert the English interest to join with her neighbours in a rebellion,† which would certainly prove fatal to her. (He moved none of his goods from his house, that there might not be the least umbrage from such an action.‡) She thanked him for his advice, and sent two of her men to guard him to his house, [who]¹ when they came there, urged him to take care to secure his goods, which he refused, for the reasons before mentioned; but desired the Indians, that if what they feared, should happen, they would take care of what he left, and directed them to a place in the woods where they should dispose of them, which they faithfully observed. He

¹ [which]

---

* The Honourable Josiah Winslow, Esq., who was afterwards commander in chief of the forces in this war. He was a son of the distinguished Mr. Edward Winslow, who was also Governour of Plymouth many years. He was born in 1629, and was the first Governor born in Newengland, which office he filled 7 years. He died 18 Dec. 1680, aged 52.

† This war was called a rebellion, because the English fancied them under the King of England, but that did not make them so. As well might emigrants from the United States land on the coast of France, and because they were disputed by the inhabitants, of their right so to do, call them rebels; yet, when the country was neither claimed nor improved, certainly, to take possession and improve, was not wrong. Our author is by no means so lavish of ill names as many early writers. Hellhounds, fiends, serpents, caitiffs, dogs, &c. were their common appellations. The ill fame of Mather, in this respect, will be celebrated as long as the marvellous contents of the Magnalia are read.

‡ This sentence was included in brackets in the copy but as I have appropriated that mark to my own use, I substitute the parenthesis

took his leave of his guard, [after bidding][1] them
tell their mistress, [that] if she continued steady in
her dependence on the English, and kept within her
own limits of Sogkonate, he would see her again
quickly; and then hastened away to Pocasset;* where
he met with Peter Nunnuit, the husband of the
Queen† of Pocasset, who was just then come over in
a canoe from Mounthope. Peter told him that there
would certainly be war, for Philip had held a dance
of several weeks continuance, and had entertained
the young men from all parts of the country. And
added, that Philip expected to be sent for to Plymouth, to be examined about Sassamon's‡ death, who
was murdered at Assawomset ponds,§ knowing himself guilty of contriving that murder. The same
Peter told him that he saw Mr. James Brown,|| of

[1] [and bid]

---

* (Tiverton shore over against the north end of Rhodeisl-
and.)

† Weetamore or Wetamoe, "Philip's near kinswoman."
Hub. 224. The same mentioned in another place, as
"Squaw Sachem of Pocasset." She was drowned in cross-
ing a river or arm of the sea at Swanzey, 6 August, 1675,
by attempting to escape from a party of English. Ib. 224.
Her head was cut off, and set upon a pole. Ibid.

‡ The same of whom the history is given in note 3 on
page 21.

§ (Middleborough.)
Three large ponds about 40 miles from Boston, and 16
from Newbedford. In passing from the latter place to the
former we have the largest on the right, which now bears the
name of Assawomset, or Assawamset, and two others on the
left. They are all very near together. The road passes between two, separated only by a narrow neck of flat land,
about a stone's throw over.

|| "One of the magistrates of Plymouth jurisdiction."
Hubbard, 12. This gentleman was very active in the war.
He was a magistrate between the years 1670 and 1675.
Morton, 208. A minister of Swanzey is mentioned by Ma-
ther in his third *clasis* of Newengland ministers by this
name.

Swanzey,* and Mr. Samuel Gorton,† who was an interpreter, and two other men,‡ who brought a letter

---

* A town on the west side of Taunton river in the bottom of Mounthope bay, about 15 miles from Taunton, and in the vicinity of Mounthope, distance by the road about 11 miles.

†Accounts of this gentleman may be seen in Morton's Memorial, 117, &c., which, perhaps, are not impartial. That author partaking of the persecuting spirit of the times, accuses him of all manner of outrages against religion and government. "Not only," he observes, "abandoning and rejecting all civil power and authority, (except moulded according to *his* own *fancy*) but belching out errours, &c." Several pages in that work are filled up to this effect. Dr. Eliot, N. E. Biog. 227, says, "It is evident that he was not so bad a man as his enemies represented." The reader is referred to that excellent work, for an interesting account of him. Allen, also, 314, seems inclined to do him justice, and is more particular. It appears evident that he was rather wild in his views of religion, and went too far, perhaps, in persuading others to fall in with him. He came to Boston in 1636, from London, and was soon suspected of heresy, on which he was examined. But from his aptness in evading questions nothing was found against him. He went to Plymouth, but did not stay long there, having got into difficulty with their minister. From thence he went to Rhodeisland of his own accord; or as some say, was banished there. Here, it is said, he underwent corporeal punishment for his contempt of civil authority. Leaving this place he went to Providence in 1649, where he was very humanely treated by Mr. Roger Williams, who also had been banished on the score of tenets. He began a settlement at Patuxet, 4 or 5 miles south of Providence in 1641, but was soon complained of to the government of Massachusetts, for encroaching upon the lands of others. The Governour ordered him to answer to the same which he refused, treating the messenger with contempt. But he was arrested, carried to Boston and had his trial. A cruel sentence was passed upon him, being confined a whole winter at Charlestown in heavy irons, and then banished out of the colony. In 1644, he went to England, and in 1648, returned to his possessions by permission of parliament.

---

‡ Who these *two men* were I have not been able to ascertain. Mention is made in the histories of this war of messengers being sent, but in none more than two, and their names are not mentioned. Two were also sent from Massachusetts. See Hub. Nar. 72, 73. Hutch. I, 262. They were sent 16 June, 1675.

from the Governour of Plymouth to Philip. He observed to him further, that the young men were very eager to begin the war, and would fain have killed Mr. Brown, but Philip prevented it; telling them that his father had charged him to show kindness to Mr. Brown. In short, Philip was forced to promise them, that, on the next Lord's day, when the English were gone to meeting they should rifle their houses, and from that time forward, kill their cattle.

Peter desired Mr. Church to go and see his wife, who was but [just] up the hill;* he went and found but few of her people with her. She said they were all gone against her will to the dances, and she much feared [that] there would be a war. Mr. Church advised her to go to the island and secure herself, and those that were with her, and send to the Governour of Plymouth, who she knew was her friend; and so left her, resolving to hasten to Plymouth, and wait on the Governour. And he was so expeditious that he was with the Governour early next morning,† though he waited on some of the magistrates by the way, who were of the council of war, and also met him at the Governour's. He gave them an account of his observations and discoveries, which confirmed their former intelligences, and hastened their preparation for defence.

Philip, according to his promise to his people, permitted them to march out of the neck‡ on the next Lord's day,§ when they plundered the nearest hou-

---

liament. He was a minister, and a man of talents and ability. His defence against the charges in Morton's Memorial, shows him to be a man of learning, and is worthy perusing. It is in Hutchinson, Hist. Mas. I, 467 to 470. He lived to an advanced age, but the time of his death is not known.

* I conclude this hill to be that a little north of Howland's ferry.
† June 16.
‡ The neck on which Bristol and Warren now are, making the ancient Pokanoket.
§ June 20. See Trumbull, Hist. Con. I, 327. Ibid. U States, I, 139.

ses that the inhabitants had deserted, but as yet offered no violence to the people, at least none were killed.* However the alarm was given by their numbers and hostile equipage, and by the prey they made of what they could find in the forsaken houses. An express came the same day to the Governour,† who immediately gave orders to the captains of the towns, to march the greatest part of their companies, and to rendezvous at Taunton on Monday night,‡ where Major Bradford was to receive them, and dispose them under Captain (now made Major) Cutworth§ of Scituate. The Governour desired Mr. Church to give them his company, and to use his interest in their behalf, with the gentlemen of Rhode-island. He complied with it, and they marched the next day. Major Bradford desired Mr. Church, with a commanded party, consisting of English and some friend Indians, to march in the front at some distance from the main body. Their orders were to keep so far before as not to be in sight of the army. And so they did, for by the way they killed a deer, flayed, roasted, and eat the most of him before the army came up with them. But the Plymouth forces soon

---

* But an Indian was fired upon and wounded, which was a sufficient umbrage for them to begin the work. See Hub. Nar. 72, and Hutch. I, 261. It appears that Philip waited for the English to begin, and to that end, had suffered his men to provoke them to it; yet, it was thought that Philip tried to restrain them from beginning so soon, as is observed in note 1 to page 17. At this time a whimsical opinion prevailed, that the side which first began would finally be conquered. Hutch. Ibid.

† In consequence of this intelligence Governour Winslow proclaimed a fast. H. Adams, 120.

‡ June 21.

§ James Cudworth, several years a magistrate of Plymouth colony. Other historians style him Captain, but do not take notice of this advancement. See Hubbard, Nar. 75, 79, 84. Also in the continuation of Morton, 208, where it appears he was an assistant in the government between 1670 and 1675.

arrived at Swanzey,* and were chiefly posted at Major Brown's† and Mr. Miles'‡ garrisons, and were there soon joined with those that came from Massachusetts, who had entered into a confederacy with their Plymouth brethren against the perfidious heathens.

The enemy, who began their hostilities with plundering and destroying cattle,§ did not long content themselves with that game ; they thirsted for English blood, and they soon broached it ; killing two men in the way not far from Mr. Miles' garrison, and

---

* Whether the Plymouth forces were at Swanzey when the first English were killed does not appear, though it is presumed that they were not. We are certain that they had sufficient time to arrive there. It appears from the text that they marched from Plymouth on Monday, which was the 21 June, and the first English were killed the 24.

The author seems to be a little before his story concerning the Massachusetts' men, for we know that they did not arrive till the 28 June, and their arrival is related before the first men were killed.

Dr. Morse, in his late history of the Revolution, has run over this history without any regard to dates. Nor has he thought it worth his while to tell us there ever was such an author as Church, but copies from him as though it were his own work, which, at best he makes a mutilated mass.

† See note 5 on page 27.

‡ The Rev. John Miles, as I find in Allen, Biog. 429, was minister of the first Baptist church in Massachusetts ; that in 1649 he was a settled minister near Swansea in South Wales. Hence, perhaps, the name of Swanzey in Mass. is derived. Mr. Miles being ejected in 1662, came to this country, and formed a church at Rehoboth. He removed to Swanzey a few years after, which town was granted to the baptists by the government of Plymouth. Hutchinson, I, 209, speaks of him as a man discovering christian unity, &c. He died in 1683.

§ It appears that an Indian was wounded while in the act of killing cattle ; or as tradition informs us, the Indian who was wounded, after killing some animals in a man's field, went to his house and demanded liquor, and being refused attempted to take it by violence, threatening at the same time to be revenged for such usage, this caused the Englishman to fire on him.

soon after eight more* at Matapoiset:† Upon whose
bodies they exercised more than brutish barbarities;
beheading, dismembering and mangling them, and
exposing them in the most inhuman manner, which
gashed and ghostly objects struck a damp on all be-
holders.‡

The enemy flushed with these exploits, grew yet
bolder, and skulking every where in the bushes, shot
at all passengers, and killed many that ventured
abroad. They came so near as to shoot two sentinels at Mr. Miles' garrison, under the very noses
of our forces. These provocations drew out [—][1]
some of Captain Prentice's troops,§ who desired
they might have liberty to go out and seek the enemy in their own quarters. Quartermasters Gill and
Belcher‖ commanded the parties drawn out, who
earnestly desired Mr. Church's company. They provided him a horse and furniture, (his own being out of
the way.) He readily complied with their desires,
and was soon mounted. This party was no sooner
over Miles' bridge,¶ but were fired upon by an am-

[1] [the resentment of]

---

* It was the same day, 24 June, on Thursday, being a fast,
appointed by the Governour of Plymouth, on hearing what
took place the 20. See H. Adam's Hist. N. England, 120.
At Rehoboth a man was fired upon the same day. Hutchinson,
I, 261.

† (In Swanzey.)
Several places bore this name. The word is now generally pronounced Matapois. It appears too, that the pronunci
ation tended thus, at first, as I find it spelt in Winslow's Narrative, Matapuyst. See Belknap, Biog. II, 292.

‡ The sight must have been dreadful, but yet, it did not
hinder the English from the like foul deeds. Weetamore's
head was cut off and set upon a pole. See note 2 on page 27.

§ Capt. Thomas Prentice of the Boston troops. Twelve
was the number that went over at this time. Hubbard, 75
Hutchinson, I, 262.

‖ Hubbard, 75, calls him Corporal Belcher. He makes no
mention of any person by the name of Gill.

¶ There is a bridge over Palmer's river, which bears this
name. It is about 4 miles north of Warren.

buscade of about a dozen Indians, as they were afterward discovered to be. When they drew off, the pilot* was mortally wounded, Mr. Belcher received a shot in his knee, and his horse was killed under him. Mr. Gill was struck with a musket ball on the side of his body; but being clad with a buff coat,† and some thickness of paper under it, it never broke his skin.‡ The troopers were surprised to see both their commanders wounded and wheeled off; but Mr. Church persuaded, at length stormed and stamped, and told them it was a shame to run, and leave a wounded man there to become a prey to the barbarous enemy; for the pilot yet sat on his horse, though amazed with the shot as not to have sense to guide him. Mr. Gill seconded him, and offered, though much disabled, to assist in bringing him off. Mr. Church asked a stranger, who gave him his company in that action, if he would go with him and fetch off the wounded man. He readily consented, and they with Mr. Gill went; but the wounded man fainted, and fell off his horse before they came to him. But Mr. Church and the stranger dismounted, took up the man, dead, and laid him before Mr. Gill on his horse. Mr. Church told the other two, [that] if they would take care of the dead man, he would go and fetch his horse back, which was going off the causeway toward the enemy; but before he got over the causeway he saw the enemy run to the right into the neck. He brought back the horse, and called earnestly and repeatedly to the army to come over and fight the enemy; and while he stood calling and persuading, the skulking enemy returned to their old stand, and all discharged their guns at him at one clap; [and] though every shot missed him, yet, one

---

* William Hammond.

† A buff coat, and kind of cuirass or breastplate of iron or steel formed their armour; swords, carabines, and pistols, their weapons.

‡ June 28. This action took place the same day that the other troops arrived

of the army on the other side of the river, received one
of the balls in his foot. Mr. Church now began, (no
succour coming to him) to think it time to retreat.
Saying, "*The Lord have mercy on us,* if such a
handful of Indians shall thus dare such an army."*

Upon this it was immediately resolved, and orders
were given to march down into the neck,† and having passed the bridge and causeway, the direction
was to extend both wings, which not being well heed-
ed by those that remained in the centre, some of
them mistook their friends for their enemies,‡ and
made a fire upon them in the right wing, and wounded that noble heroick youth, Ensign Savage, in the
thigh,§ but it happily proved but a flesh wound. They
marched until they came to the narrow of the neck,
at a place called Keekamuit,‖ where they took down

---

* Thus ended the 28 June, 1675, according to Hubbard,
75 ; but by the text, the next transaction would seem under
the same date, which from the fact that most of the army did
not arrive until after noon, and that the action did not take
place until it had arrived, it is plain that it was not. Hutchinson, I, 262, is as indistinct with regard to the dates in
question, as our author, but Holmes considered it as I do.
Annals, I, 421. The next morning, Hubbard, 75, says, that
the Indians, at half a mile's distance, shouted twice or
thrice, and 9 or 10 showing themselves at the bridge, the
army immediately went in pursuit of them.

† June 29.

‡ I cannot find as any historian takes notice of this bad
management of the army. The reason is obvious as Hubbard says nothing of it, whom they all follow. Hence it appears that Savage was wounded by his own companions, and
not by 10 or 12 of the enemy discharging upon him at once.
See next note.

§ "He had at that time one bullet lodged in his thigh,
another shot through the brim of his hat, by ten or twelve
of the enemy discharging upon him together, while he boldly held up his colours in the front of his company."
Hubbard, 76. Our author or Mr. Hubbard is in a great
mistake about the manner in which he was wounded, but the
former ought not to be mistaken.

‖ (Upper part of Bristol.)
Now the upper part of Warren, which has been taken

the heads of eight Englishmen that were killed at the head of Matapoiset neck, and set upon poles, after the barbarous manner of those savages. There Philip had staved all his drums and conveyed all his canoes to the east side of Matapoiset river. Hence it was concluded by those, that were acquainted with the motions of those people, that they had quitted the neck. Mr. Church told them that Philip was doubtless gone over to Pocasset side to engage those Indians in a rebellion with him, which they soon found to be true. The enemy were not really beaten out of Mounthope neck, though it was true [that] they fled from thence; yet it was before any pursued them. It was but to strengthen themselves, and to gain a more advantageous post. However, some, and not a few, pleased themselves with the fancy of a mighty conquest.

A grand council was held, and a resolve passed, to build a fort there, to maintain the first ground they had gained, by the Indians leaving it to them. And to speak the truth, it must be said, that as they gained not that field by their sword, nor their bow, so it was rather their fear than their courage that obliged them to set up the marks of their conquest.*

Mr. Church looked upon it, and talked of it with contempt, and urged hard the pursuing [of] the enemy on Pocasset side; and with the greater earnestness; because of the promise made to Awashonks, before mentioned.

The council adjourned themselves from Mount-

---

from Bristol. It is called on the map of Rhodeisland, Kickemuet, or rather the bay which makes this neck on one side, is so called. Warren river makes the other side.

*Major Savage and Major Cudworth commanded the forces in this expedition, at whom, of course, this reflection is directed. But chiefly, I suppose, at Major Cudworth: For I find, Hubbard, 79, that Captain Cudworth, as he denominates him, "left a garrison of 40 men upon Mounthope neck," which is all that he says about this fort.

hope to Rehoboth,* where Mr. Treasurer Southworth, being weary of his charge of Commissary
General, (provision being scarce and difficult to
be obtained for the army,† that now lay still to cover the people from nobody, while they were building a fort for nothing) retired, and the power and
trouble of that post was left to Mr. Church, who
still urged the commanding officers to move over to
Pocasset side, to pursue the enemy and kill Philip,
which would in his opinion be more probable to keep
possession of the neck, than to tarry to build a fort.‡

He was still restless on that side of the river, and
the rather, because of his promise to the squaw Sachem of Sogkonate. And Captain Fuller§ also urged the same, until at length there came further or-

---

* A town in Massachusetts, about 10 miles from where they then were, and about 38 from Boston.

† Hubbard says, 77, that the forces under Major Savage returned to Swanzey, and those under Capt. Cudworth pass-
ed over to Rhodeisland the same day, as the weather looked likely to be tempestuous, and that night there fell abundance of rain. But it is presumed that Captain Cudworth soon returned to build said fort, as he arrived at Swanzey the 5 July.

‡ While these things were passing, Capt. Hutchinson was despatched with a letter from the Governour of Massachusetts, bearing date July 4, 1675, constituting him commis-
sioner to treat with the Narragansets, who now seem openly to declare for Philip. He arrived the 5 at Swanzey, and on the 6, a consultation was held, wherein it was resolved "to treat with the Narragansets sword in hand." Accordingly the forces marched into their country, and after several cere-
monious days, a treaty, as long as it was useless, was signed on the 15. It may be seen at large in Hubbard, Nar. 81 to 83, and Hutchinson, I, 263, 264. By which the Narragan-
sets agreed, to harbour none of Philip's people, &c.; all which was only forced upon them, and they regarded it no longer than the army was present. The army then returned to Taunton, 17 June.

§ I learn nothing more of this gentleman than is found in this history. The name is common in Massachusetts and elsewhere. He had 6 files each containing 6 men, therefore their whole number consisted of 36 men only.

ders* concerning the fort, and withal an order for Captain Fuller with six files to cross the river to the side so much insisted on, and to try if he could get speech with any of the Pocasset or Sogkonate Indians, and that Mr. Church should go [as] his second.

Upon the Captain's receiving his orders, he asked Mr. Church whether he were willing to engage in this enterprise; to whom it was indeed too agreeable to be declined; though he thought the enterprise was hazardous enough for them to have [had] more men assigned them. Captain Fuller told him, that for his own part, he was grown ancient and heavy, [and] he feared the travel and fatigue would be too much for him. But Mr. Church urged him, and told him [that] he would cheerfully excuse him his hardship and travel, and take that part to himself, if he might but go; for he had rather do any thing in the world, than to stay there to build the fort.

Then they drew out the number assigned them, and marched the same night† to the ferry,‡ and were

---

* From Major Cudworth, who did not go with the rest of the army into the country of the Narragansets. Hub. 84.

† No author that I have seen, excepting Mr. Hubbard, fixes any date to this memorable part of Philip's War. Neither Hutchinson nor Trumbull takes any notice of it. Hubbard, 84, says, "Upon Thursday, July 7, Captain Fuller and Lieutenant Church went into Pocasset to seek after the enemy," &c. But he is in an errour about the day of the week or month, and perhaps both; for I find that the 7 July falls on Wednesday; an errour which might easily have happened in some former edition of his Narrative. Though this scrutiny may seem unimportant, yet, the transaction, it must be allowed, merits particular attention; for history without chronology may be compared to the trackless desert over which we may wander in vain for relief. Most authors since Mr. Hubbard's time, pass lightly over this event, and either think it not worth fixing a date to, or doubting the authority of Mr. Hubbard. But I am induced to believe, that the day of the month is right, and that the day of the week is wrong. If this be the case, we are able to fix the date of the battle of the Peasfield on July 8.

‡ Bristol ferry.

transported to Rhodeisland, from whence, the next
night they got passage over to Pocasset side in Rhodeisland boats, and concluded there to dispose themselves in two ambuscades before day, hoping to surprise some of the enemy by their falling into one or
other of their ambushments. But Captain Fuller's
party being troubled with the *epidemical* plague of
lust after tobacco, must needs strike fire to smoke
it.* And thereby discovered themselves to a party
of the enemy coming up to them, who immediately
fled with great precipitation.

This ambuscade drew off about break of day, perceiving [that] they were discovered, the other continued in their post until the time assigned them,
and the light and heat of the sun rendered their sta-
tion both insignificant and troublesome, and then returned unto the place of rendezvous; where they
were acquainted with the other party's disappointment, and the occasion of it. Mr. Church calls for
the breakfast he had ordered to be brought over in
the boat, but the man that had the charge of it, confessed that he was asleep when the boat's men called him, and in haste came away and never thought
of it. It happened that Mr. Church had a few cakes
of rusk in his pocket, that Madam Cranston, † (the

---

* It is customary with many to this day in Rhodeisland, to
use this phrase. If a person tells another that he smoked tobacco at any particular time, he will say that he *smoked it*,
or "*I have smokt it.*"

† I am sorry to acknowledge the want of information of so
conspicuous a character as a Governour of Rhodeisland, but
the histories of Newengland do not tell us there ever was
such a Governour. Probably the town of Cranston perpetu-
ates his name. From Allen, Biog. 196, it appears that Mr.
William Coddington was Governour this year, 1675; yet
there may be no mistake in the text, though this name has
been written with variation. From Trumbull's Conn. I,
356, I find that "JOHN CRANSTON, Esq., Governour of
Rhodeisland, [in 1679] held a court in Narraganset, in September, and made attempts to introduce the authority and
officers of Rhodeisland, into that part of Connecticut. The
general assembly therefore, in October, protested against

Governour's Lady of Rhodeisland) gave him when he came off the island, which he divided among the company, which was all the provisions they had.

Mr. Church after their slender breakfast, proposed to Captain Fuller, that he would march in quest of the enemy, with such of the company as would be willing to march with him, which he complied with, though with a great deal of scruple; because of his small numbers, and the extreme hazard he foresaw must attend them.*

But some of the company reflected upon Mr. Church, that notwithstanding his talk on the other side of the river, he had not shown them any Indians since they came over; which now moved him to tell them, that, if it were their desire to see Indians, he believed he should now soon show them what they should say was enough.

The number allowed him† soon drew off to him, which could not be many; because their whole company consisted of no more than thirty-six.

They moved towards Sogkonate, until they came to the brook‡ that runs into Nunnaquahqat§ neck where they discovered a fresh and plain track, which

---

nis usurpation, and declared his acts to be utterly void." Thus the spirit of feeling between the two colonies at this period is discovered.

*Captain Fuller had not proceeded far, before he fell in with a large number of the enemy, but fortunately he was in the vicinity of the water, and more fortunately, near an old house, in which he sheltered himself and men until a vessel discovered and conveyed them off, with no other loss, than having two men wounded. He had 17 men in his company.

† Nineteen. Hubbard, 85, says, that Mr. Church had not above 15 men.

‡ This brook is that which empties into the bay nearly a mile southward from Howland's ferry. The road to Little Compton, here, follows the shore of the bay, and crosses said brook where it meets the bay.

§ Now called Quaucut, a small strait near the brook just mentioned.

they concluded to be from the great pine swamp, about a mile from the road that leads to Sogkonate. "Now," says Mr. Church, to his men, "if we follow this track, no doubt but we shall soon see Indians enough." They expressed their willingness to follow the track, and moved [on] in it; but [they] had not gone far, before one of them narrowly escaped being bit with a rattlesnake; and the woods that the track led them through was haunted much with those snakes, which the little company seemed more to be afraid of, than the black serpents they were in quest of; and therefore bent their course another way to a place where they thought it probable to find some of the enemy. Had they kept the track to the pine swamp, they had been certain of meeting Indians enough, but not so certain that any of them should have returned to give [an] account how many.

Now they passed down into Punkatees* neck, and in their march discovered a large wigwam full of Indian truck, which the soldiers were for loading themselves with, until Mr. Church forbid it; telling them they might expect soon to have their hands full and business without caring for plunder. Then crossing the head of the creek into the neck, they again discovered fresh Indian tracks; [which had] very lately passed before them into the neck. They then got privately and undiscovered unto the fence of Captain Almy's† peas field, and divided into two parties; Mr. Church keeping the one party with

---

* A point of land running south nearly two miles between the bay and Little Compton, and a little more than a mile wide. On Lockwood's map of Rhodeisland it is called Puncatest. It is the southern extremity of Tiverton, and has been known by the name of Pocasset neck.

† Captain John Almy, who lived on Rhodeisland; the same, I presume, mentioned in the beginning of this history. The land is now owned by people of the same name, and Mr. Sanford Almy, an aged gentleman, lives near the spot.

himself, sent the other with Lake,* who was acquainted with the ground, on the other side. Two Indians were soon discovered coming out of the peas field towards them, when Mr. Church and those that were with him, concealed themselves from them by falling flat on the ground, but the other division, not using the same caution, was seen by the enemy, which occasioned them to run, which, when Mr. Church perceived, he showed himself to them, and called; telling them he desired but to speak with them, and would not hurt them. But they ran and Church pursued. The Indians climbed over a fence, and one of them facing about, discharged his piece, but without effect, on the English. One of the English soldiers ran up to the fence and fired upon him that had discharged his piece, and they concluded by the yelling they heard, that the Indian was wounded. But the Indians soon got into the thickets, whence they saw them no more for the present.

Mr. Church then marching over a plane piece of ground where the woods were very thick on one side, ordered his little company to march at a double distance to make as big a show, (if they should be discovered,) as might be. But before they saw any body they were saluted with a volley of fifty or sixty guns. Some bullets came very surprisingly near Mr. Church, who starting, looked behind him to see what was become of his men, expecting to have seen half of them dead; but seeing them all upon their legs, and briskly firing at the smokes of the enemies' guns; (for that was all that was then to be seen.)† He blessed God, and called to his men

---

* As the name of Lake is not mentioned any where else in this history, I cannot determine who this was.

† This was indeed very remarkable, as it appears that nothing prevented the Indians from taking deliberate aim. The truth of the text must not be doubted, but certainly Jove never worked a greater miracle in favour of the Trojans at the siege of Troy, than Hesper now did for our heroes.

not to discharge all their guns at once, lest the enemy should take the advantage of such an opportunity to run upon them with their hatchets.

Their next motion was immediately into the pea field.* When they came to the fence, Mr. Church bid as many as had not discharged their guns to clap under the fence and lie close, while the others, at some distance in the field, stood to charge ; hoping, that if the enemy should creep to the fence, (to gain a shot at those that were charging their guns,) they might be surprised by those that lie under the fence. But casting his eyes to the side of the hill above them, the hill seemed to move, being covered over with Indians, with their bright guns glittering in the sun, and running in a circumference with a design to surround them.

Seeing such multitudes surrounding him and his little company, it put him upon thinking what was become of the boats that were ordered to attend him, and looking up, he spied them ashore at Sandy-point,† on the island side of the river,‡ with a number of horse and foot by them, and wondered what should be the occasion ; until he was afterwards informed that the boats had been over that morning from the island, and had landed a party of men at Fogland, that were designed in Punkatees neck to fetch off some cattle and horses, but were am-

---

* (Tiverton shore about half a mile above Fogland ferry.) The situation of Punkatees is given in a preceding note. It contains nearly two square miles, and it is sufficient to know that it contained the ground on which this battle was fought.

† There are two Sandy points on the Rhodeisland shore, one above and the other below Fogland ferry; this was that above. Fogland ferry connects the island with Punkatees and is near the middle of it.

‡ The bay is meant. It being narrow, or from three fourths to a mile wide, is sometimes called a river, and in the old charters, Narraganset river. See Douglass, I, 398.

buscaded, and many of them wounded by the enemy.*

Now our gentleman's courage and conduct were both put to the test. He encouraged his men, and orders some to run and take a wall for shelter before the enemy gained it. It was time for them now to think of escaping if they knew which way. Mr. Church orders his men to strip to their white shirts, that the islanders might discover them to be Englishmen, and then orders three guns to be fired distinctly, hoping [that] it might be observed by their friends on the opposite shore. The men that were ordered to take the wall being very hungry, stopped a while among the peas to gather a few, being about four rods from the wall. The enemy from behind, hailed them with a shower of bullets. But soon all but one came tumbling over an old-hedge, down the bank, where Mr. Church and the rest were, and told him, that his brother, B. Southworth,† who was the man that was missing, was killed; that they saw him fall. And so they did indeed see him fall, but it was without a shot, and lay no longer than till he had an opportunity to clap a bullet into one of the enemies' foreheads, and then came running to his company.

The meanness of the English powder was now their greatest misfortune. When they were immediately upon this beset with multitudes of Indians, who possessed themselves of every rock, stump, tree or fence, that was in sight, firing upon them without

---

* It is mentioned in a later part of this history, that Mr. Church's servant was wounded at Pocasset, while there after cattle. This is the time alluded to. Hubbard, 86, says that " five men coming from Rhodeisland, to look up their cattle upon Pocasset neck, were assaulted by the same Indians; one of the five was Captain Church's servant, who had his leg broken in the skirmish, the rest hardly escaping with their lives;" and, that " this was the first time that ever any mischief was done by the Indians upon Pocasset neck." This was on the same day of the battle of Punkatees.

† Brother in law to Mr. Church.

ceasing; while they had no other shelter but a small bank, and bit of a water fence.* And yet, to add to the disadvantage of this little handful of distressed men, the Indians also possessed themselves of the ruins of a stone house, that overlooked them. So that, now, they had no way to prevent lying quite open to some or other of the enemy, but to heap up stones before them, as they did; and still bravely and wonderfully defended themselves against all the numbers of the enemy.

At length came over one of the boats from the island shore, but the enemy plied their shot so warmly to her, as made her keep at some distance. Mr. Church desired them to send their canoe ashore, to fetch them on board; but no persuasions nor arguments could prevail with them to bring their canoe to shore; which some of Mr. Church's men perceiving, began to cry out, for God's sake to take them off, for their ammunition was spent! &c. Mr. Church being sensible of the danger of the enemy's hearing their complaints, and being made acquainted with the weakness and scantiness of their ammunition, fiercely called to the boat's master, and bid him either send his canoe ashore, or else be gone presently, or he would fire upon him.

Away goes the boat, and leaves them still to shift for themselves. But then another difficulty arose; the enemy, seeing the boat leave them, were reanimated, and fired thicker and faster than ever. Upon which, some of the men, that were lightest of foot, began to talk of attempting an escape by flight, until Mr. Church solidly convinced them of the impracticableness of it, and encouraged them yet. [He] told them, that he had observed so much of the remarkable, and wonderful providence of God, [in]

---

* This indeed will compare with Lovewell's Fight. That hero, to prevent being quite encompassed, retreated to the shore of a pond The particulars of which will be found in the continuation of this history. See Appendix, XI.

hitherto preserving them, that it encouraged him to believe, with much confidence, that God would yet preserve them ; that not a hair of their heads should fall to the ground ; bid them be patient, courageous, and prudently sparing of their ammunition, and he made no doubt but they should come well off yet, &c. [Thus] until his little army again resolved, one and all, to stay with, and stick by him. One of them, by Mr. Church's order, was pitching a flat stone up on end before him in the sand, when a bullet from the enemy with a full force, struck the stone while he was pitching it on end, which put the poor fellow to a miserable start, till Mr. Church called upon him to observe how God directed the bullets, that the enemy could not hit him when in the same place, [and] yet could hit the stone as it was erected.

While they were thus making the best defence they could against their numerous enemies, that made the woods ring with their constant yelling and shouting. And night coming on, somebody told Mr. Church, [that] they spied a sloop up the river as far as Goldisland,* that seemed to be coming down towards them. He looked up and told them, that, succour was now coming, for he believed it was Captain Golding,† whom he knew to be a man for business, and would certainly fetch them off if he came. The wind being fair, the vessel was soon with them, and Captain Golding it was. Mr. Church (as soon as they came to speak with one another) desired him to come to anchor at such a distance from the shore, that he might veer out his cable, and ride afloat; and let slip his canoe, that it might

---

* A very small ledgy island a little to the south of the stone bridge, near the middle of the stream, and about 4 or 5 miles from where they were.

† I find nothing relating to this gentleman excepting what is found in this history. We may infer that he was a man of worth and confidence, by Mr. Church's entrusting him with an important post at the fight when Philip was killed.

drive a shore; which directions Captain Golding observed. But the enemy gave him such a warm salute, that his sails, colours and stern were full of bullet holes.

The canoe came ashore, but was so small that she would not bear above two men at a time; and when two were got aboard they turned her loose to drive a shore for two more. And the sloop's company kept the Indians in play the while. But when at last it came to Mr. Church's turn to go aboard, he had left his hat and cutlass at the well, where he went to drink when he first came down; he told his company, [that] he would never go off and leave his hat and cutlass for the Indians, [that] they should never have that to reflect upon him. Though he was much dissuaded from it, yet he would go and fetch them. He put all the powder he had left into his gun, (and a poor charge it was) and went presenting his gun at the enemy, until he took up what he went for. At his return he discharged his gun at the enemy, to bid them farewell for that time; but had not powder enough to carry the bullet half way to them. Two bullets from the enemy struck the canoe as he went on board, one grazed the hair of his head a little before, another stuck in a small stake that stood right against the middle of his breast.*

Now this gentleman with his *army*, making in all twenty men, himself and his pilot being numbered with them, got all safe on board, after six hours engagement with three hundred Indians; [of] whose numbers we were told afterwards by some of them-

---

* The lofty and elegant lines of Barlow, on the conduct of Gen. Putnam at the battle of Bunker's hill, will admirably apply to our hero.

"There strides bold Putnam, and from all the plains
Calls the tired troops, the tardy rear sustains,
And mid the whizzing balls that skim the lowe
Waves back his sword, defies the following foe."

Columbiad, B. V. 562, &c.

selves.* A deliverance which that good gentleman often mentions to the glory of God, and his protecting providence.

The next day,† meeting with the rest of his little company,‡ whom he had left at Pocasset, (that had also a small skirmish with the Indians and had two men wounded) they returned to the Mounthope garrison, which Mr. Church used to call the losing fort.

Mr. Church then returned to the island, to seek provision for the army. [There he] meets with Alderman,§ a noted Indian, that was just come over from the squaw Sachem's cape of Pocasset, having deserted from her, and brought over his family, who gave him an account of the state of the Indians, and where each of the Sagamore's headquarters was. Mr. Church then discoursed with some, who knew the spot well, where the Indians said Weetamore's‖ headquarters were, and offered their service to pilot him [to it.]

With this news he hastened to the Mounthope garrison, [and] the army expressed their readiness to embrace such an opportunity.

All the ablest soldiers were now immediately drawn off, equipped and despatched upon this design, under the command of a certain officer.¶ And having marched about two miles, viz., until they came to

---

* Hubbard 85, says that there were seven or eight scores. Mather, following him, says there were "an hundred and almost five times fifteen terrible Indians." Magnalia, II, 488.

† July 19.

‡ On Rhodeisland. Mr. Church and his company were transported there, as were Capt. Fuller and his company before. See note 1 on page 39.

§ The Indian that killed Philip

‖ (Squaw Sachem of Pocasset.) An account of this "old Queen" has been given. See note 2 on page 27.

¶ I have not learned this officer's name, but it was Capt. Henchman's Lieutenant.

the cove that lies southwest from the Mount where orders were given for a halt. The commander in chief told them [that] he thought it proper to take advice before he went any further; called Mr. Church and the pilot and asked them how they knew that Philip and all his men were not by that time got to Weetamore's camp; or that all her own men were not by that time returned to her again, with many more frightful questions. Mr. Church told him [that] they had acquainted him with as much as they knew, and that for his part he could discover nothing that need to discourage them from proceeding; that he thought it so practicable, that he with the pilot, would willingly lead the way to the spot, and hazard the brunt. But the chief commander insisted on this, that the enemy's numbers were so great, and he did not know what numbers more might be added unto them by that time; and his company so small, that he could not think it practicable to attack them; adding moreover, that if he were sure of killing all the enemy and knew that he must lose the life of one of his men in the action, he would not attempt it. "Pray sir, then," replied Mr. Church, [—][1] "lead your company to yonder windmill on Rhodeisland, and there they will be out of danger of being killed by the enemy, and we shall have less trouble to supply them with provisions."* But return he would and did unto the garrison until more strength came to them, and a sloop to transport them to Fallriver,† in order to visit Weetamore's camp.

[1] [Please to.]

---

*The action related in the next paragraph was not until they returned; though it might be understood that Church went " out on a discovery" before.

† (South part of Freetown.)
It is in the town of Troy, which was taken from Freetown. Fallriver is a local name, derived from a stream that empties into the bay about a mile above Tiverton line. Probably no place in the United States contains so many factories in so small a compass as this.

Mr. Church, one Baxter, and Captain Hunter, an Indian, proffered to go out on the discovery on the left wing, which was accepted. They had not marched above a quarter of a mile before they started three of the enemy. Captain Hunter wounded one of them in the knee, who when he came up [to him] he discovered to be his near kinsman. The captive desired favour for his squaw, if she should fall into their hands, but asked none for himself; excepting the liberty of taking a whiff of tobacco; and while he was taking his whiff his kinsman, with one blow of his hatchet, despatched him.

Proceeding to Weetamore's camp they were discovered by one of the enemy, who ran in and gave information. Upon which a lusty young fellow left his meat upon his spit,* running hastily out, told his companions [that] he would kill an Englishman before he ate his dinner; but failed of his design; being no sooner out than shot down. The enemies' fires, and what shelter they had, were by the edge of a thick cedar swamp, into which on this alarm they betook themselves, and the English as nimbly pursued; but were soon commanded back by their chieftain, [but not until][1] they were come within [the] hearing of the cries of their women and children; and so ended that exploit. But returning to their sloop the enemy pursued them, and wounded two of their men. The next day they returned to the Mounthope garrison.†

[1] [after]

---

*(Probably a wooden spit.)

† These operations took up about four or five days, hence we have arrived to the 13 or 14 July. In the course of which time, fourteen or fifteen of the enemy were killed. See Hubbard, 87. Holmes, I, 422. These individual efforts were of far more consequence than the manœuvres of the main army during the same time; yet Hutchinson, H. Adams, and some others since, thought them not worth mentioning.

C

PHILIP'S WAR.

Soon after this was Philip's headquarters visited[*] by some other English forces, but Philip, and his gang had the very fortune to escape, that Weetamore and hers (but now mentioned) had. They took into a swamp, and their pursuers were commanded back.

After this Dartmouth's[†] distresses required succour, [a] great part of the town being laid desolate, and many of the inhabitants killed. The most of Ply-

---

[*] A particular account of this affair from our author, would have been gratifying. But most other historians before and since him, have been elaborate upon it.

In consequence of the intelligence gained by Mr. Church, the army, after finishing the treaty with the Narragansets, before named, moved to Taunton, where they arrived the 17 July, in the evening; and on the 18, marched to attack Philip, who was now in a great swamp, adjacent to, and on the east side of Taunton river. The army did not arrive until late in the day, but soon entered resolutely into the swamp. The underwood was thick, and the foe could not be seen. The first that entered were shot down, but the rest rushing on, soon forced them from their hiding places, and took possession of their wigwams, about 100 in number. Night coming on, each was in danger from his fellow; firing at every bush that seemed to shake. A retreat was now ordered. Concluding that Philip was safely hemmed in, the Massachusetts forces marched to Boston, and the Connecticut troops, being the greatest sufferers, returned home; leaving those of Plymouth to starve out the enemy. Trumbull's Connecticut, I, 332. Ibid. U. S. I, 140. This movement of the army has been very much censured. Had they pressed upon the enemy the next day, it is thought they would have been easily subdued. But Philip and his warriours, on the 1 August, before day, passed the river on rafts, and in great triumph, marched off into the country of the Nipmucks. About 16 of the English were killed. Ibid. Mather, II, 488, says that Philip left a hundred of his people behind who fell into the hands of the English. It is said that Philip had a brother killed in this fight, who was a chief Captain, and had been educated at Harvard College. Hutch. I, 265.

[†] That part of Dartmouth which was destroyed is about 5 miles S. W. from Newbedford, and known by the name of Aponaganset. The early histories give us no particulars about the affair, and few mention it at all. Many of the inhabitants moved to Rhodeisland. Middleborough, then called Nemasket, about this time was mostly burned; probably, while the treaty was concluding with the Narragansets.

mouth forces were ordered thither. And coming to Russell's garrison* at Ponaganset,† they met with a number of the enemy, that had surrendered themselves prisoners on terms promised by Captain Eels of the garrison, and Ralph Earl,‡ who persuaded them (by a friend Indian he had employed) to come in. And had their promise to the Indians been kept, and the Indians fairly treated, it is probable that,

---

* The cellars of this old garrison are still to be seen. They are on the north bank of Aponaganset about a mile from its mouth. I was informed by an inhabitant on the spot, that considerable manœuvring went on here in those days. The Indians had a fort on the opposite side of the river, and used to show themselves, and act all manner of mockery, to aggravate the English; they being at more than a common gunshot off. At one time one made his appearance, and turned his backside in defiance, as usual; but some one having an uncommonly long gun fired upon him and put an end to his mimickry.

A similar story is told by the people of Middleborough, which took place a little north of the town house, across the Nemasket. The distance of the former does not render the story so improbable as that of the latter, but circumstances are more authentick. The gun is still shown which performed the astonishing feat. The distance, some say is nearly half a mile, which is considerable ground of improbability. That a circumstance of this kind occurred at both these places, too, is a doubt. But it is true that a fight did take place across the river at Middleborough. The Indians came to the river and burned a grist mill which stood near the present site of the lower factory, and soon after drew off. The affair has been acted over by the inhabitants as a celebration not many years since.

† (In Dartmouth.)
The word is generally pronounced as it is spelled in the text, but is always, especially of late, written Aponaganset. Mr. Douglass, it appears learned this name Polyganset, when he took a survey of the country. See his Summary, I, 403.

‡ I can find no mention of these two gentlemen in any of the histories. But their names are sufficiently immortalized by their conduct in opposing the diabolical acts of government for selling prisoners as slaves. It is possible that they might decline serving any more in the war, after being so much abused; and hence were not noticed by the historians, who also pass over this black page of our history as lightly as possible.

most, if not all, the Indians in those parts had soon followed the example of those, who had now surrendered themselves, which would have been a good step towards finishing the war. But in spite of all that Captain Eels, Church or Earl could say, argue, plead or beg, somebody else that had more power in their hands, improved it. And without any regard to the promises made them on their surrendering themselves, they were carried away to Plymouth, there sold, and transported out of the country, being about eight score persons.* An action so hateful to Mr. Church, that he opposed it, to the loss of the good will and respects of some that before were his good friends.

But while these things were acting at Dartmouth, Philip made his esaape;† leaving his country, fled over Taunton river, and Rehoboth plain, and Patuxet‡ river, where Captain Edmunds§ of Providence, made some spoil upon him, and had probably done more, but was prevented by the coming of a superiour officer, that put him by.‖

---

*With regret it is mentioned that the venerable John Winthrop was Governour of Connecticut, (Connecticut and Newhaven now forming but one colony) the Hon. John Leverett of Massachusetts, and the Hon. Josiah Winslow of Plymouth. Rhodeisland, because they chose freedom rather than *slavery*, had not been admitted into the Union. From this history it would seem that one Cranston was Governour of Rhodeisland at this time; but that colony appears not to be implicated in this as well as many other acts of maleadministration. See note 2 on page 38.

† An account of which is given in note 1, page 50.

‡ Douglass wrote this word Patuket, as it is now pronounced. Summary, I, 400. It is now often written Patuxet. It is Blackstone river, or was so called formerly.

§ I find no other account of this officer in the Indian wars, only what is hinted at in this history; from which it appears that he was more than once employed, and was in the eastern war.

‖ Hubbard, 91, says that Philip had about thirty of his party killed; but he takes no notice of Capt. Edmunds' being *put by*. He said that Capt. Henchman came up to them,

PHILIP'S WAR. 53

And now another fort was built at Pocasset,* that proved as troublesome and chargeable as that at Mounthope; and the remainder of the summer was improved in providing for the forts and forces there maintained; while our enemies were fled some hundreds of miles into the country near as far as Albany.†

---

but not till the skirmish was over. "But why Philip was followed no further," he says, is better to suspend than too critically to inquire into." Hence we may conclude that the pursuit was countermanded by Capt. Henchman, who when too late followed after the enemy without any success.

* The fort here meant was built to prevent Philip's escape from the swamp before mentioned. See note 1, on page 50. Mr. Church appears early to have seen the folly of fort building under such circumstances. While that at Mounthope was building, he had seen Philip gaining time; and while this was building to confine him to a swamp, he was marching off in triumph.

† Here appears a large chasm in our history including about four months, namely, from the escape of Philip on the 1 August, to December; during which time many circumstances transpired worthy of notice, and necessary to render this history more perfect. Mr. Church appears to have quitted the war, and is, perhaps, with his family.

Philip having taken up his residence among the Nipmucks or Nipnets, did not fail to engage them in his cause.

On the 14 July a party killed 4 or 5 people at Mendon a town 37 miles southwest of Boston.

August 2, Capt. Hutchinson with 20 horsemen went to renew the treaty with those Indians at a place appointed, near Quabaog, (now Brookfield) a town about 60 miles nearly west from Boston; but on arriving at the place appointed, the Indians did not appear. So he proceeded 4 or 5 miles beyond, towards their chief town, when all at once, some hundreds of them fired upon the company. Eight were shot down, and eight others were wounded. Among the latter was Capt. Hutchinson who died soon after. The remainder escaped to Quabaog, and the Indians pursued them. But the English arrived in time to warn the inhabitants of the danger, who with themselves crowded into one house. The other houses (about 20) were immediately burned down. They next besieged the house containing the inhabitants (about 70) and the soldiers. This they exerted themselves to fire also,

And now strong suspicions began to arise of the Narraganset* Indians, that they were ill affected and

with various success for two days, and on the third they nearly effected their object by a stratagem. They filled a cart with combustibles and set it on fire, and by means of splicing poles together had nearly brought the flames in contact with the house, when Major Willard arrived with 48 dragoons and dispersed them. See American Ann. I, 423, 424.

The Indians about Hadley, who had hitherto kept up the show of friendship, now deserted their dwellings and drew off after Philip. Toward the last of August, Capt. Beers and Capt. Lothrop pursued and overtook them, and a fierce battle was fought, in which 10 of the English and 26 Indians were killed.

September 1, they burned Deerfield and killed one of the inhabitants. The same day (being a fast) they fell upon Hadley while the people were at meeting, at which they were overcome with confusion. At this crisis, a venerable gentleman in singular attire appeared among them, and putting himself at their head, rushed upon the Indians and dispersed them, then disappeared. The inhabitants thought an angel had appeared, and led them to victory. But it was General Goffe, one of the Judges of King Charles I, who was secreted in the town. See President Stiles' history of the Judges, 109, and Holmes, I, 424.

About 11 September Capt. Beers with 36 men went up the river to observe how things stood at a new plantation called Squakeag, now Northfield. The Indians a few days before (but unknown to them) had fallen upon the place and killed 9 or 10 persons, and now laid in ambush for the English, whom it appears they expected. They had to march nearly 30 miles through a hideous forest. On arriving within three miles of the place, they were fired upon by a host of enemies, and a large proportion of their number fell. The others gained an eminence and fought bravely till their Captain was slain, when they fled in every direction. Sixteen only escaped. Hubbard, 107.

On the 18th following, as Capt. Lothrop with 80 men was guarding some carts from Deerfield to Hadley, they were fallen

---

*It was believed that the Indians generally returned from the western frontier along the Connecticut, and took up their winter quarters among the Narragansets; but whether Philip did is uncertain. Some suppose that he visited the Mohawks and Canada Indians for assistance.

designed mischief. And so the event soon discovered. The next winter they began their hostilities upon the English. The united colonies then agreed to send an army to suppress them: Governour Winslow to command the army.*

He undertaking the expedition, invited Mr. Church to command a company, [—]¹ which he declined;

¹ [in the expedition]

---

fallen upon, and, including teamsters, 90 were slain; 7 or 8 only escaped. Ibid. 108.

October 5, the Springfield Indians having been joined by about 300 of Philip's men began the destruction of Springfield. But the attack being expected, Major Treat was sent for, who was then at Westfield, and arrived in time to save much of the town from the flames, but, 32 houses were consumed. Holmes, I, 425.

October 19, Hatfield was assaulted on all sides by 7 or 800 Indians, but there being a considerable number of men well prepared to receive them, obliged them to flee without doing much damage. A few out buildings were burned, and some of the defenders killed, but we have no account how many. Holmes, I. 425, says this affair took place at Hadley; but Hubbard whom he cites, 116, says it was at Hatfield. The places are only separated by a bridge over the Connecticut, and were formerly included under the same name.

Mr. Hoyt in his Antiquarian Researches, 136, thinks that it was in this attack that Gen. Goffe made his appearance, because Mr. Hubbard takes no notice of an attack upon that place in Sept. 1675, which, if there had been one, it would not have escaped his notice. But this might have been unnoticed by Mr. Hubbard as well as some other affairs of the war.

Thus are some of the most important events sketched in our hero's absence, and we may now add concerning him what Homer did of Achilles' return to the siege of Troy.

Then great Achilles, terror of the plain,
Long lost to battle, shone in arms again.
Iliad, II, B. XX, 57.

*It was to consist of 1000 men and what friendly Indians would join them. Massachusetts was to furnish 527, Plymouth 158, Connecticut 315. Major Robert Treat with those of Connecticut, Major Bradford with those of Plymouth, and Major Samuel Appleton with those of Massachusetts. The whole under Gen. Josiah Winslow. American Annals, I, 426.

craving excuse from taking [a] commission, [but] he promises to wait upon him as a Reformado [a volunteer] through the expedition. Having rode with the General to Boston, and from thence to Rehoboth, upon the General's request he went thence the nearest way over the ferries, with Major Smith,* to his garrison in the Narraganset country, to prepare and provide for the coming of General Winslow, who marched round through the country with his army proposing by night to surprise Pumham,† a certain Narraganset sachem, and his town; but being aware of the approach of our army, made their escape into the deserts‡. But Mr. Church meeting with fair winds, arrived safe at the Major's garrison in the evening,§ and soon began to inquire after the enemy's resorts, wigwams or sleeping places; and having gained some intelligence, he proposed to the Eldridges and some other brisk hands that he met with, to attempt the surprising of some of the enemy, to make a present of, to the General, when he should arrive, which might advantage his design. Being brisk blades they readily complied with the motion, and were soon upon their march. The night was very cold, but blessed with the moon. Before

---

*This gentleman, Mr. Hubbard informs us, Nar. 128, lived in Wickford where the army was to take up its head-quarters. Wickford is about 9 miles N. W. from Newport on Narraganset bay.

† (Sachem of Shawomot or Warwick.)
This Sachem had signed the treaty in July, wherein such great faith and fidelity were promised. See note 3 on page 36. A few days before the great swamp fight at Narraganset Capt. Prentice destroyed his town after it was deserted. But in July, 1676, he was killed by some of the Massachusetts men, near Dedham. A grandson of his was taken before this, by a party under Capt. Denison, who was esteemed the best soldier and most warlike of all the Narraganset chiefs. Trumbull, I, 345.

‡ It appears that all did not escape into the deserts. The heroick Capt. Mosely captured 36 on his way to Wickford.

§ December 11.

the day broke they effected their exploit; and, by
the rising of the sun, arrived at the Major's garrison,
where they met the general, and presented him with
eighteen of the enemy, [which] they had captivated.
The General, pleased with the exploit, gave them
thanks particularly to Mr. Church, the mover and
chief actor of the business. And sending two of
them (likely boys) [as] a present to Boston; [and]
smiling on Mr. Church, told him, that he made no
doubt but his faculty would supply them with Indian
boys enough before the war was ended.

Their next move was to a swamp,* which the Indians had fortified with a fort.† Mr. Church rode in
the General's guard when the bloody engagement

---

*Hubbard, 136, says that the army was piloted to this place
by one Peter, a fugitive Indian, who fled from the Narragansets,
upon some discontent, and to him they were indebted, in a great
measure for their success. How long before the army would
have found the enemy, or on what part of the fort they would
have fallen, is uncertain. It appears that had they come upon
any other part, they must have been repulsed. Whether this
Peter was the son of Awashonks, or Peter Nunnuit, the husband
of Weetamore, the Queen of Pocasset, is uncertain. But Mr.
Hubbard styles him a fugitive from the Narragansets. If he
were a Narraganset, he was neither.

† Before this, on the 14, a scout under Sergeant Bennet killed
two and took four prisoners. The rest of the same company,
in ranging the country, came upon a town, burned 150 wigwams,
killed 7 of the enemy and brought in eight prisoners. On
the 15, some Indians came under the pretence of making
peace, and on their return killed several of the English, who
were scattered on their own business. Captain Mosely, while
escorting Maj. Appleton's men to quarters, was fired upon
by 20 or 30 of the enemy from behind a stone wall, but
were immediately dispersed, leaving one dead. On the 16,
they received the news that Jerry Bull's garrison at Petty-
quamscot, was burned, and fifteen persons killed. On the 18,
the Connecticut forces arrived, who on their way had taken and
killed 11 of the enemy. The united forces now set out, Dec.
19, for the headquarters of the enemy. The weather was
severely cold and much snow upon the the ground. They
arrived upon the borders of the swamp about one o'clock. Hubbard, 128 to 130.

began. But being impatient of being out of the heat of the action, importunately begged leave of the General, that he might run down to the assistance of his friends. The General yielded to his request, provided he could rally some hands to go with him. Thirty men immediately drew out and followed him. They entered the swamp, and passed over the log, that was the passage into the fort, where they saw many men and several valiant Captains lie slain.* Mr. Church spying Captain Gardner of Salem, amidst the wigwams in the east end of the fort, made towards him; but on a sudden, while they were looking each other in the face, Captain Gardner settled down. Mr. Church stepped to him, and seeing the blood run down his cheek lifted up his cap, and calling him by his name, he looked up in his face but spake not a word; being mortally shot through the head. And observing his wound, Mr. Church found the ball entered his head on the side that was next the upland, where the English entered the swamp. Upon which, having ordered some care to be taken of the Captain, he despatched information to the General, that the best and forwardest of his army, that hazarded their lives to enter the fort upon the muzzles of the enemy's guns, were shot in their backs, and killed by them that lay behind. Mr. Church with his small company, hastened out of the fort (that the English were now possessed of) to get a shot at the Indians that were in the swamp, and kept firing upon them. He soon met with a broad and bloody track where the enemy had fled with their wounded men. Following hard in the track, he soon spied one of the enemy, who clapped his gun across his breast, made towards Mr. Church, and beckoned to him with his hand. Mr. Church immediately commanded no man to hurt him, hop-

---

*Six Captains were klled. Captains Davenport, Gardiner and Johnson of Massachusetts; Gallop, Siely and Marshall of Connecticut. No mention is made that any officers were killed belonging to Plymouth.

ing by him to have gained some intelligence of the enemy, that might be of advantage. But it unhappily fell out, that a fellow that had lagged behind, coming up, shot down the Indian; to Mr. Church's great grief and disappointment. But immediately they heard a great shout of the enemy, which seemed to be behind them or between them and the fort; and discovered them running from tree to tree to gain advantages of firing upon the English that were in the fort. Mr. Church's great difficulty now was how to discover himself to his friends in the fort; using several inventions, till at length he gained an opportunity to call to, and informed a Sergeant in the fort, that he was there and might be exposed to their shots, unless they observed it. By this time he discovered a number of the enemy, almost within shot of him, making towards the fort. Mr. Church and his company were favoured by a heap of brush that was between them, and the enemy, and prevented their being discovered to them. Mr. Church had given his men their particular orders for firing upon the enemy. And as they were rising up to make their shot, the aforementioned Sergeant in the fort, called out to them, for God's sake not to fire, for he believed they were some of their friend Indians. They clapped down again, but were soon sensible of the Sergeant's mistake. The enemy got to the top of the tree, the body whereof the Sergeant stood upon, and there clapped down out of sight of the fort; but all this while never discovered Mr. Church, who observed them to keep gathering unto that place until there seemed to be a formidable black heap of them. "Now brave boys," said Mr. Church to his men, "if we mind our hits we may have a brave shot, and let our sign for firing on them, be their rising to fire into the fort." It was not long before the Indians rising up as one body, designing to pour a volley into the fort, when our Church nimbly started up, and gave them such a round volley, and unexpected clap on their backs, that they, who escaped with their lives, were so surprised, that they scampered, they knew not whither themselves. About a dozen of them ran right over the log into the fort, and took into a sort of hovel that was built with poles, after the manner of a corn crib. Mr. Church's men having their cartridges fixed, were soon ready to obey his orders, which were immediately to charge and run [—][1] upon the hovel and overset it; calling as he ran on, to some that were in the fort, to assist him in oversetting it. They no sooner came to face the enemy's shelter, but Mr. Church discovered that one of them had found a hole to point his gun through right at him. But however [he] encouraged his company, and ran right on, till he was struck with three bullets; one in his thigh, which was near half cut off as it glanced on the joint of his hip bone; another through the gatherings of his breeches and drawers with a small flesh wound; a third pierced his pocket, and wounded a pair of mittens that he had borrowed of Captain Prentice; being wrapped up together, had the misfortune of having many holes cut through them with one bullet. But however he made shift to keep on his legs, and nimbly discharged his gun at them that had wounded him. Being disabled now to go a step, his men would have carried him off, but he forbid their touching of him, until they had perfected their project of oversetting the enemy's shelter; bid them run, for now the Indians had no guns charged. While he was urging them to run on, the Indians began to shoot arrows, and with one pierced through the arm of an Englishman that had hold of Mr. Church's arm to support him. The English, in short, were discouraged and drew back. And by this time the English people in the fort had begun to set fire to the wigwams and houses in the fort, which Mr. Church laboured hard to prevent. They told him

[1] [on]

[that] they had orders from the General to burn them. He begged them to forbear until he had discoursed with the General. And hastening to him, he begged to spare the wigwams, &c., in the fort from fire. [And] told him [that] the wigwams were musket proof; being all lined with baskets and tubs of grain and other provisions, sufficient to supply the whole army, until the spring of the year, and every wounded man might have a good warm house to lodge in, who otherwise would necessarily perish with the storms and cold; and moreover that the army had no other provisions to trust unto or depend upon; that he knew that the Plymouth forces had not so much as one [biscuit][1] left, for he had seen their last dealt out, &c.* The General advising a few words with the gentlemen that were about him moved towards the fort, designing to ride in himself and bring in the whole army; but just as he was entering the swamp one of his Captains met him, and asked him, whither he was going? He told him "Into the fort." The Captain laid hold of his horse and told him, [that] his life was worth an hundred of theirs, and [that] he should not expose himself. The General told him, that, he supposed the brunt was over, and that Mr. Church had informed him that the fort was taken, &c.; and as the case was circumstanced, he was of the mind, that it was most practicable for him and his army to shelter themselves in the fort. The Captain in a great heat replied, that Church lied; and told the General, that, if he moved another step, towards the fort he would shoot his horse under him. Then [bristled][2] up

[1] [biskake]   [2] [brusled]

* Thus the heroick Church discovered not only great bravery in battle, but judgment and forethought. Had his advice been taken, no doubt many lives would have been saved. It may be remarked, that notwithstanding Mr. Church so distinguished himself in this fight, his name is not mentioned by our chief historians.

another gentleman, a certain Doctor,* and opposed Mr. Church's advice, and said, [that] if it were complied with, it would kill more men than the enemy had killed. "For (said he) by tomorrow the wounded men will be so stiff, that there will be no moving of them." And looking upon Mr. Church, and seeing the blood flow apace from his wounds, told him, that if he gave such advice as that was, he should bleed to death like a dog, before they would endeavour to stanch his blood. Though after they had prevailed against his advice they were sufficiently kind to him. And burning up all the houses and provisions in the fort, the army returned the same night in the storm and cold. And I suppose that every one who is acquainted with that night's march, deeply laments the miseries that attended them; especially the wounded and dying men.† But it mercifully came to pass that Captain Andrew Belcher‡ arrived at Mr. Smith's that very night from Boston with a vessel laden with provisions for the army, which must otherwise have perished for want.

Some of the enemy that were then in the fort have since informed us that, near a third of the Indians belonging to all the Narraganset country, were kill-

* I have not been able to learn the name of the beforementioned Captain nor Doctor. Perhaps it is as well if their memories be buried in oblivion. Trumbull says that, they had the best surgeons which the country could produce. Hist. Con. I, 340. In another place, I, 346, Mr. Gershom Bulkley, he says, "was viewed one of the greatest physicians and surgeons then in Connecticut."

† What rendered their situation more intolerable, was, beside the severity of the cold, a tremendous storm filled the atmosphere with snow; through which they had 18 miles to march before they arrived at their headquarters. See Hist. Connecticut, I, 340.

‡ The father of Governour Belcher. He lived at Cambridge, and was one of his Majesty's council. No one was more respected for integrity, and it is truly said that he was "an ornament and blessing to his country." He died October 31, 1728, aged 71. Eliot, 52.

ed by the English, and by the cold of that night;* that they fled out of their fort so hastily, that they carried nothing with them, that if the English had kept in the fort, the Indians would certainly have been necessitated, either to surrender themselves to them, or to have perished by hunger, and the severity of the season.†

Some time after this fort fight, a certain Sogkonate Indian, hearing Mr. Church relate the manner of his being wounded, told him, [that] he did not know but he himself was the Indian that wounded him, for that he was one of that company of Indians that Mr. Church made a shot upon, when they were rising to make a shot into the fort. They were in number about sixty or seventy that just then came down from Pumham's town‡ and never before then fired a gun against the English. That when Mr.

---

* Mr. Hubbard, 135, mentions, that one Potock, a great counsellor among them, confessed on being taken, that the Indians lost 700 fighting men, besides 300, who died of their wounds. Many old persons, children and wounded, no doubt perished in the flames. But letters from the army, at the time, may be seen in Hutchinson, I, 272, 273, in which the enemy's loss is not so highly rated. They compare better with the account given by our author in the next note.

† (The swamp fight happened on December 19,* 1675, in which about 50 English were killed in the action, and died of their wounds; and about 300 or 350 Indians, men, women and children were killed, and as many more captivated.† It is said 500 wigwams were burned with the fort, and 200 more in other parts of Narraganset. The place of the fort was an elevated ground, or piece of upland, of, perhaps, 3 or 4 acres, in the middle of a hideous swamp, about 7 miles nearly due west from Narraganset, south ferry.‡)

‡ What is now Warwick. See note 2, page 56.

* The old copy of this history, from which I print this, gives the date, Dec. 29, but it must be a misprint.

† Perhaps later writers are more correct with regard to the loss of the English, than our author. It is said that there were above 80 slain, and 150 wounded, who afterwards recovered. Hist. Con. I, 340.

‡ The swamp where this battle was fought is in Southkingston, Rhode Island, situated as mentioned above.

Church fired upon them he killed fourteen dead upon the spot, and wounded a greater number than he killed. Many of which died afterwards of their wounds, in the cold and storm [of] the following night.

Mr. Church was moved with other wounded men, over to Rhodeisland, where in about three months' time, he was in some good measure recovered of his wounds, and the fever that attended them; and then went over to the General* to take his leave of him, with a design to return home.† But the Gene-

---

* General Winslow, with the Plymouth and Massachusetts forces, remained in the Narraganset country most of the winter, and performed considerable against the enemy. The Connecticut men under Major Treat, being much cut to pieces, returned home.

† While our hero is getting better of his wounds we will take a short view of what is transacting abroad.

The enemy, toward the end of January, left their country and moved off to the Nipmucks. A party, in their way, drove off 15 horses, 50 cattle and 200 sheep, from one of the inhabitants of Warwick. On the 10 Feb., several hundreds of them fell upon Lancaster; plundered and burned a great part of the town, and killed or captivated forty persons. (Philip commanded in this attack, it was supposed.) Feb. 21, nearly half of the town of Medfield was burned, and on the 25, seven or eight buildings were also burned at Weymouth. March 13, Groton was all destroyed excepting four garrison houses. On the 17, Warwick had every house burned save one. On the 26, Marlborough was nearly all destroyed, and the inhabitants deserted it. The same day Capt. Pierce of Scituate with fifty English and twenty friendly Indians, was cut off with most of his men. (For the particulars of this affair see note further onward.) On the 28, forty houses and thirty barns were burned at Rehoboth; and the day following, about 30 houses in Providence. The main body of the enemy was supposed now to be in the woods between Brookfield and Marlborough, and Connecticut river. Capt Denison of Connecticut with a few brave volunteers performed signal services. In the first of April he killed and too 44 of the enemy, and before the end of the month 76 mor. were killed and taken, all without the loss of a man. In the beginning of April the Wamesit Indians did some mischief at Chelmsford, on Merrimack river, to which it appears they had been provoked. On the 17, the remaining houses at

rat's great importunity again persuaded him to accompany him in a long march* into the Nipmuck† country, though he had then tents in his wounds, and so lame as not [to be] able to mount his horse without two men's assistance.

In this march, the first thing remarkable, was, they came to an Indian town, where there were many wigwams in sight, but an icy swamp, lying between them and the wigwams, prevented their running at once upon it as they intended. There was much firing upon each side before they passed the swamp. But at length the enemy all fled, and a certain Mohegan, that was a friend Indian, pursued and seized one of the enemy that had a small wound in his leg, and brought him before the General, where he was examined. Some were for torturing him to bring him

---

Marlborough were consumed. The next day, 18 April, they came furiously upon Sudbury. (Some account of which will be given in an ensuing note.) Near the end of April, Scituate about 30 miles from Boston, on the bay, had 19 houses and barns burned. The inhabitants made a gallant resistance and put the enemy to flight. May 8, they burned 17 houses and barns at Bridgewater, a large town about 20 miles south of Boston. Mather, Magnalia, II, 497, says that, "not an inhabitant was lost by this town during the war, neither young nor old; that when their dwellings were fired at this time, God, from heaven, fought for them with a storm of lightning, thunder and rain, whereby a great part of their houses were preserved." On the 11, the town of Plymouth had 16 houses and barns burned; and two days after 9 more. Middleborough, 38 miles from Boston, had its few remaining houses burned the same day.

These were the most distressing days that Newengland ever beheld. Town after town fell a sacrifice to their fury. All was fear and consternation. Few there were, who were not in mourning for some near kindred, and nothing but horrour stared them in the face. But we are now to see the affairs of Philip decline.

* I cannot find as any other historian has taken notice of this expedition of the commander in chief. It appears from what is above stated that it was in March, 1676.

† (Country about Worcester, Oxford, Grafton, Dudley, &c.)

to a more ample confession of what he knew concerning his countrymen. Mr. Church, verily believing [that] he had been ingenuous in his confession, interceded and prevailed for his escaping torture. But the army being bound forward in their march, and the Indian's wound somewhat disenabling him for travelling, it was concluded [that] he should be knocked on the head. Accordingly he was brought before a great fire, and the Mohegan that took him was allowed, as he desired to be, his executioner. Mr. Church taking no delight in the sport, framed an errand at some distance among the baggage horses, and when he had got ten rods, or thereabouts, from the fire, the executioner fetching a blow with a hatchet at the head of the prisoner, he being aware of the blow, dodged his head aside, and the executioner missing his stroke, the hatchet flew out of his hand, and had like to have done execution where it was not designed. The prisoner upon his narrow escape broke from them that held him, and notwithstanding his wound, made use of his legs, and happened to run right upon Mr. Church, who laid hold on him, and a close scuffle they had; but the Indian having no clothes on slipped from him and ran again, and Mr. Church pursued [him,][1] although being lame there was no great odds in the race, until the Indian stumbled and fell, and [then] they closed again—scuffled and fought pretty smartly, until the Indian, by the advantage of his nakedness, slipped from his hold again, and set out on his third race, with Mr. Church close at his heels, endeavouring to lay hold on the hair of his head, which was all the hold could be taken of him. And running through a swamp that was covered with hollow ice; it made so loud a noise that Mr. Church expected (but in vain) that some of his English friends would follow the noise and come to his assistance. But the Indian happened to run athwart a large tree that lay

[1] [the Indian]

fallen near breast high, where he stopped and cried out aloud for help. But Mr. Church being soon upon him again, the Indian seized him fast by the hair of his head, and endeavoured by twisting to break his neck. But though Mr. Church's wounds had somewhat weakened him, and the Indian a stout fellow, yet he held him in play and twisted the Indian's neck as well, and took the advantage of many opportunities, while they hung by each other's hair, gave him notorious bunts in the face with his head. But in the heat of the scuffle they heard the ice break, with somebody's coming apace to them, which when they heard, Church concluded there was help for one or other of them, but was doubtful which of them must now receive the fatal stroke—anon somebody comes up to them, who proved to be the Indian that had first taken the prisoner; [and] without speaking a word, he felt them out, (for it was so dark he could not distinguish them by sight, the one being clothed and the other naked) he felt where Mr. Church's hands were fastened in the Netop's* hair and with one blow settled his hatchet in between them, and [thus] ended the strife. He then spoke to Mr. Church and hugged him in his arms, and thanked him abundantly for catching his prisoner. [He then]¹ cut off the head of his victim and carried it to the camp, and [after] giving an account to the rest of the friend Indians in the camp how Mr. Church had seized his prisoner, &c., they all joined in a mighty shout.

Proceeding in this march they had the success of killing many of the enemy; until at length their provisions failing, they returned home.

King Philip† (as was before hinted) was fled to a

¹ [and]

---

* The Netop Indians were a small tribe among the Sogkonates.

† It was supposed by many that Philip was at the great swamp fight at Narraganset in December, 1675. See note 1

place called Scattacook,* between York and Albany, where the Moohags† made a descent upon him and killed many of his men, which moved him from thence.‡

His next kennelling place was at the falls§ of Connecticut river, where, sometime after Captain Turner found him, [and] came upon him by night, killed him a great many men, and frightened many more into the river, that were hurled down the falls and drowned.‖

---

* It is above Albany, on the east side of the north branch of the Hudson, now called Hoosac river, about 15 miles from Albany. Smith wrote this word Scaghtahook. History N. York, 307.

† (Mohawks.)
This word according to Roger Williams, is derived from the word *moho*, which signifies to eat. Or Mohawks signified cannibals or man eaters among the other tribes of Indians. Trumbull, U. States, I, 47. Hutchinson, I, 405. This tribe was situated along the Mohawk river, from whom it took its name, and was one of the powerful Fivenations, who in 1713, were joined by the Tuskarora Indians, a large tribe from N. Carolina, and thence known by the name of the Sixnations. Williamson, N. Carolina, I, 203. Hon. De Witt Clinton, in N. Y. Hist. Soc. Col. II, 48, says the Tuskaroras joined the other nations in 1712.

‡ Philip despairing of exterminating the English with his Newengland Indians resorted to the Mohawks to persuade them to engage in his cause. They not being willing, he had recourse to a foul expedient. Meeting with some Mohawks in the woods, hunting, he caused them to be murdered; and then informed their friends, that the English had done it. But it so happened that one, which was left for dead, revived and returned to his friends, and informed them of the truth. The Mohawks in just resentment fell upon him and killed many of his men. Adams, Hist. N. Eng. 125.

§ (Above Deerfield.)
It has been suggested, and it is thought very appropriately to call that cataract, where Capt. Turner destroyed the Indians, Turner's Falls. See Antiquarian Researches, 131.

‖ Philip with a great company of his people had taken a stand at the fall in Connecticut river for the convenience of getting a supply of fish, after the destruction of their provisions at the great swamp fight in Narraganset. Some

PHILIP'S WAR. 69

Philip got over the river, and on the back side of Wetuset* hills, meets with all the remnants of the Narraganset and Nipmuck† Indians, that were there gathered together, and became very numerous; and [then] made their descent on Sudbury‡ and the adjacent parts of the country, where they met with,

---

prisoners deserted and brought news to Hadley, Hatfield and Northampton of the Indians' situation at the falls. On the 18 May, 160 men under Capt. Turner arrived near their quarters at day break. The enemy were in their wigwams asleep, and without guards. The English rushed upon them and fired as they rose from sleep, which so terrified them that they fled in every direction: crying out "Mohawks! Mohawks!" Some ran into the river, some took canoes, and in their fright forgot the paddles, and were precipitated down the dreadful fall and dashed in pieces. The enemy is supposed to have lost 300. The English having finished the work, began a retreat; but the Indians, on recovering from their terror fell upon their rear, killed Capt. Turner and 38 of his men. See American Annals, I, 430. Why is the name of Turner not found in our Biographical Dictionaries?

*In the north part of the present town of Princetown in Worcester county, about 50 miles W. of Boston. Mr. Hubbard wrote this word Watchuset, and Dr. Morse, Wachusett, and calls it a mountain. See Univ. Gaz. But in this, as well as many other words, the easiest way is the best way; hence Wachuset is to be preferred.

† (About Rutland.)
It was just said that the Nipmuck country was about Worcester, Oxford, &c. See note 2 on page 65. Nipmuck was a general name for all Indians beyond the Connecticut toward Canada.

‡ On the 27 March, 1676, some persons of Marlborough joined others of Sudbury, and went in search of the enemy. They came upon nearly 300 of them before day asleep by their fires, and within half a mile of a garrison house. The English, though but 40 in number, ventured to fire upon them; and before they could arouse and escape, they had several well directed fires, killing and wounding about 30. On 18 April, as has been before noted, they furiously fell upon Sudbury, burned several houses and barns and killed several persons. Ten or twelve persons that came from Concord, 5 miles distant, to assist their friends, were drawn into an ambush, and all killed or taken. Hubbard, 182, 184.

and swallowed up [the] valiant Captain Wadsworth* and his company; and many other doleful desolations in those parts. The news whereof coming to Plymouth, and they expecting [that,] probably, the enemy would soon return again into their colony, the council of war were called together, and Mr. Church was sent for to them; being observed by the whole colony to be a person extraordinarily qualified for, and adapted to the affairs of war. It was proposed in council, that lest the enemy in their return, should fall on Rehoboth, or some other of their out towns, a company consisting of sixty or seventy men, should be sent into those parts, and [that] Mr. Church [be] invited to take the command of them. He told them that if the enemy returned into that colony again, they

---

* Capt. Samuel Wadsworth, father of president Wadsworth of Harvard College. Capt. Wadsworth was sent from Boston with 50 men to relieve Marlborough. After marching 25 miles, they were informed that the enemy had gone toward Sudbury; so without stopping to take any rest, they pursued after them. On coming near the town, a party of the enemy were discovered, and pursued about a mile into the woods, when on a sudden they were surrounded on all sides by 500 Indians, as was judged. No chance of escape appeared. This little band of brave men now resolved to fight to the last man. They gained an eminence, which they maintained for some time; at length, night approaching, they began to scatter, which gave the enemy the advantage, and nearly every one was slain. This was a dreadful blow to the country. It is not certain that any ever escaped to relate the sad tale. President Wadsworth erected a monument where this battle was fought with this inscription.

"Captain Samuel Wadsworth of Milton, his Lieutenant Snarp of Brookline, Captain Broclebank of Rowley, with about Twenty Six* other souldiers, fighting for the defence of their country, were slain by the Indian enemy April 18th, 1676, and lye buried in this place."

"This monument stands to the west of Sudbury causeway, about one mile southward of the church in old Sudbury, and about a quarter of a mile from the great road, that leads from Worcester to Boston." Holmes, I, 429. Sudbury is about 22 miles from Boston.

* *Supposed to be the number of bodies found.*

might reasonably expect that they would come very numerous, and if he should take the command of men he should not lie in any town or garrison with them, but would lie in the woods as the enemy did—and that to send out such small companies against such multitudes of the enemy that were now mustered together, would be but to deliver so many men into their hands, to be destroyed, as the worthy Captain Wadsworth and his company were. His advice upon the whole was, that, if they sent out any forces, to send no less than three hundred soldiers; and that the other colonies should be asked to send out their quotas also; adding, that, if they intended to make an end of the war by subduing the enemy, they must make a business of the war as the enemy did; and that for his own part, he had wholly laid aside all his own private business and concerns, ever since the war broke out.* He told them that, if they would send forth such forces as he should direct [them] to, he would go with them for six weeks march, which was long enough for men to be kept in the woods at once; and if they might be sure of liberty to return in such a space, men would go out cheerfully; and he would engage [that] one hundred and fifty of the best soldiers should immediately list, voluntarily, to go with him, if they would please to add fifty more; and one hundred of the friend Indians. And with such an army, he made no doubt, but he might do good service, but on other terms he did not incline to be concerned.

Their reply was, that, they were already in debt, and so big an army would bring such a charge upon them, that they should never be able to pay. And as for sending out Indians, they thought it no ways advisable; and in short, none of his advice practicable.

* It will be discoverable in almost every step onward, how shamefully Mr. Church was treated by government for all his services.

Now Mr. Church's consort, and his then only son were till this time* remaining at Duxbury; and his fearing their safety there, (unless the war were more vigorously engaged in) resolved to move to Rhode-island, though it was much opposed, both by government and relations. But at length the Governour, considering that he might be no less serviceable, by being on that side of the colony, gave his permit, and wished [that] he had twenty more as good men to send with him.

Then preparing for his removal, he went with his small family to Plymouth to take leave of their friends, where they met with his wife's parents, who much persuaded that she might be left at Mr. Clark's garrison, (which they supposed to be a mighty safe place) or at least that she might be there, until her soon expected lying in was over; (being near her time.) Mr. Church no ways inclining to venture her any longer in those parts, and no arguments prevailing with him, he resolutely set out for Taunton, and many of their friends accompanied them. There they found Captain Pierce† with a commanded

---

* The beginning of March, 1676.

† This gentleman belonged to Scituate, as is seen in note to page 64. I have learned no particulars of him, except what are furnished in the Indian wars. It appears that he was now on his march into the Narraganset country, having heard that many of the enemy had collected at Pawtuxet, a few miles to the southward of Providence. He being a man of great courage, and willing to engage the enemy on any ground, was led into a fatal snare. On crossing the Pawtuxet river he found himself encircled by an overwhelming number. He retreated to the side of the river to prevent being surrounded; but this only alternative failed: For the enemy crossing the river above, came upon their backs with the same deadly effect as those in front. Thus they had to contend with tripple numbers, and a double disadvantage.— Means was found to despatch a messenger to Providence for succour, but through some unacountable default in him, or them to whom it was delivered, none arrived until too late. The scene was horrid beyond description! Some say that all the English were slain, others, that one only escaped, which

party, who offered Mr. Church to send a relation of his with some others to guard him to Rhodeisland. But Mr. Church thanked him for his respectful offer, but for some good reasons refused to accept it. In short, they got safe to Captain John Almy's* house upon Rhodeisland where they met with friends and good entertainment. But by the way let me not forget this remarkable providence, viz , that within twentyfour hours, or thereabouts, after their arrival at Rhodeisland, Mr. Clark's garrison, that Mr. Church was so much importuned to leave his wife and children at, was destroyed by the enemy.†

Mr. Church being at present disabled from any particular service in the war, began to think of some other employ. But he no sooner took a tool to cut

---

was effected as follows. A friendly Indian pursued him with an uplifted tomahawk, in the face of the enemy, who considering his fate certain, and that he was pursued by one of their own men, made no discovery of the stratagem, and both escaped. Another friend Indian seeing that the battle was lost, blackened his face with powder and ran among the enemy, whom they took to be one of themselves, who also were painted black, then presently escaped into the woods. Another was pursued, who hid behind a rock, and his pursuer lay secreted near to shoot him when he ventured out. But he behind the rock put his hat or cap upon a stick, and raising it up in sight, the other fired upon it. He dropping his stick ran upon him before he could reload his gun and shot him dead. See Hubbard, Nar. 151, &c. It appears that Canonchet, a Narraganset chief, who afterwards fell into the hands of the brave Capt. Denison commanded in this battle. See Hist. Connect. 344.

* See note 2 on page 40.

† On the 12 March Mr. Clark's house was assaulted by the Indians, who after barbarously murdering 11 persons, belonging to two families, set it on fire. Mr. Hubbard, 155, says, that "The cruelty was the more remarkable, in that they had often received much kindness from the said Clark." Philip is supposed to have conducted this affair. About the time that that chief fell, 200 Indians delivered themselves prisoners at Plymouth, 3 of whom were found to have been among those who murdered Mr. Clark's family and were executed. The rest were taken into favour. Ibid. 216.

a small stick, but he cut off the top of his fore finger, and the next to it half off; upon which he smilingly said, that he thought he was out of his way to leave the war, and resolved he would [go] to war again.

Accordingly his second son being born on the 12th of May, and his wife and son [likely]¹ to do well, Mr. Church embraces the opportunity of a passage in a sloop bound to Barnstable, [which]² landed him at Sogkonesset,* from whence he rode to Plymouth, and arrived there the first Tuesday in June.†

The General Court then sitting, welcomed him, and told him [that] they were glad to see him alive. He replied, [that] he was as glad to see them alive; for he had seen so many fires and smokes towards their side of the country, since he left them, that he could scarce eat or sleep with any comfort, for fear they had all been destroyed. For all travelling was stopped, and no news had passed for a long time together.

He gave them an account,‡ that the Indians had made horrid desolations at Providence, Warwick, Pawtuxet, and all over the Narraganset country; and that they prevailed daily against the English on that side of the country. [He] told them [that] he longed to hear what methods they designed [to take] in the war. They told him [that] they were par-

¹ [like]   ² [who]

---

* Known now by the name of Wood's hole. It is in the town of Falmouth, not far to the eastward of Sogkonate point. Douglass wrote this name Soconosset, and Hutchinson Sucanesset. A small clan of Indians resided here from whom it took its name.

† Namely the 8.

‡ We should not suppose that this was the first intelligence that the people of Plymouth received of the destruction of those places, as this visit was nearly 3 months after the destruction of Warwick, Providence, &c., and about 4 from the cutting off of Capt. Pierce; yet it might be the case.

ticularly glad that providence had brought him there at that juncture; for they had concluded the very next day to send out an army of two hundred men; two thirds English, and one third Indians; in some measure agreeable to his former proposal—expecting Boston and Connecticut to join with their quotas.

In short, it was so concluded, and that Mr. Church should return to the island, and see what he could muster there, of those who had moved from Swanzey, Dartmouth, &c.; so returned the same way [that] he came. When he came to Sogkonesset, he had a sham put upon him about a boat [which] he had bought to go home in, and was forced to hire two of the friend Indians to paddle him in a canoe from Elizabeth's* to Rhodeisland.

It fell out, that as they were on their voyage passing by Sogkonate point,† some of the enemy were upon the rocks a fishing. He bid the Indians that managed the canoe, to paddle so near the rocks, as that he might call to those Indians; [and] told them, that he had a great mind ever since the war broke out to speak with some of the Sogkonate Indians, and that they were their relations, and therefore they need not fear their hurting of them. And he added, that, he had a mighty conceit, that if he could get a fair opportunity to discourse [with] them, that he could draw them off from Philip, for he knew [that] they never heartily loved him. The enemy hallooed, and made signs for the canoe to come to them; but when they approached them they skulked and hid in the clefts of the rocks. Then Mr. Church ordered the canoe to be paddled off again, lest, if he came too near, they should fire upon him. Then the Indians appearing again, beckoned and

---

* From Woods hole or Sogkonesset to this island is 1 mile

† A little north of this point is a small bay called Church's cove, and a small cape about 2 miles further north bears the name of Church's point.

called in the Indian language, and bid them come ashore, for they wanted to speak with [them.]¹ The Indians in the canoe answered them again, but they on the rocks told them, that the surf made such a noise against the rocks, [that] they could not hear any thing they said. Then Mr. Church by signs with his hands, gave [them] to understand, that he would have two of them go down upon the point of the beach. (A place where a man might see who was near him.) Accordingly two of them ran along the beach, and met him there without their arms; excepting, that one of them had a lance in his hand. They urged Mr. Church to come ashore, for they had a great desire to have some discourse with him. He told them, [that] if he, that had his weapon in his hand, would carry it up some distance upon the beach, and leave it, he would come ashore and discourse [with] them. He did so, and Mr. Church went ashore, hauled up his canoe, ordered one of his Indians to stay by it, and the other to walk above on the beach, as a sentinel, to see that the coasts were clear. And when Mr. Church came up to the Indians, one of them happened to be honest George, one of the two that Awashonks formerly sent to call him to her dance, and was so careful to guard him back to his house again. [This was] the last Sogkonate Indian he spoke with before the war broke out. He spoke English very well. Mr. Church asked him where Awashonks was? [He said]² "In a swamp about three miles off." Mr. Church asked him what it was [that] he wanted, that he hallooed and called him ashore? He answered, that he took him for Church as soon as he heard his voice in the canoe, and that he was very glad to see him alive; and he believed his mistress would be as glad to see him, and speak with him. He told him further, that he believed she was not fond of maintaining a war with the English, and that she had left Philip and did not

¹ [him]   ² [He told him]

PHILIP'S WAR. 77

intend to return to him any more. He was mighty
earnest with Mr. Church to tarry there while he
would run and call her; but he told him "No, for
he did not know but the Indians would come down
and kill him before he could get back again." He
said that, if Mounthope, or Pocasset Indians could
catch him, he believed they would knock him on the
head; but all Sogkonate Indians knew him very well,
and he believed none of them would hurt him. In
short, Mr. Church refused, then, to tarry; but promised that he would come over again and speak with
Awashonks, and some other Indians that he had a
mind to talk with.

Accordingly he [directed]¹ him to notify Awashonks, her son Peter,* their chief Captain, and one
Nompash† (an Indian that Mr. Church had, formerly, a particular respect for) to meet him two days
after, at a rock at the lower end of Captain Rich-
mond's‡ farm, which was a very noted place. And
if that day should prove stormy, or windy, they were
to expect him the next moderate day; Mr. Church
telling George, that he would have him come with
the persons mentioned, and no more. They gave
each other their hands upon it, [and] parted.

Mr. Church went home, and the next morning to
Newport; and informed the government of what had
passed between him and the Sogkonate Indians; and
desired their permit for him, and Daniel Wilcox§ (a

¹ [appointed]

---

* See note 1, on page 57.

† In another place his name is spelt Numposh. He was
Captain of the Sogkonate or Seconate Indians in "the first
expedition east."

‡ This rock is near the water a little north of where they
then were.

§ The fatal 10 November, 1825, allows me only to say of
this person that descendants in the fourth generation (I
think) are found in Newbedford. See page iv, of my preface.

man that well understood the Indian language,) to go over to them. They told him, that they thought he was mad; after such service as he had done, and such dangers that he [had] escaped, now to throw away his life; for the rogues would as certainly kill him as ever he went over. And utterly refused to grant his permit, or to be willing that he should run the risk.

Mr. Church told them, that it ever had been in his thoughts, since the war broke out, that if he could discourse the Sogkonate Indians, he could draw them off from Philip, and employ them against him; but could not, till now, never have an opportunity to speak with any of them, and was very loath to lose it, &c. At length they told him, [that] if he would go, it should be only with the two Indians that came with him; but they would give him no permit under their hands.

He took his leave of them, resolving to prosecute his design. They told him, they were sorry to see him so resolute, nor if he went did they ever expect to see his face again.

He bought a bottle of rum, and a small roll of tobacco, to carry with him, and returned to his family.

The next day, being the day appointed for the meeting, he prepared two light canoes for the design, and his own man with the two Indians for his company. He used such arguments with his tender and now almost broken hearted wife, from the experience of former preservations, and the prospect of the great service he might do, (might it please God to succeed his design, &c.,) that he obtained her consent to his attempt. And committing her, the babes, and himself to heaven's protection, he set out.

They had, from the shore, about a league to paddle. Drawing near the place, they saw the Indians sitting on the bank, waiting for their coming. Mr

Church sent one of his Indians ashore in one of the canoes to see whether they were the same Indians whom he had appointed to meet him, and no more: And if so, to stay ashore and send George to fetch him. Accordingly George came and fetched Mr. Church ashore, while the other canoe played off to see the event, and to carry tidings, if the Indians should prove false.

Mr. Church asked George whether Awashonks and the other Indians [that] he appointed to meet him were there? He answered [that] they were. He then asked him if there were no more than they, whom he appointed to be there? To which he would give no direct answer. However, he went ashore; when he was no sooner landed, but Awashonks and the rest that he had appointed to meet him there, rose up and came down to meet him; and each of them successively gave him their hands, and expressed themselves glad to see him, and gave him thanks for exposing himself to visit them. They walked together about a gun shot from the water, to a convenient place to sit down, where at once rose up a great body of Indians, who had lain hid in the grass, (that was [as] high as a man's waist) and gathered round them, till they had closed them in; being all armed with guns, spears, hatchets, &c. with their hairs trimmed, and faces painted, in their warlike appearance.

It was doubtless somewhat surprising to our gentleman at first, but without any visible discovery of it, after a small silent pause on each side, he spoke to Awashonks, and told her, that George had informed him that she had a desire to see him, and discourse about making peace with the English. She answered "Yes." "Then," said Mr. Church, "it is customary when people meet to treat of peace, to lay aside their arms, and not to appear in such hostile form as your people do." [He] desired of her, that if they might talk about peace, which he desired they might, her men might lay aside their arms, and appear more treatable. Upon which there began a considerable noise and murmur among them in their own language, till Awashonks asked him what arms they should lay down, and where? He (perceiving the Indians looked very surly and much displeased) replied, "Only their guns at some small distance, for formality's sake." Upon which with one consent, they laid aside their guns and came and sat down.

Mr. Church pulled out his *calabash*, and asked Awashonks whether she had lived so long at Wetuset,* as to forget to drink occapeches?† and drinking to her, he perceived that she watched him very diligently, to see (as he thought) whether he swallowed any of the rum. He offered her the shell, but she desired him to drink again first. He then told her, [that] there was no poison in it; and pouring some into the palm of his hand, sipped it up. And took the shell and drank to her again, and drank a good swig, which indeed was no more than he needed. Then they all standing up, he said to Awashonks, "You wont drink for fear there should be poison in it," and then handed it to a little ill looking fellow, who catched it readily enough, and as greedily would have swallowed the liquor when he had it at his mouth. But Mr. Church catched him by the throat, and took it from him, asking him whether he intended to swallow shell and all? and then handed it to Awashonks. She ventured to take a good hearty dram, and passed it among her attendants.

The shell being emptied, he pulled out his tobacco; and having distributed it, they began to talk.

Awashonks demanded of him the reason, why he had not (agreeable to his promise when she saw him

---

* Wachuset. See note 1, on p. 69.

† Commonly heard as though written *okape*, or *ochape*.

last) been down at Sogkonate before now? Saying, that probably if he had come then, according to his promise, they had never joined with Philip against the English.

He told her [that] he was prevented by the war's breaking out so suddenly; and yet, he was afterwards coming down, and came as far as Punkatees, where a great many Indians set upon him, and fought him a whole afternoon, though he did not come prepared to fight, [and] had but nineteen men with him, whose chief design was to gain an opportunity to discourse some Sogkonate Indians. Upon this there at once arose a mighty murmur, confused noise and talk among the fierce looking creatures, and all rising up in a hubbub. And a great surly looking fellow took up his tomhog, or wooden cutlass to kill Mr. Church, but some others prevented him.

The interpreter asked Mr. Church, if he understood what it was that the great fellow (they had hold of) said? He answered him "No." "Why" said the interpreter, "he says [that] you killed his brother at Punkatees, and therefore he thirsts for your blood." Mr. Church bid the interpreter tell him that his brother began first; that if he had kept at Sogkonate, according to his desire and order, he should not have hurt him.

Then the chief Captain commanded silence; and told them that they should talk no more about old things, &c., and quelled the tumult, so that they sat down again, and began upon a discourse of making peace with the English. Mr. Church asked them what proposals they would make, and on what terms they would break their league with Philip? Desiring them to make some proposals that he might carry to his masters; telling them that it was not in his power to conclude a peace with them, but that he knew that if their proposals were reasonable, the government would not be unreasonable; and that he would use his interest with the government for them; and to encourage them to proceed, put them in mind that the Pequots* once made war with the English, and that after they subjected themselves to the English, the English became their protectors, and defended them against other nations† that would otherwise have destroyed them, &c.

After some further discourse and debate he brought them at length to consent, that if the government of Plymouth would firmly engage to them, that they and all of them, and their wives and children should have their lives spared, and none of them transported out of the country, they would subject themselves to them, and serve them, in what they were able.

Then Mr. Church told them, that he was well satisfied the government of Plymouth would readily concur with what they proposed, and would sign their articles. And complimenting them upon it, how pleased he was with the thoughts of their return, and of the former friendship that had been between them, &c.

The chief Captain rose up, and expressed the great value and respect he had for Mr. Church; and bowing to him, said, "Sir, if you will please to accept of me and my men, and will head us, we will fight for you, and will help you to Philip's head before the Indian corn be ripe." And when he had ended, they all expressed their consent to what he said, and told Mr. Church [that] they loved him, and were willing to go with him, and fight for him as long as the English had one enemy left in the country.

Mr. Church assured them, that if they proved as good as their word, they should find him theirs, and their children's fast friend. And (by the way) the friendship is maintained between them to this day.‡

---

* See a history of this war in the Appendix, No. IV.

† The Narragansets. See first note to Philip's war.

‡ 1716. They consisted now, probably of no more than 200 persons.

Then he proposed unto them, that they should choose five men to go strait with him to Plymouth. They told him "No, they would not choose, but he should take which five he pleased." Some compliments passed about it, at length it was agreed, [that] they should choose three, and he two. Then he agreed that he would go back to the island that night, and would come to them the next morning, and go through the woods to Plymouth. But they afterwards objected, [for][1] his travelling through the woods would not be safe for him; [that] the enemy might meet with them and kill him, and then they should lose their friend and the whole design [would be] ruined beside. And therefore proposed that he should come in an English vessel, and they would meet him, and come on board at Sogkonate point, and sail from thence to Sandwich, which in fine was concluded upon.

So Mr. Church promising to come as soon as he could possibly obtain a vessel, and then they parted.

He returned to the island and was at great pains and charge to get a vessel; but with unaccountable disappointments, sometimes by the falseness, and sometimes by the faintheartedness of men that he bargained with, and something by wind and weather, &c.: Until at length Mr. Anthony Low* put in to the harbour with a loaded vessel bound to the westward, and being made acquainted with Mr Church's case, told him, that he had so much kindness for him, and was so pleased with the business he was engaged in, that he would run the venture of his vessel and cargo to wait upon him.

Accordingly, next morning they set sail with a wind that soon brought them to Sogkonate point. But coming there they met with a contrary wind, and a great swelling sea.

[1] [that]

---

* After much search I can ascertain nothing of this person. The name is common in our country at this day.

The Indians were there waiting upon the rocks, but had nothing but a miserable broken canoe to get aboard in; yet Peter Awashonks ventured off in it, and with a great deal of difficulty and danger got aboard. And by this time it began to rain and blow exceedingly, and forced them up the sound; and then [they] went away through Bristol ferry, round the island to Newport, carrying Peter with them.

Then Mr. Church dismissed Mr. Low, and told him, that inasmuch as Providence opposed his going by water, and he expected that the army would be up in a few days, and probably, if he should be gone at that juncture, it might ruin the whole design; [he] would therefore yield his voyage.

Then he writ the account of his transactions with the Indians, and drew up the proposals, and articles of peace, and despatched Peter with them to Plymouth, that his honour the Governour, if he saw cause, might sign them.

Peter was sent over to Sogkonate on Lord's day* morning, with orders to take those men that were chosen to go down, or some of them, at least, with him. The time being expired that was appointed for the English army to come, there was great looking for them. Mr. Church, on the Monday morning, (partly to divert himself after his fatigue, and partly to listen for the army) rode out with his wife, and some of his friends to Portsmouth,† under a pretence of cherrying; but came home without any news from the army. But by midnight, or sooner, he was roused with an express from Major Bradford, who was arrived with the army at Pocasset, to whom he forthwith repaired,‡ and informed him of the

---
* July 9.

† The island of Rhodeisland is divided into 3 towns; Newport in the south, Middletown, and Portsmouth in the north.

‡ July 11.

whole of his proceedings with the Sogkonate Indians.

With the Major's consent and advice, he returned again next morning to the island in order to go over that way to Awashonks, to inform her that the army was arrived, &c.

Accordingly from Sachueeset neck* he went in a canoe to Sogkonate. [He] told her that Major Bradford was arrived at Pocasset with a great army, whom he had informed of all the proceedings with her; that if she would be advised, and observe order, she nor her people need not to fear being hurt by them; told her [that] she should call all her people down into the neck, lest if they should be found straggling about, mischief might light on them; that on the morrow they would come down and receive her and give her farther orders.

She promised to get as many of her people together as possibly she could; desiring Mr. Church to consider that it would be difficult for to get them together at such short warning.

Mr. Church returned to the island and to the army the same night.

The next morning† the whole army marched towards Sogkonate, as far as Punkatees, and Mr. Church with a few men went down to Sogkonate to call Awashonks and her people, to come up to the English camp. As he was going down they met with a Pocasset Indian, who had killed a cow, and got a quarter of her on his back, and her tongue in his pocket. [He]¹ gave them an account, that he came from Pocasset two days since in company with his mother, and several other Indians, now hid in a swamp above Nonquid.‡ Disarming of him, he sent him by two men to Major Bradford, and proceeded

¹ [who]

---

* (The southeast corner of Rhodeisland.)
† July 13 ‡ (In Tiverton.)

to Sogkonate. They saw several Indians by the way skulking about but let them pass.

Arriving at Awashonks camp, [he] told her [that] he was come to invite her and her people up to Punkatees,* where Major Bradford now was with the Plymouth army, expecting her and her subjects to receive orders, until further order could be had from the government. She complied, and soon sent out orders for such of her subjects as were not with her, immediately to come in. And by twelve o'clock of next day, she with most of her number appeared before the English camp at Punkatees. Mr. Church tendered [himself to] the Major to serve under his commission, provided the Indians might be accepted with him, to fight the enemy. The Major told him, [that] his orders were to improve him if he pleased, but as for the Indians he would not be concerned with them. And presently gave forth orders for Awashonks, and all her subjects, both men, women and children, to repair to Sandwich;† and to be there upon peril, in six days. Awashonks and her chiefs gathered round Mr. Church, (where he was walked off from the rest) [and] expressed themselves concerned that they could not be confided in, nor improved. He told them, [that] it was best to obey orders, and that if he could not accompany them to Sandwich, it should not be above a week before he would meet them there; that he was confident the Governour would commission him to improve them.

The Major hastened to send them away with Jack Havens (an Indian who had never been in the wars) in the front, with a flag of truce in his hand.

---

* (Adjoining Fogland ferry.)
The geography of this place, with respect to extent and situation, has been given on page 40, note 1.

† A town between Plymouth and Barnstable, on Cape Cod. If the Major were arbitrary in giving this order, he was liberal with the time, as the distance was not above 50 miles by way of Plymouth, and perhaps no more than 30 through the woods.

They being gone, Mr. Church by the help of his
man Toby, (the Indian whom he had taken prisoner
as he was going down to Sogkonate) took said Toby's mother, and those that were with her, prisoners.

Next morning the whole army moved back to Pocasset. This Toby informed them that there were
a great many Indians gone down to Wepoiset* to
eat clams; (other provisions being very scarce with
them) that Philip himself was expected within three
or four days at the same place. Being asked what
Indians they were? he answered, "Some Weetamore's Indians; some Mounthope Indians; some
Narraganset Indians; and some other upland Indians; in all, about three hundred."

The Rhodeisland boats, by the Major's order,
meeting them at Pocasset, they were soon embarked.
It being just in the dusk of the evening, they could
plainly discover the enemies' fires at the place the
Indian directed to, and the army concluded no other,
but [that] they were bound directly thither, until
they came to the north end of the island and heard
the word of command for the boats to bear away.

Mr. Church was very fond of having this probable
opportunity of surprising that whole company of Indians embraced; but orders, it was said must be
obeyed, which were to go to Mounthope, and there
to fight Philip.

This with some other good opportunities of doing
spoil upon the enemy, being unhappily missed,† Mr.
Church obtained the Major's consent to meet the
Sogkonate Indians, according to his promise. He was
offered a guard to Plymouth, but chose to go with
one man only, who was a good pilot.

About sunset,‡ he, with Sabin§ his pilot, mounted

---

* In Swanzey.

† The cause of this ill timed manœuvre of the army must
remain a mystery. ‡ July 20.

§ As this name does not occur any where else in this history, it is not probable that he served regularly in that capacity

their horses at Rehoboth, where the army now was, and by two hours by sun next morning, arrived safe at Plymouth. And by that time they had refreshed themselves, the Governour and Treasurer* came to town. Mr. Church gave them a short account of the affairs of the army, &c. His honour was pleased to give him thanks for the good and great service he had done at Sogkonate; [and] told him, [that] he had confirmed all that he had promised Awashonks, and had sent the Indian back again that [had] brought his letter.† He asked his honour whether he had any thing later from Awashonks? He told him [that] he had not. Whereupon he gave his honour an account of the Major's orders relating to her and hers, and what discourse had passed *pro* and *con*, about them; and that he had promised to meet them, and that he had encouraged them that he thought he might obtain of his honour a commission to lead them forth to fight Philip. His honour smilingly told him, that he should not want commission if he would accept it, nor yet good Englishmen enough to make up a good army.

But in short he told his honour [that] the time had expired that he had appointed to meet the Sogkonates at Sandwich. The Governour asked him when he would go? He told him, that afternoon by his honour's leave. The Governour asked him how many men he would have with him? He answered, not above half a dozen; with an order to take more at Sandwich, if he saw cause, and horses provided. He no sooner moved it, but had his number of men tendering to go with him; among [whom]¹ were Mr.

¹ [which]

---

* Mr. Southworth.

† This letter contained an answer to the account of his meeting Awashonks, before related, which was sent from the island by Peter.

Jabez Howland,* and Nathaniel Southworth.† They
went to Sandwich that night, where Mr. Church (with
need enough) took a nap of sleep. The next morning, with about sixteen or eighteen men, he proceeded as far as Agawom,‡ where they had great expectation of meeting the Indians, but met them not.
His men being discouraged, about half of them returned. Only half a dozen stuck by him, and promised so to do until they should meet with the Indians.

When they came to Sippican§ river, Mr. Howland began to tire, upon which Mr. Church left him
and two more, for a reserve, at the river; that if he
should meet with enemies, and be forced back, they
might be ready to assist them in getting over the
river. Proceeding in their march, they crossed
another river, and opened a great bay,‖ where they
might see many miles along shore, where were sands
and flats; and hearing a great noise below them, towards the sea, they dismounted their horses; left
them, and creeped among the bushes, until they
came near the bank, and saw a vast company of In-

---

* Little more than the pages of this history furnish, am I
able to communicate of the worthy Howland. More, but
for the fatal winds, or more fatal flames of Courtstreet might
have been told. He was a son of the venerable John Howland of Carver's family, (whose name is the 13th to that
memorable instrument, or first foundation of government in
Newengland, which may be seen in Appendix, III, with the
other signers.) As I am informed by my worthy friend, Mr.
Isaac Howland of Westport, who is also a descendant.

† This gentleman was with Mr. Church in his first and
second expeditions to the eastward, as will be seen in those
expeditions. I learn nothing more of him.

‡ A small river in Rochester. Several places were known
by this name. Our Plymouth fathers proposed to go to a
place about twenty leagues to the northward, known to them
by the name of Agawam, (now Ipswich.) Morton, 20.

§ (Rochester.)

‖ Buzzard's bay.

dians, of all ages and sexes; some on horseback running races; some at football; some catching eels and flat fish in the water; some clamming, &c.; but, which way, with safety, to find out what Indians they were, they were at a loss.

But at length, retiring into a thicket, Mr. Church hallooed to them. They soon answered him, and a couple of smart young fellows, well mounted, came upon a full career to see whom it might be that called, and came just upon Mr. Church before they discovered him. But when they perceived themselves so near Englishmen, and armed, were much surprised; and tacked short about to run as fast back as they came forward, until one of the men in the bushes called to them, and told them his name was Church, and [they] need not fear his hurting of them. Upon which after a small pause, they turned about their horses, and came up to him. One of them that could speak English, Mr. Church took aside and examined; who informed him, that the Indians below were Awashonks and her company, and that Jack Havens was among them; whom Mr. Church immediately sent for to come to him, and ordered the messenger to inform Awashonks that he was come to meet her. Jack Havens soon came, and by that time Mr. Church had asked him a few questions, and had been satisfied by him, that it was Awashonks and her company that were below, and that Jack had been kindly treated by them, a company of Indians all mounted on horseback, and well armed, came riding up to Mr. Church, but treated him with all due respects. He then ordered Jack to go [and] tell Awashonks, that he designed to sup with her in the evening, and to lodge in her camp that night. Then taking some of the Indians with him, he went back to the river to take care of Mr. Howland.

Mr. Church having a mind to try what mettle he was made of, imparted his notion to the Indians that were with him, and gave them directions how to act their parts. When he came pretty near the place, he and his Englishmen pretendedly fled, firing on their retreat towards the Indians that pursued them, and they firing as fast after them. Mr. Howland being upon his guard, hearing the guns, and by and by seeing the motion both of the English and Indians, concluded [that] his friends were distressed, and was soon on the full career on horseback to meet them; [when]¹ he [perceived]² their laughing, [and] mistrusted the truth.

As soon as Mr. Church had given him the news, they hastened away to Awashonks. Upon their arrival, they were immediately conducted to a shelter open on one side whither Awashonks and her chiefs soon came, and paid their respects; and the multitudes gave shouts as made the heavens to ring.

It being now about sunsetting, or near the dusk of the evening, the Netops* came running from all quarters loaden with the tops of dry pines, and the like combustible matter, making a huge pile thereof, near Mr. Church's shelter, on the open side thereof. But by this time supper was brought in, in three dishes; viz., a curious young bass in one dish; eels and flat fish in a second; and shell fish in a third. But neither bread nor salt to be seen at table. But by that time supper was over, the mighty pile of pine knots and tops, &c., was fired; and all the Indians, great and small, gathered in a ring round it, Awashonks, with the oldest of her people, men and women mixed, kneeling down, made the first ring next the fire; and all the lusty stout men,

¹ [until]   ² [perceiving]

* This name is used by our author, I suspect, in the same sense as other writers use that of *sannop*. See Winthrop's Journal, sub anno 1630, and Hubbard, Nar. 30, where it appears to be an Indian word employed by the sachems as a common name for their men. The latter author spelt it sannap. Nipnet was a general name for all inland Indians between the Massachusetts and Connecticut river. Ibid. 15.

standing up, made the next, and then all the rabble in a confused crew, surrounded, on the outside.

Then the chief Captain stepped in between the rings and the fire, with a spear in one hand, and a hatchet in the other; danced round the fire, and began to fight with it; making mention of all the several nations and companies of Indians in the country, that were enemies to the English. And at naming of every particular tribe of Indians, he would draw out and fight a new firebrand; and at finishing his fight with each particular firebrand, would bow to him, and thank him; and when he had named all the several nations and tribes, and fought them all, he stuck down his spear and hatchet, and came out, and another stept in, and acted over the same dance, with more fury, if possible, than the first; and when about half a dozen of their chiefs had thus acted their parts, the Captain of the guard stept up to Mr. Church, and told him, [that] they were making soldiers for him, and what they had been doing was all one [as] swearing of them. And having in that manner engaged all the stout lusty men, Awashonks and her chiefs came to Mr. Church, and told him, that now they were all engaged to fight for the English, and [that] he might call forth all, or any of them, at any time, as he saw occasion, to fight the enemy. And [then] presented him with a very fine firelock.

Mr. Church accepts their offer, drew out a number of them, and set out next morning before day for Plymouth, where they arrived the same day.

The Governour being informed of it, came early to town* next morning;† and by that time, he had Englishmen enough to make a good company, when joined with Mr. Church's Indians, that offered their

---

* The Governour resided at Marshfield a few miles north of Plymouth.

† July 23.

voluntary service, to go under his command in quest of the enemy. The Governour then gave him a commission which is as follows.

"Captain BENJAMIN CHURCH, you are hereby nominated, ordered, commissioned, and empowered to raise a company of volunteers of about two hundred men, English and Indians; the English not exceeding the number of sixty, of which company, or so many of them as you can obtain, or shall see cause at present to improve, you are to take the command, conduct, and to lead them forth now and hereafter, at such time, and unto such places within this colony, or elsewhere within the confederate colonies, as you shall think fit; to discover, pursue, fight, surprise, destroy, or subdue our Indian enemies, or any part or parties of them, that by the providence of God you may meet with, or them, or any of them, by treaty and composition to receive to mercy, if you see reason, (provided they be not murderous rogues, or such as have been principal actors in those villanies.) And forasmuch as your company may be uncertain, and the persons often changed, you are also hereby empowered with the advice of your company, to choose and commissionate a Lieutenant, and to establish Sergeants, and Corporals as you see cause And you herein improving your best judgment and discretion, and utmost ability, faithfully to serve the interest of God, his Majesty's interest, and the interest of the colony; and carefully governing your said company at home and abroad. These shall be unto you full and ample commission, warrant and discharge. Given under the publick seal, this 24th day of July, 1676.

Per JOS. WINSLOW, *Governour*."

Receiving commission, he marched the same night into the woods, got to Middleborough* before day;

---

* About 15 miles from Plymouth. The fruitful waters in this town and the plenty of game in its woods, caused it to be a principal residence for Indians. Mourt says (in Prince,

and as soon as the light appeared, took into the woods and swampy thickets, towards a place where they had some reason to expect to meet with a parcel of Narraganset Indians, with some others that belonged to Mounthope. Coming near to where they expected them, Captain Church's Indian scout discovered the enemy; and well observing their fires, and postures, returned with the intelligence to their Captain; who gave such directions for the surrounding of them, as had the desired effect; surprising them from every side, so unexpectedly, that they were all taken, not so much as one escaped.*

And upon a strict examination, they gave intelligence of another parcel of the enemy, at a place called Munponset pond.† Captain Church hastening with his prisoners through the woods to Plymouth,

---

Chron. 191,) "thousands of men have lived here, who died of the great plague, about 3 years before our arrival." It was subject to Massassoit, and was first visited by the English, 3 July, 1621. Mr. Edward Winslow, and Mr. Stephen Hopkins passed through there, on their way to visit Massassoit. They saw the bones of many that died of the plague, where their habitations had been. Ibid. Relicks of antiquity are often found to this day. A gentleman lately digging to set posts for a front yard, near the town house, discovered an Indian sepulchre. It contained a great quantity of beads of different kinds, with many other curiosities. A remnant of a tribe of Indians now lives on the northeast side of the great Assawomset. They have mixed with the blacks, and none remain of clear blood. The last that remained unmixed, was a man who died a few years since, at the age, it was supposed, of 100 years. He went by the name of Cymon. What is known of the troubles of the inhabitants in this war is found scattered through Mr. Hubbard's Narrative, in Bachus' Hist. Middleborough, and note 1, for page 51, of this work.

* We have to regret that our author does not tell us the number which he took, and the place where he took them. But his indefinite mode of writing, may, in part, be accounted for, by the consideration, that it is given after nearly forty years, mostly from recollection; especially this part of the history.

† A small pond in the north part of the present town of

disposed of them all, excepting, only one, Jeffrey, who proving very ingenuous and faithful to him, in informing where other parcels of Indians harboured, Captain Church promised him, that if he continued to be faithful to him, he should not be sold out of the country, but should be his waiting man, to take care of his horse, &c.; and accordingly he served him faithfully as long as he lived.

But Captain Church was forthwith sent out again, and the terms for his encouragement being concluded on, viz., that the country should find them ammunition and provision, and have half the prisoners and arms [that] they took: The Captain and his English soldiers to have the other half of the prisoners and arms; and the Indian soldiers the loose plunder. Poor encouragement! But after some time it was mended.

They soon captivated the Munponsets,* and brought them in, not one escaping.

This stroke he held several weeks, never returning empty handed. When he wanted intelligence of their kenneling places, he would march to some place, likely to meet with some travellers or ramblers, and scattering his company, would lie close; and seldom lay above a day or two, at most, before some of them would fall into their hands; whom he would compel to inform where their company were. And so by his method of secret and sudden surprises, took great numbers of them prisoners.

The government observing his extraordinary courage and conduct, and the success from heaven†

---

* A small tribe of Indians that resided near Munponset pond.

† Whether Heaven had any thing to do with making slaves of the Indians after they were made prisoners, may be doubted by scepticks, on the same principles that every feeling man now doubts of the justness of our southern brethren to make slaves of Negroes. But to the commendation of our hero be it spoken, that his voice was always against en

added to it, saw cause to enlarge his commission;
gave him power to raise and dismiss his forces, as he
should see occasion; to commissionate officers under him, and to march as far as he should see cause,
within the limits of the three united colonies; to receive to mercy, give quarter, or not; excepting some
particular and noted murderers, viz., Philip, and all
that were at the destroying of Mr. Clark's garrison,
and some few others.

Major Bradford being now at Taunton with his
army, and wanting provisions, some carts were ordered from Plymouth for their supply, and Captain
Church to guard them. But he obtaining other
guards for the carts, as far as Middleborough, ran
before with a small company, hoping to meet with
some of the enemy; appointing the carts and their
guards to meet with them at Nemascut,* about an
hour after sun's rising, next morning.

He arrived there about the breaking of the daylight, and discovered a company of the enemy; but
his time was too short to wait for gaining advantage,
and therefore ran right in upon them, surprised and
captivated about sixteen of them, who upon examination, informed that Tispaquin† a very famous Cap-

---

slaving mankind. What greater proof can we have of his
humanity, considering the age in which he lived? See page
52, and note 1.

* (Near Raynham.)
That part of Middleborough along the river of that name.
This name like many others was written differently by the
early contemporary writers. It is generally spelt Namasket;
but more properly Nemasket. Holmes, I, 211, from 1 Mass.
Hist. Coll. III, 148, says, it was that part of Middleborough,
which the English first planted. Hutchinson, I, 262, says,
that Philip sometimes resided here. See note 1, on page 93.
Savage, in Winthrop, I, 55, says, "This name belonged to
part of the tract now included in Middleborough; but the
lines of Indian geography were probably not very precise, or
are forgotten."

† He was at the destroying of Mr. Clark's house at Plymouth. After his wife and child were taken by Captain
Church, he came and delivered himself up at Plymouth, as a

tain among the enemy was at Assawompset* with a numerous company.

But the carts must now be guarded, and the opportunity of visiting Tispaquin must now be laid aside; the carts are to be faithfully guarded, lest Tispaquin should attack them.

Coming towards Taunton, Captain Church taking two men with him, made all speed to the town. And coming to the river side, he hallooed, and inquiring of them that came to the river, for Major Bradford or his Captains. He was informed [that] they were in the town, at the tavern. He told them of the carts that were coming, that he had the cumber of guarding them, which had already prevented his improving opportunities of doing service; prayed, therefore, that a guard might be sent over to receive the carts, that he might be at liberty—refusing all invitations and persuasions to go over to the tavern to visit the Major. He at length obtained a guard to receive the carts, by whom also he sent his prisoners to be conveyed with the carts, to Plymouth; directing them not to return by the way they came, but by Bridgewater.

---

prisoner of war; but was afterward barbarously *murdered* by the *government* for his confidence in them, as will be seen in the progress of this history.

To do justice in some degree, to the memory of the numerous race of human beings, who have left this delightful country to us, a biographical work should be written, containing as much of the lives and actions as can now be found, of such of those natives, whose names have come down to us. The author of these notes has taken some steps toward that end, which would be freely contributed to assist an able hand in the undertaking. Should no other attempt it, some years to come may produce it from his pen.

* (In Middleborough.)

This word again occurs in the course of a few paragraphs and is there spelt right. It must have been inattention that caused the difference in its orthography, as well as in many others. The country around the ponds bore the name of Assawomset. See note 4, on page 27. In modern writers we see it sometimes spelt as above.

E

Hastening back, he proposed to camp that night at Assawomset neck.* But as soon as they came to the river that runs into the great pond,† through the thick swamp at the entering of the neck, the enemy fired upon them, but hurt not a man. Captain Church's Indians ran right into the swamp, and fired upon them, but it being in the dusk of the evening, the enemy made their escape in the thickets.

The Captain then moving about a mile into the neck, took the advantage of a small valley to feed his horses. Some held the horses by the bridles, the rest on the ground, looked sharp out for the enemy, [who were] within hearing on every side, and some very near. But in the dead of the night the enemy being out of hearing, or still, Captain Church moved out of the neck (not the same way he came in, lest he should be ambuscaded) towards Cushnet,‡ where all the houses were burnt. And crossing Cushnet river,§ being extremely fatigued with two nights' and one day's ramble without rest or sleep. And observing good forage for their horses, the Captain concluded upon baiting, and taking a nap. Setting six men to watch the passage of the river; two to

---

* A short distance below or to the south of Sampson's Tavern. The "thick swamp," next mentioned, remains to this time.

† The Assawomset.

‡ (In Dartmouth.)
Newbedford has been since taken from Dartmouth. The part where Newbedford now is was meant.

§ The river on which Newbedford stands is called Cushnet. Dr. Douglass wrote this word Accushnot. Summary, I, 403. And I think, that if we write Aponaganset, we should also write Accushnot, or rather Accushnet. But he wrote Polyganset. Ibid. See note 2, on page 51, of this history. The most ancient way of writing those names, in general, is to be preferred; for it is the most direct road to uniformity, and consistency. Two very desirable and agreeable attendants to be met with in language; yet, the writer of these notes is very sensible of his failures in these as well as other respects.

watch at a time, while the others slept, and so to take their turns, while the rest of the company went into a thicket to sleep under a guard of two sentinels more. But the whole company being very drowsy, soon forgot their danger, and were fast asleep, sentinels and all. The Captain first awakes, looks up, and judges he had slept four hours; which being longer than he designed, immediately rouses his company, and sends away a file to see what was become of the watch, at the passage of the river; but they no sooner opened the river in sight, but they discovered a company of the enemy viewing of their tracks, where they came into the neck. Captain Church, and those with him, soon dispersed into the brush, on each side of the way, while the file sent, got undiscovered to the passage of the river, and found their watch all fast asleep. But these tidings thoroughly awakened the whole company.

But the enemy giving them no present disturbance, they examined their [knapsacks,][1] and taking a little refreshment, the Captain ordered one party to guard the horses, and the other to scout, who soon met with a track, and following of it, they were brought to a small company of Indians, who proved to be Littleeyes,* and family, and near relations, who were of Sogkonate, but, had forsaken their countrymen, upon their making peace with the English. Some of Captain Church's Indians asked him, if he did not know this fellow? [and] told him, "This is the rogue that would have killed you at Awashonks' dance." And signified to him, that now he had an opportunity to be revenged on him. But the Captain told them, [that] it was not Englishmen's fashion to seek revenge; and that he should have the quarter the rest had.

Moving to the river side, they found an old canoe,

---

[1] [snapsacks.]

---

* See page 25.

with which the Captain ordered Littleeyes and his company to be carried over to an island,* telling him, [that] he would leave him on that island until he returned. And lest the English should light on them, and kill them, he would leave his cousin Lightfoot† (whom the English knew to be their friend) to be his guard. Littleeyes expressed himself very thankful to the Captain.

He leaving his orders with Lightfoot, returns to the river side, towards Ponaganset, to Russel's orchard.‡ [On] coming near the orchard they clapped into a thicket, and there lodged the rest of the night without any fire. And upon the morning light's appearing, moved towards the orchard, [and] discovered some of the enemy, who had been there the day before, and had beat down all the apples, and carried them away; discovered also where they had lodged that night, and saw the ground, where they set their baskets, [was] bloody; being, as they supposed, and as it was afterwards discovered, [—][1] with the flesh of swine, &c., which they had killed that day. They had lain under the fences without any fires, and seemed by the marks [which] they left behind them, to be very numerous; perceived also by the dew on the grass, that they had not been long gone, and therefore, moved apace in pursuit of them.

Travelling three miles or more, they came into the country road where the tracks parted. One parcel

[1] [to be]

---

* What, I suspect, is now called Palmer's island. There are others further out, which from their distance, it is thought unlikely that they went down so far.

† Cousin to Littleeyes. He was a valuable and faithful servant to Church, and is notorious for his exploits in the eastern wars.

‡ This orchard stood just in the rear of the old garrison before mentioned. See note 2, on page 50. The remains of which were to be seen within the age of some recently living.

steered towards the west end of the great cedar swamp, and the other to the east end. The Captain halted, and told his Indian soldiers, that they had heard, as well as he, what some men had said at Plymouth, about them, &c.; that now was a good opportunity for each party to prove themselves. The track being divided, they should follow one and the English the other, being equal in number. The Indians declined the motion, and were not willing to move any where without him; said [that] they should not think themselves safe without him. But the Captain insisting upon it, they submitted. He gave the Indians their choice, to follow which track they pleased. They replied, that they were light and able to travel, therefore, if he pleased, they would take the west track. And appointing the ruins of John Cook's house at Cushnet, for the place to meet at, each company set out briskly to try their fortunes.

Captain Church, with his English soldiers, followed their track until they came near entering a miry swamp, when the Captain heard a whistle in the rear; (which was a note for a halt) and looking behind him, he saw William Fobes* start out of the company, and made towards him, who hastened to meet him as fast as he could. Fobes told him [that] they had discovered abundance of Indians, and if he pleased to go a few steps back, he might see them himself. He did so, and saw them across the swamp; observing them, he perceived [that] they were gathering whortleberries, and they had no apprehensions of their being so near them. The Captain supposed them to be chiefly women, and therefore calling one Mr. Dillano, who was acquainted with the ground, and the Indian language, and another named Mr.

---

*Perhaps *Forbes* would have been the proper way of spelling this name. He went commissary with Church in his third eastern expedition.

Barns.* With these two men he takes right through the swamp, as fast as he could, and orders the rest to hasten after them.

Captain Church with Dillano and Barns, having good horses, spurred on and were soon amongst the thickest of the Indians, and out of sight of their own men. Among the enemy was an Indian woman, who with her husband had been driven off from Rhodeisland, notwithstanding they had a house upon Mr. Sanford's land, and had planted an orchard before the war; yet the inhabitants would not be satisfied, till they were sent off. Captain Church with his family, living then at the said Sanford's, came acquainted with them, who thought it very hard to turn off such old quiet people. But in the end it proved a providence, and an advantage to him and his family, as you may see afterwards.

This Indian woman knew Captain Church, and as soon as she knew him, held up both her hands, and came running towards them, crying aloud, "Church! Church! Church!" Captain Church bid her stop the rest of the Indians, and tell them, [that] the way to save their lives, was, not to run, but yield themselves prisoners, and he would not kill them. So with her help, and Dillano's, who could call to them in their own language, many of them stopped and surrendered themselves, others scampering and casting away their baskets, &c., betook themselves to the thickets; but Captain Church being on horseback, soon came up with them, and laid hold of a gun that was in the hand of one of the foremost of the company, pulled it from him, and told him he must go back. And when he had turned them, he began to look about him to see where he was, and what was become of his company; hoping they

¹ [and]

---

* Of this person as well as Dillano and Fobes, after considerable pains and search, I can tell nothing. The names are common in the old colony.

might be all as well employed as himself. But he could find none but Dillano, who was very busy gathering up prisoners. The Captain drove his that he had stopped, to the rest; inquiring of Dillano for their company, but could have no news of them; [and][1] moving back, picked up now and then a sculking prisoner by the way.

When they came near the place where the first started the Indians, they discovered their company standing in a body together, and had taken some few prisoners; when they saw their Captain, they hastened to meet him. They told him [that] they found it difficult getting through the swamp, and neither seeing nor hearing any thing of him, they concluded [that] the enemy had killed him, and were at a great loss what to do.

Having brought their prisoners together, they found [that] they had taken and killed sixty-six of their enemy. Captain Church then asked the old squaw, what company they belonged unto? She said, [that] they belonged part to Philip, and part to Qunnappin* and the Narraganset sachem;† discovered

[1] [but]

---

* An old Queen among the Narragansets, says Hutch. I, 263. Trum. I, 347, says that Magnus an old Narraganset Queen was killed 3 July. It is possible that both names meant the same person. She signed the treaty in June, of which mention has been made. In Hutchinson, the name is spelt Quaiapen, and in Hubbard, Quenoquin, and by a writer in N. H. Hist. Col. III, 108, Quannopin. But these names may not all mean the same person, as the author last cited, says, that Mrs. Rowlandson, wife of the minister of Lancaster, when taken was sold to Quannopin whose wife was a sister to Philip's wife. The same writer observes, on page 141, that one of Quannopin's wives' name was [Wittimore. She could not be the same that was drowned near Swanzey, for that was before Mrs. R. was taken. See note 2, on page 27.

† Who is meant by this Narraganset sachem, it is difficult to determine. There were six that subscribed the treaty in June. Canonchet, who was noted for his enmity to the Eng-

also upon her declaration, that both Philip and Quannapin were about two miles off, in the great cedar swamp. He inquired of her what company they had with them. She answered, "Abundance of Indians." The swamp, she said, was full of Indians from one end unto the other, that were settled there; [and] that there were near an hundred men, [who] came from the swamp with them, and left them upon that plain to gather whortleberries, and promised to call them as they came back out of Sconticut neck,* whither they went to kill cattle and horses for provisions for the company.

She perceiving Captain Church move towards the neck, told him, [that] if they went that way they would be killed. He asked her where about they crossed the river? She pointed to the upper passing place. Upon which Captain Church passed over so low down, as he thought it not probable [that] they should meet with his track in their return, and hastened towards the island, where he left Littleeyes with Lightfoot. Finding a convenient place by the river side for securing his prisoners, Captain Church and Mr. Dillano went down to see what was become of Captain Lightfoot, and the prisoners left in his charge.

Lightfoot seeing and knowing them, soon came over with his broken canoe, and informed them, that

---

lish, but it could not be he, because he was taken by the Connecticut volunteers the first week in April, 1676, according to Hubbard, 158, and it was now July; Canonicus, who was killed by the Mohawks, in June; Mattatoag, of whom we hear nothing; Ninigret, who did not join with the rest in the war; and Pumham, who was killed in the woods near Dedham, about the last week in July, as before observed, and who it is possible this might be. He must have been a very old man, as I presume he is the same who sold land to Mr. Samuel Gorton about 1643, and became dissatisfied and complained of him to the court. See Savage's Winthrop, II, 120.

* The point of land opposite Newbedford where the village of Fairhaven now is.

he had seen that day about one hundred men of the enemy go down into Sconticut neck, and that they were now returning again. Upon which they three ran down immediately to a meadow where Lightfoot said [that] the Indians had passed, where they not only saw their tracks, but also them. Whereupon they lay close, until the enemy came into the said meadow, and the foremost set down his load, and halted until all the company came up, and then took up their loads and marched again the same way that they came down into the neck, which was the nearest way unto their camp. Had they gone the other way, along the river, they could not have missed Captain Church's track, which would doubtless have exposed them to the loss of their prisoners, if not of their lives.

But as soon as the coast was clear of them, the Captain sends his Lightfoot to fetch his prisoners from the island, while he and Mr. Dillano returned to the company; sent part of them to conduct Lightfoot and his company to the aforesaid meadow, where Captain Church and his company met them. Crossing the enemy's track they made all haste until they got over Mattapoiset river,* near about four miles beyond the ruins of Cook's house, where he appointed to meet his Indian company, whither he sent Dillano with two more to meet them; ordering them that if the Indians were not arrived to wait for them.

Accordingly, finding no Indians there, they waited until late in the night, when they arrived with their booty. They despatched a post to their Captain, to give him an account of their success, but the day broke before they came to him. And when they had compared successes, they very remarkably found that the number that each company had taken and

---

* (In Rochester.)
Quite a small stream, to the east of which is the village of this name, though now usually pronounced Mattapois. See note 2, on page 32.

slain was equal. The Indians had killed three of
the enemy, and taken sixty-three prisoners, as the
English had done before them.

Both the English and Indians were surprised at
this remarkable providence, and were both parties
rejoicing at it; being both before afraid of what
might have been the unequal success of the parties.
But the Indians had the fortune to take more arms
than the English.

They told the Captain, that they had missed a
brave opportunity by parting; [that] they came upon
a great town of the enemy, viz., Captain Tyasks'*
company; (Tyasks was the next man to Philip) that
they fired upon the enemy before they were discovered, and ran upon them with a shout; [and] the men
ran and left their wives and children, and many of
them their guns. They took Tyasks' wife and son,
and thought, that if their Captain and the English
company had been with them, they might have taken
some hundreds of them; and now they determined
not to part any more.

That night, Philip sent (as afterwards they found
out) a great army to waylay Captain Church at the
entering on of Assawomset neck, expecting [that] he
would have returned the same way [that] he went in;
but that was never his method to return the same way
that he came; and at this time going another way,
he escaped falling into the hands of his enemies.
The next day they went home by Scipican,† and got
well with their prisoners to Plymouth.

---

*In another place, Annawon is called the next man to Philip,
or his chief Captain. Hubbard spelt his name Tiashq, and
informs us that he surrendered himself to the English in June;
but this could not be the case, as it was now near the end of
July, if the Indians knew the company to be Tyasks'. Though
nothing is said in the text that we might be positive that Tyasks
was there, yet Hubbard says that his "wife and child" were taken
first. Nar. 230.

† A small river in Rochester. Near its mouth is the little
village of Scipican, 4 miles to the eastward of Mattapoiset.

He soon went out again, and this stroke he drove many weeks. And when he took any number of prisoners, he would pick out some that he took a fancy to, and would tell them, [that] he took a particular fancy to them, and had chosen them for himself to make soldiers of; and if any would behave themselves well, he would do well by them, and they should be his men, and not sold out of the country. If he perceived [that] they looked surly, and his Indian soldiers called them treacherous dogs, as some of them would sometimes do, all the notice he would take of it, would only be to clap them on the back, and tell them, "Come, come, you look wild and surly, and mutter, but that signifies nothing; these my best soldiers, were, a little while ago, as wild and surly as you are now; by that time you have been but one day along with me, you will love me too, and be as brisk as any of them." And it proved so; for there was none of them, but (after they had been a little while with him, and seen his behaviour, and how cheerful and successful his men were) would be as ready to pilot him to any place where the Indians dwelt or haunted, (though their own fathers, or nearest relations should be among them) or to fight for him, as any of his own men.

Captain Church was, in two particulars, much advantaged by the great English army* that was now

---

*I cannot learn as this "great army" was in much active service about this time. But the Connecticut soldiers were very active. A party under Capt. Denison took prisoner Canonchet, or Nanunttenoo, as he was last called, "the chief sachem of all the Narragansets," who had come down from the Nipmuck country to get seed corn to plant the deserted settlements on Connecticut river. Canonchet was near Pautucket river with a company of his men, and while secure in his tent, and was relating over his exploits against the English, Denison came upon him. He fled with all haste, but as he was crossing the river, a misstep brought his gun under water, and retarded his progress. One Monopoide, a Pequot, being swift of foot, first came up with him. He made no resistance, though he was a man of great

abroad. One was, that they drove the enemy down to that part of the country, viz., to the eastward of Taunton river, by which his business was nearer home. The other was, that when he fell on with a push upon any body of the enemy, (were they never so many) they fled, expecting the great army. And his manner of marching through the woods was such, [that][1] if he were discovered, they appeared to be more than they were; for he always marched at a wide distance one from another, partly for their safety: And this was an Indian custom to march thin and scattered.

Captain Church inquired of some of the Indians that were become his soldiers, how they got such advantage, often, of the English in their marches through the woods? They told him, that the In-

[1] [as]

---

strength. A young Englishman next came up, and asked him some questions, but he would make no answer. At length, casting a look of neglect on his youthful face, said, in broken English, "You too much child; no understand matters of war— Let your Captain come; him I will answer." He would not accept of his life when offered him; and when told that he was to die, said, "He liked it well; that he should die before his heart was soft, or he had spoken any thing unworthy of himself. He was afterward shot at Stonington. And by Autumn, this with other volunteer companies killed and took 230 of the enemy, and 50 muskets; these exploits were continued until the Narragansets were all driven out of the country, except Ninigret. Trumbull, I, 343 to 345. The regular soldiers under Major Talcot marched into the Nipmuck's country, where at one time they killed and took 52 of the enemy. This was in the beginning of June. On 12 June they came upon about 700 Indians, who were furiously besieging Hadley, whom they immediately dispersed. On their return to the Narraganset country they came upon the main body of the enemy near a large cedar swamp, who mostly fled into it. But being surrounded, 171 were killed and taken. Among them was Magnus, the old Queen of Narraganset. Near Providence they made prisoners, and killed 67; and soon after 60 more on their return to Connecticut. Holmes, I, 431 to 433. See note 1, on page 103.

dians gained great advantage of the English by two things; [they]¹ always took care in their marches and fights, not to come too thick together; but the English always kept in a heap together; [so] that it was as easy to hit them, as to hit a house. The other was, that if at any time they discovered a company of English soldiers in the woods, they knew that there were all, for the English never scattered, but the Indians always divided and scattered.

Captain Church [being] now at Plymouth, something or other happened that kept him at home a few days, until a post came to Marshfield on the Lord's* day morning, informing the Governour, that a great army of Indians were discovered, who it was supposed were designing to get over the river towards Taunton or Bridgewater,† to attack those towns that lay on that side [of] the river. The Governour hastened to Plymouth, raised what men he could by the way, came to Plymouth in the beginning of the forenoon exercise, sent for Captain Church out of the meeting house, gave him the news, and desired him immediately to rally what of his company he could, and what men he had raised should join them.

The Captain bestirs himself, but found no bread in the store house, and so was forced to run from house to house to get household bread for their march. But this nor any thing else prevented his marching by the beginning of the afternoon exercise. Marching with what men‡ were ready, he took with him the post that came from Bridgewater to pilot him to the place where he thought he might meet with the enemy.

¹ [the Indians]

---

* July 30, 1676.

† This word in the text was given uniformly without the first *e*.

‡ He had "about 30 Englishmen and 20 reconciled Indians." Hubbard, Nar. 223.

In the evening they heard a smart firing at a distance from them, but it being near night, and the firing but of short continuance, they missed the place, and went into Bridgewater town. It seems [that] the occasion of the firing was, that Philip, finding that Captain Church made that side of the country too hot for him, designed to return to the other side of the country that he came last from. And coming to Taunton river with his company, they felled a great tree across the river, for a bridge to pass over on. And just as Philip's old uncle Akkompoin,* and some other of his chiefs were passing over the tree, some brisk Bridgewater lads had ambushed them, fired upon them, and killed the old man, and several others, which put a stop to their coming over the river that night.†

Next morning, Captain Church moved very early with his company, which was increased by many of Bridgewater, that enlisted under him for that expedition; and by their piloting, soon came very still to the top of the great tree, which the enemy had fallen across the river, and the Captain spied an Indian sitting on the stump of it on the other side of the river, and he clapped his gun up, and had doubtless despatched him, but that one of his own Indians called hastily to him, not to fire, for he believed it was one of their own men. Upon which the Indian upon the stump, looked about, and Captain Church's Indian seeing his face, perceived his mistake, for he knew him to be Philip; clapped up his gun and fired, but it was too late; for Philip immediately threw himself off the stump, leaped down a bank on the other side of the river and made his escape.‡

---

* This might be a brother of Massassoit, but we hear of none but Quadequinah.

† Hubbard places the date of this action on the 31; but according to our author it was on Sunday, and Sunday was the 30.

‡ He had not long before cut off his hair that he might not be known. Hubbard.

Captain Church, as soon as possible got over the river, and scattered in quest of Philip and his company; but the enemy scattered and fled every way. [—]¹ He picked up a considerable many of their women and children, among which were Philip's wife and son; [the son]² about nine years old. Discovering a considerable new track along the river, and examining the prisoners, found [that] it was Qunnapin and the Narragansets, that were drawing off from those parts towards the Narraganset country. He inquired of the prisoners, whether Philip was gone in the same track? They told him that they did not know; for he fled in a great fright when the first English gun was fired, and [that] they had none of them seen or heard any thing of him since.

Captain Church left part of his company there to secure the prisoners [which] they got, and to pick up what more they could find, and with the rest of his company hastened in the track of the enemy to overtake them, if it might be before they got over the river; and ran some miles along the river, until he came to a place where the Indians had waded over; and he with his company waded over after them, up to the armpits; being almost as wet before with sweat as the river could make them. Following about a mile further, and not overtaking them, and the Captain being under [a] necessity to return that night to the army, came to a halt; told his company [that] he must return to his other men. His Indian soldiers moved for leave to pursue the enemy, (though he returned); [they] said [that] the Narragansets were great rogues, and [that] they wanted to be revenged on them for killing some of their relations; named Tockamona, (Awashonks' brother) and some others. Captain Church bade them go and prosper, and made Lightfoot their chief, and gave him the title of Captain. Bid them go and quit themselves like men. And away they scampered like so many horses.

Next morning* early they returned to their Captain, and informed him that they had come up with the enemy, and killed several of them, and brought him thirteen of them prisoners. [They] were mighty proud of their exploit, and rejoiced much at the opportunity of avenging themselves.† Captain Church sent the prisoners to Bridgewater, and sent out his scouts to see what enemies or tracks they could [find.] Discovering some small tracks, he followed them, found where the enemy had kindled some fires, and roasted some flesh, &c., but had put out their fires and were gone.

The Captain followed them by the track, putting his Indians in the front; some of which were such as he had newly taken from the enemy, and added to his company. [He] gave them orders to march softly, and upon hearing a whistle in the rear, to sit down, till further order; or, upon discovery of any of the enemy, to stop; for his design was, if he could discover where the enemy were, not to fall upon them (unless necessitated to it) until next morning. The Indians in the front came up with many women and children, and others that were faint and tired, and so not able to keep up with the company. These gave them an account, that Philip with a great number of the enemy, was a little before.

Captain Church's Indians told the others, [that] they were their prisoners, but if they would submit to order, and be still, no one should hurt them. They being their old acquaintance, were easily persuaded to conform. A little before sunset there was a halt in the front, until the Captain came up. They told him [that] they discovered the enemy. He ordered them to dog them, and watch their motion till it was dark. But Philip soon came to a stop, and fell to breaking and chopping wood, to

---

* August 1st.
† Mr. Hubbard takes no notice of this exploit.

make fires; and a great noise they made. Captain Church draws his company up in a ring, and sat down in the swamp without any noise or fire.

The Indian prisoners were much surprised to see the English soldiers; but the Captain told them, [that] if they would be quiet, and not make any disturbance or noise, they should meet with civil treatment; but if they made any disturbance, or offered to run, or make their escape, he would immediately kill them all; so they were very submissive and obsequious.

When the day broke, Captain Church told his prisoners, that his expedition was such, at [that]¹ time, that he could not afford them any guard; told them, [that] they would find it to be [to] their interest, to attend the orders he was now about to give them; which were, that when the fight was over, which they now expected, or as soon as the firing ceased, they must follow the track of his company, and come to them. (An Indian is next to a blood hound to follow a track.) He said to them, it would be in vain for them to think of disobedience, or to gain any thing by it; for he had taken and killed a great many of the Indian rebels, and should, in a little time kill and take all the rest, &c.

By this time it began to be [as]² light as the time that he usually chose to make his onset. He moved, sending two soldiers before, to try, if they could privately discover the enemy's postures. But very unhappily it fell out, that [at] the very same time, Philip had sent two of his [men] as a scout upon his own track, to see if none dogged [him.]³ [They]⁴ spied the two Indian men, [—]⁵ turned short about, and fled with all speed to their camp, and Captain Church pursued as fast as he could. The two Indians set a yelling and howling, and made the most hideous noise they could invent, soon gave the alarm to Philip and his camp, who all fled at the first tid-

¹ [this]   ² [so]   ³ [them]   ⁴ [who]   ⁵ [and]

ings; left their kettles boiling, and meat roasting upon their wooden spits, and ran into a swamp,* with no other breakfast, than what Captain Church afterwards treated them with.

Captain Church pursuing, sent Mr. Isaac Howland† with a party on one side of the swamp, while himself with the rest, ran on the other side, agreeing to run on each side, until they met on the further end. Placing some men in secure stands at that end of the swamp where Philip entered, concluding that if they headed him, and beat him back, that he would take back in his own track. Captain Church and Mr. Howland soon met at the further end of the swamp, (it not being a great one) where they met with a great number of the enemy, well armed, coming out of the swamp. But on sight of the English, they seemed very much surprised and tacked short. Captain Church called hastily to them, and said, [that] if they fired one gun they were all dead men; for he would have them to know that he had them hemmed in with a force sufficient to command them; but if they peaceably surrendered, they should have good quarter,‡ &c. They seeing the Indians and English come so thick upon them, were so surprised, that many of them stood still and let the English come and take the guns out of their hands, when they were both charged and cocked.

Many, both men, women and children of the enemy, were imprisoned at this time; while Philip,

---

*This swamp was on the west side of Taunton river, in Mattapoiset neck in Swanzey.

† A brother to Jabez Howland before mentioned, and son of the first John Howland, whose name lives among the celebrated FORTY ONE. See note 1, page 89.

‡ We may conclude that Mr. Hubbard is more correct in his account of this affair than our author; he says, that one of Church's Indians called to them in their own language, &c., which from the circumstance that Mr. Church could not speak Indian, is creditable. Nar. 223.

Tispaquin, Totoson,* &c., concluded that the English would pursue them upon their tracks, so were waylaying [them]¹ at the first end of the swamp; hoping thereby to gain a shot upon Captain Church, who was now better employed in taking prisoners, and running them into a valley, in form something [—]² like a punch bowl; and appointing a guard of two files, treble armed with guns taken from the enemy.

But Philip having waited all this while in vain, now moves on after the rest of his company to see what was become of them. And by this time Captain Church had got into the swamp ready to meet him, and as it happened made the first discovery. clapped behind a tree, until Philip's company came pretty near, and then fired upon them; killed many of them, and a close skirmish followed. Upon this Philip having grounds sufficient to suspect the event of his company that went before them, fled back upon his own track; and coming to the place where the ambush lay, they fired on each other, and one Lucas of Plymouth, not being so careful as he might have been about his stand, was killed by the Indians.

In this swamp skirmish Captain Church, with his two men who always ran by his side, as his guard, met with three of the enemy, two of which surrendered themselves, and the Captain's guard seized them, but the other, being a great, stout, surly fellow,

¹ [their tracks]   ² [shaped]

---

* A son of the noted Sam Barrow. Totoson, as will presently be seen, died of grief for the destruction of his family, and loss of his country. He was one of the six Narraganset sachems that subscribed the treaty in July, 1675. His principal place of resort was in Rochester, on the left of the main road as you pass from the village of Rochester to Mattapoiset, and about two miles from the latter. It was a piece of high ground in a large swamp, connected to the high land by a narrow neck, over which, all had to pass to visit him. The road passes near where this neck joins the high ground. *MS. Recollections.*

with his two locks tied up with red, and a great rattlesnake's skin hanging to the back part of his head, (who Captain Church concluded to be Totoson) ran from them into the swamp. Captain Church in person pursued him close, till coming pretty near up with him, presented his gun between his shoulders, but it missing fire, the Indian perceiving it, turned and presented at Captain Church, [but his gun][1] missing fire also; (their guns taking wet with the fog and dew of the morning) [and][2] the Indian turning short for another run, his foot tripped in a small grape vine, and he fell flat on his face. Captain Church was by this time up with him, and struck the muzzle of his gun, an inch and a half, into the back part of his head, which despatched him without another blow.* But Captain Church looking behind him, saw Totoson, the Indian whom he thought he had killed, come flying at him like a dragon; but this happened to be fair in sight of the guard that were set to keep the prisoners, who, spying Totoson and others that were following him, in the very seasonable juncture made a shot upon them, and rescued their Captain; though he was in no small danger from his friends' bullets; for some of them came so near him that he thought he felt the wind of them.

The skirmish being over, they gathered their prisoners together, and found the number that they had killed and taken, was one hundred and seventy-three, (the prisoners which they took over night included) who after the skirmish, came to them as they were ordered.†

Now having no provisions but what they took from

[1] [and]   [2] [but]

---

* It cannot, now, be ascertained who this Indian warriour was, but his bravery was not unequal, perhaps, to numberless *civilized* warriours whose individual fame has filled far bulkier books than this.

† These exploits took up two days, namely the 2, and 3 August.

the enemy, they hastened to Bridgewater, sending an express before to provide for them, their company being now very numerous.*

The gentlemen of Bridgewater met Captain Church with great expressions of honour and thanks, and received him and his army with all due respect and kind treatment.

Captain Church drove his prisoners (that night) into Bridgewater pound, and set his Indian soldiers to guard them. They being well treated with victuals and drink, they had a merry night, and the prisoners laughed as loud as the soldiers; not being so treated [for] a long time before.

Some of the Indians now said to Captain Church, "Sir, you have now made Philip ready to die, for you have made him as poor and miserable as he used to make the English; for you have now killed or taken all [of] his relations; that they believed he would now soon have his head, and that this bout had almost broken his heart,"

The next day† Captain Church moved, and arrived with all his prisoners safe at Plymouth. The great English army was now at Taunton, and Major Talcot,‡ with the Connecticut forces, being in these parts of the country, did considerable spoil upon the enemy.

---

* Church had but about 80 Englishmen and 20 reconciled Indians, says Hubbard, 223, as before noted; and that he took about 153 prisoners. It is probable that he is a little out of the way in the former, as well as the latter part of the statement.

† August 14.

‡ Major John Talcot. It is to be regretted that we have no account of this military chieftain in a biographical work. There are many of this class, which, should they receive a small part of the attention bestowed on some obscure characters, would add much to the value of such works. I have little information of Major Talcot, except what is contained in the valuable History of Connecticut. In note 1, on page 107, a few of his exploits are sketched; but about this time he was as busy as Church, and performed very signal

Now Captain Church being arrived at Plymouth received thanks from the government for his good service, &c. Many of his soldiers were disbanded, and he thought to rest himself awhile; being much fatigued, and his health impaired, by excessive heats and colds, wading through rivers, &c. But it was not long before he was called upon to rally, upon advice that some of the enemy were discovered in Dartmouth woods.

He took his Indians and as many English volunteers as presented to go with him; scattering into small parcels, Mr. Jabez Howland (who was now, and often, his Lieutenant, and a worthy good soldier) had the fortune to discover and imprison a parcel of the enemy. In the evening they met together at an appointed place, and by examining the prisoners they gained intelligence of Totoson's haunt.* And being brisk in the morning, they soon gained an advantage of Totoson's company,† though he himself,

---

services. After he had recruited his men at home a short time, he received intelligence that a large body of Indians were fleeing to the westward. Major Talcot overtook them near the close of the third day, between Westfield and Albany on the west side of Housatonick river. On the following morning he divided his men into two parties; one was to cross the river and come upon their front, at the same time the other fell upon their rear. This well concerted plan came near being ruined; as the first party were crossing the river they were discovered by one of the enemy who was out, fishing. He hallooed, "Awannux! Awannux!" and was immediately shot down. This surprised the enemy, and the gun was taken for the signal to begin the onset by the other party, who discharged upon them as they were rising from sleep. All that were not killed or wounded fled into the woods which were very thick, and the pursuit was given up. Forty-five of the enemy were killed and taken, among the former was the sachem of Quabaog. The army now returned. The Major had at first 350 men beside friendly Indians.

* See note on page 115.

† Hubbard, Nar. 232, says that about fifty were taken at this time.

with his son about eight years old, made their escape, and one old squaw with them, to Agawom,* his own country. But Sam Barrow,† as noted a rogue as any among the enemy, fell into the hands of the English at this time. Captain Church told him, that because of his inhuman murders and barbarities, the Court had allowed him no quarter, but was to be forthwith put to death; and therefore he was to prepare for it. Barrow replied, that the sentence of death against him was just, and that indeed he was ashamed to live any longer, and desired no more favour, than to smoke a whiff of tobacco before his execution. When he had taken a few whiffs, he said, he was ready; upon which one of Captain Church's Indians sunk his hatchet into his brains.

The famous Totoson arriving at Agawom,‡ his son,§ which was the last that was left of the family, (Captain Church having destroyed all the rest) fell sick. The wretch reflecting upon the miserable condition he had brought himself into, his heart became a stone within him, and [he] died. The old squaw flung a few leaves and brush over him, came into Sandwich, and gave this account of his death; and offered to show them where she left his body; but never had the opportunity, for she immediately fell sick and died also.

---

* In Rochester.

† I find nothing more recorded of Barrow, than what is here given. It appears that he had been a noted villain, and perhaps his sentence was just. But he was an old man, and would have died soon enough without murdering. No doubt he made great efforts to redeem his sinking country, an account of which cannot be had at this day, which with many others we have greatly to lament the loss of with the generations to come.

‡ (Several places were called Agawom; [or Agawam] as at Ipswich and Springfield; this Agawom lies in Wareham.)

It is probable that Totoson had other places of resort as well as in Rochester, but that described in note on page 115, is supposed to be the principal.

§ Totoson, son of Sam Barrow, is meant.

Captain Church being now at Plymouth again, weary and worn, would have gone home to his wife and family, but the government being solicitous to engage him in the service until Philip was slain; and promising him satisfaction and redress for some mistreatment that he had met with, he fixes for another expedition.

He had soon volunteers enough to make up the company he desired, and marched through the woods, until he came to Pocasset. And not seeing or hearing of any of the enemy, they went over the ferry to Rhodeisland, to refresh themselves. The Captain with about half a dozen in his company, took horses and rode about eight miles down the island, to Mr. Sanford's, where he had left his wife.* [She][1] no sooner saw him, but fainted with surprise; and by that time she was a little revived, they spied two horsemen coming a great pace. Captain Church told his company, that "Those men (by their riding) come with tidings." When they came up, they proved to be Major Sanford,† and Captain Golding. [They][2] immediately asked Captain Church, what he would give to hear some news of Philip? He replied, that [that] was what he wanted. They told him, [that] they had rode hard with some hopes of overtaking him, and were now come on purpose to inform him, that there were just now tidings from Mounthope. An Indian came down from thence (where Philip's camp now was) [—][3] to Sandy point, over against Trip's, and hallooed, and made signs to

[1] [who]   [2] [who]   [3] [on]

---

* This was on the 11 August.

† The same very probably, who arrested Sir Edmund Andros at R. I. in 1689. Andros was then a prisoner at the castle in Boston harbour, when his servant, by the assistance of Bacchus, caused the sentinel to let him stand in his stead, and Sir Edmund escaped. Hutchinson, I, 349. The name is not uniformly spelt. In the text of Hutchinson, the first *d* is omitted, as in our text page 102, but in his Index two *des* are used.

be fetched over. And being fetched over, he reported, that he was fled from Philip, " who (said he) has killed my brother just before I came away, for giving some advice that displeased him."* And said, [that] he was fled for fear of meeting with the same his brother had met with. Told them also, that Philip was now in Mounthope neck. Captain Church thanked them for their good news, and said, [that] he hoped by to-morrow morning to have the rogue's head. The horses that he and his company came on, standing at the door, (for they had not been unsaddled) his wife must content herself with a short visit, when such game was ahead. They immediately mounted, set spurs to their horses, and away.

The two gentlemen that brought him the tidings, told him, [that] they would gladly wait upon him to see the event of the expedition. He thanked them, and told them, [that] he should be as fond of their company as any men's; and (in short) they went with him. And they were soon at Trip's ferry, (with Captain Church's company) where the deserter was. [He]¹ was a fellow of good sense, and told his story handsomely. He offered Captain Church, to pilot him to Philip, and to help to kill him, that he might revenge his brother's death. Told him, that Philip was now upon a little spot of upland, that was in the south end of the miry swamp, just at the foot of the mount, which was a spot of ground that Captain Church was well acquainted with.

By that time they were over the ferry, and came near the ground, half the night was spent. The Captain commands a halt, and bringing the company together, he asked Major Sanford's and Captain Golding's advice, what method [it] was best to take in making the onset; but they declined giving him any

¹ [who]

---

* Mr. Hubbard says that it was for advising him to make peace with the English.

advice; telling him, that his great experience and success forbid their taking upon them to give advice. Then Captain Church offered Captain Golding [—][1] the honour (if he would please accept of it) to beat up Philip's headquarters. He accepted the offer and had his allotted number drawn out to him, and the pilot. Captain Church's instructions to him were, to be very careful in his approach to the enemy, and be sure not to show himself, until by daylight they might see and discern their own men from the enemy; told him also, that his custom in like cases, was, to creep with his company, on their bellies, until they came as near as they could; and that as soon as the enemy discovered them, they would cry out, and that was the word for his men to fire and fall on. [He] directed him, [that] when the enemy should start and take into the swamp, [that] they should pursue with speed; every man shouting and making what noise [he][2] could; for he would give orders to his ambuscade to fire on any that should come silently.

Captain Church knowing that it was Philip's custom to be foremost in the flight, went down to the swamp, and gave Captain Williams of Scituate the command of the right wing of the ambush, and placed an Englishman and an Indian together behind such shelters of trees, &c., [as][3] he could find, and took care to place them at such distance, that none might pass undiscovered between them; charged them to be careful of themselves, and of hurting their friends, and to fire at any that should come silently through the swamp. But [it] being somewhat farther through the swamp than he was aware of, he wanted men to make up his ambuscade.

Having placed what men he had, he took Major Sanford by the hand, [and] said, "Sir I have so placed them that it is scarce possible Philip should escape them." The same moment a shot whistled

[1] [that he should have]   [2] [they]   [3] [that]

over their heads, and then the noise of a gun towards
Philip's camp. Captain Church, at first, thought
[that] it might be some gun fired by accident; but
before he could speak, a whole volley followed, which
was earlier than he expected. One of Philip's gang
going forth to ease himself, when he had done, looked round him, and Captain Golding thought [that]
the Indian looked right at him, (though probably it
was but his conceit) so fired at him; and upon his
firing, the whole company that were with him fired
upon the enemy's shelter, before the Indians had
time to rise from their sleep, and so over shot them.
But their shelter was open on that side next the
swamp, built so on purpose for the convenience of
flight on occasion. They were soon in the swamp,
but Philip the foremost, who started at the first gun,
threw his *petunk* and powderhorn over his head,
catched up his gun, and ran as fast as he could
scamper, without any more clothes than his small
breeches and stockings; and ran directly on two of
Captain Church's ambush. They let him come fair
within shot, and the Englishman's gun missing fire,
he bid the Indian fire away, and he did so to [the]
purpose; sent one musket bullet through his heart,
and another not above two inches from it. He fell
upon his face in the mud and water, with his gun under him.*

---

*Thus fell the celebrated King Philip, the implacable enemy
of civilization. Never, perhaps, did the fall of any prince or
warriour afford so much space for solid reflection. Had the
resources of this hero been equal to those of his enemies, what
would have been their fate? This exterminating war had not been
known to millions! How vast the contrast! when this country
is viewed in its present populous and flourishing state, extending
over thousands of miles, and the sound of civilization emanating
from every part; and when presented to the imagination in the
days of Philip; with only here and there a solitary dwelling,
surrounded with an endless wilderness.

Before the fall of Philip, the Indians for some time had been
loosing ground, and were considered as nearly subdued,

By this time the enemy perceived [that] they were waylaid on the east side of the swamp, [and] tacked short about. One of the enemy, who seemed to be a great, surly old fellow; hallooed with a loud voice, and often called out, "*Iootash, Iootash.*"* Captain Church called to his Indian, Peter, and asked him, who that was that called so? He answered, that it was old Annawon,† Philip's great Captain; calling

---

but this event clearly decided their fate; doubts were no longer entertained of their appearing formidable. To this memorable and important event, we are able to fix the date, with that certainty, which adds lustre to the pages of history. Other historians agree that it was on the 12 August, and this history clearly indicates that it was on the morning of a certain day, which, therefore, falls on Saturday morning, 12 August, 1676. Mr. Hubbard, Nar. 226, says, "With Philip at this time fell five of his trustiest followers." To know their names would be a relief.

* This is evidently a word of three syllables, and is very easy to pronounce. It should be thus divided, *I-oo-tash*; giving the second syllable the same sound that *oo* has in *moose, mood*, &c. Why Dr. Morse should alter this word to Tootash, I cannot account. It is certainly an unwarrantable deviation and should not be countenanced. See Annals of the American Revolution, 53, and the edition of 1820 of his Hist. N. England.

† This word also, the author of the Annals of the American Revolution has thought proper to alter to Anawon; this, however, is less important than that mentioned in the last note, but should not be warranted. Some contend that its termination should be written *wan*, as being more agreeable to analogy. I cannot think that it is; because the author, without doubt, intended by the termination *won*, to convey the sound of *wun*, and not that heard in *swan*.

What is preserved of this warriour is found in this history. His principal camp was in Squannaconk swamp, in Rehoboth, where he was taken by Church, as will presently be seen. In a preceding page, Tyasks was called the next man to Philip; but, that Annawon stood in that place, is evident from his being possessed of that chief's royalties after he was killed. Mr. Hubbard says that a son of Philip's chief Captain was killed when Philip was. But as it is not possible for me to ascertain with certainty who he means by Philip's chief Captain, we cannot tell whether he were a son of Annawon or not; but it appears quite probable to me that he was.

on his soldiers to stand to it, and fight stoutly. Now the enemy finding that place of the swamp which was not ambushed, many of them made their escape in the English tracks.

The man that had shot down Philip, ran with all speed to Captain Church, and informed him of his exploit, who commanded him to be silent about it and let no man more know it, until they had driven the swamp clean. But when they had driven the swamp through, and found [that] the enemy had escaped, or at least, the most of them, and the sun now up, and so the dew gone, that they could not easily track them, the whole company met together at the place where the enemy's night shelter was, and then Captain Church gave them the news of Philip's death. Upon which the whole army gave three loud huzzas.

Captain Church ordered his body to be pulled out of the mire to the upland. So some of Captain Church's Indians took hold of him by his stockings, and some by his small breeches, (being otherwise naked) and drew him through the mud to the upland; and a doleful, great, naked, dirty beast he looked like.* Captain Church then said, that forasmuch as he had caused many an Englishman's body to be unburied, and to rot above ground, that not one of his bones should be buried. And calling his old Indian executioner, bid him behead and quarter him. Accordingly he came with his hatchet and stood over him, but before he struck he made a small speech directing it to Philip, [which was, that][1] " he had been a very great man, and had made many a man afraid of him, but so big as he was, he would now

[1] [and said]

---

* How natural is the propensity of man, to exult in the fall of his enemy! However great or brave, if the great disposer of events renders him unprofitably so, no allowance is made in the day of victory, though the honour of the conqueror is measured by that of his foe.

chop him in pieces."* And so he went to work and did as he was ordered.†

Philip having one very remarkable hand, being much scarred, occasioned by the splitting of a pistol in it formerly, Captain Church gave the head and that hand to Alderman,‡ the Indian who shot him, to show to such gentlemen as would bestow gratuities upon him; and accordingly he got many a penny by it.

This being on the last day of the week, the Captain with his company, returned to the island, [and] tarried there until Tuesday ;§ and then went off and ranged through all the woods to Plymouth, and received their premium, which was thirty shillings per head, for the enemies which they had killed or taken, instead of all wages; and Philip's head went at the same price. Methinks it is scanty reward, and poor encouragement; though it was better than [it][1] had

[1] [what]

---

* Dr. Morse in copying from this history, quotes the above speech thus; "You have been one very great man. You have made many a man afraid of you. But so big as you be, I will chop you in pieces."

† Being quartered he was hanged up, and his head carried in triumph to Plymouth. Magnalia, II, 498, 499. " That very night [previous to his death] Philip had been dreaming that he was fallen into the hands of the English; and now just as he was telling his dream, with advice unto his friends to fly for their lives, lest the knave who had newly gone from them should show the English how to come at them, Captain Church, with his company, fell in upon them." Ibid. Perhaps this story deserves as much credit as that on page 20, note 1. Mr. Hubbard, no doubt heard this part of the story, but perhaps not having as much faith in dreams as the author of the Magnalia, thought proper to omit it.

‡ This was the same Indian, whose brother was killed, and who informed the English where to find Philip. Trumbull, Hist. Con. I, 349.

§ August 15.

been some time before. For this march they received *four shillings and sixpence* a man, which was all the reward they had, except the honour of killing Philip. This was in the latter end* of August, 1676.

Captain Church had been but a little while at Plymouth, before a post from Rehoboth came to inform the Governour, that old Annawon, Philip's chief Captain, was with his company ranging about their woods, and was very offensive and pernicious to Rehoboth and Swanzey. Captain Church was immediately sent for again, and treated with to engage in one expedition more. He told them, [that] their encouragement was so poor, he feared [that] his soldiers would be dull about going again. But being a hearty friend to the cause, he rallies again, goes to Mr. Jabez Howland, his old Lieutenant, and some of his soldiers that used to go out with him; told them how the case was circumstanced, and that he had intelligence of old Annawon's walk and haunt, and wanted hands to hunt him. They did not want much entreating, but told him, [that] they would go with him as long as there was an Indian left in the woods. He moved and ranged through the woods to Pocasset.

It being the latter end of the week, he proposed to go on to Rhodeisland, and rest until Monday: but on the Lord's day morning,† there came a post to inform the Captain, that early the same morning, a canoe with several Indians in it, passed from Prudence island‡ to Poppasquash§ neck. Captain Church thought if he could possibly surprise them,

---

* The reason of this anachronism is explained in note 1, on page 94.

† August 20.

‡ A long and crooked Island on the west side of Rhodeisland, extending from near the centre of Rhodeisland to Warwick neck, in length about 6 miles.

§ (On the west side of Bristol.)
And separated from it by Bristol bay.

[that] he might probably gain some intelligence of more game; therefore he made all possible speed after them. The ferry boat being out of the way he made use of canoes. But by that time they had made two freights, and had got over about fifteen or sixteen of his Indians, the wind sprung up with such violence that canoes could no more pass.* The Captain seeing it was impossible for any more of his soldiers to come to him, he told his Indians, [that] if they were willing to go with him, he would go to Poppasquash, and see if they could catch some of the enemy Indians. They were willing to go, but were sorry [that] they had no English soldiers.† So they marched through the thickets that they might not be discovered, until they came unto the salt meadow, to the northward of Bristol town, that now is, [when][1] they heard a gun; the Captain looked about, not knowing but it might be some of his own company in the rear. So halting till they all came up, he found [that] it was none of his own company that fired.

Now, though he had but a few men, [he] was minded to send some of them out on a scout. He moved it to Captain Lightfoot to go with three [others][2] on a scout; he said [that] he was willing, provided the Captain's man, Nathaniel (which was an Indian they had lately taken) might be one of them, because he was well acquainted with the

[1] [then]   [2] [more]

---

* This event was but a few days more than one hundred years before the celebrated passage of Washington over the Delaware to attack the Hessians at Trenton, which has been so beautifully described by Barlow. See his Columbiad, B. vi. line 91 to 214. Perhaps this expedition of the heroick Church, in the small days of Newengland was of as much consequence as greater ones were a century after. It is not impossible, but that another Barlow may arise and sing over the events of these days of yore A vast theme for a poet!

† They had one or more Englishmen in the company as will appear presently.

neck, and coming lately from among them, knew how to call them.

The Captain bid him choose his three companions, and go; and if they came across any of the enemy, not to kill them if they could possibly take them alive, that they might gain intelligence concerning Annawon. The Captain with the rest of his company moved but a little way further toward Poppasquash, before they heard another gun, which seemed to be the same way with the other, but further off; but they made no halt until they came unto the narrow of Poppasquash neck; where Captain Church left three men more to watch, [and see] if any should come out of the neck, and to inform the scout, when they returned, which way he was gone.

He parted the remainder of his company, half on one side of the neck, and the other with himself went on the other side, [—]¹ until they met; and meeting neither with Indians nor canoes, returned big with expectations of tidings by their scout. But when they came back to the three men at the narrow of the neck, they told their Captain [that] the scout, [had]² not returned, [and] had heard nor seen any thing of them. This filled them with thoughts of what should become of them. By that time they had sat and waited an hour longer, it was very dark, and they despaired of their returning to them.

Some of the Indians told their Captain, [that] they feared his new man, Nathaniel, had met with his old Mounthope friends, and [—]³ turned rogue. They concluded to make no fires that night, (and indeed they had no great need of any) for they had no victuals to cook, [—]⁴ not so much as a morsel of bread with them.

They took up their lodgings scattering, that if possibly their scout should come in the night, and whistle, (which was their sign) some or other of them might hear them. They had a very solitary, hun-

¹ [of the neck]   ² [was]   ³ [was]   ⁴ [had]

gry night; and as soon as the day broke,* they drew off through the brush to a hill without the neck. And looking about them they espied one Indian man come running somewhat towards them. The Captain ordered one man to step out and show himself. Upon this the Indian ran right to him, and who should it be but Captain Lightfoot, to their great joy. Captain Church asked him what news? He answered, "Good news;" [that] they were all well, and had catched ten Indians; and that they guarded them all night in one of the flankers of the old English garrison;† that their prisoners were part of Annawon's company, and that they had left their families in a swamp above Mattapoiset neck.‡ And as they were marching towards the old garrison, Lightfoot gave Captain Church a particular account of their exploit, viz.; that presently after they left him, they heard another gun, which seemed toward the Indian burying place; and moving that way, they discovered two of the enemy flaying of a horse. The scout clapping into the brush, Nathaniel bid them sit down, and he would presently call all the Indians thereabout unto him. They hid, and he went a little distance back from them, and set up his note and howled like a wolf. One of the two immediately left his horse, and came running to see who was there; but Nathaniel howling lower and lower, drew him in between those that lay in wait for him, who seized him. Nathaniel continuing the same note, the other left the horse also, following his mate, and met with the same. When they caught these two, they examined them apart and found them

---

* Monday August 28.

† This was the fort that was built in June, 1675, which Church so much disapproved of. See page 35. It was probably of more service now than it had ever been before, if we judge from any account since given.

‡ (In Swanzey. There is another Mattapoiset in Rochester.)

to agree in their story; that there were eight more
of them [who came]¹ down into the neck to get
provisions, and had agreed to meet at the burying
place that evening. These two being some of Nathaniel's old acquaintance, he had great influence
upon them, and with his enticing story, (telling what
a brave captain he had, how bravely he lived since
he had been with him, and how much they might
better their condition by turning to him, &c.,) per
suaded and engaged them to be on his side, which,
indeed, now began to be the better side of the hedge.
They waited but a little while before they espied the
rest of theirs coming up to the burying place, and
Nathaniel soon howled them in, as he had done their
mates before.

When Captain Church came to the garrison, he
met his Lieutenant,* and the rest of his company.
And then making up good fires they fell to roasting
their horse beef, enough to last them a whole day,
but had not a morsel of bread, though salt they had,
(which they always carried in their pockets, [and]
which at this time was very acceptable to them.)

Their next motion was towards the place where
the prisoners told them [that] they had left their
women and children, and surprised them all; and
some others that [had]² newly come to them. And
upon examination they held to one story, that it was
hard to tell where to find Annawon, for he never
roosted twice in a place.

Now a certain Indian soldier, that Captain Church
had gained over to be on his side, prayed that he
might have liberty to go and fetch in his father, who,
he said, was about four miles from that place, in a
swamp, with no other than a young squaw. Captain
Church inclined to go with him, thinking [that] it
might be in his way to gain some intelligence of
Annawon; and so taking one Englishman and a few

¹ [come]   ² [were]

---

* Mr. Jabez Howland

Indians with him, leaving the rest there, he went with his new soldier to look [after] his father.

When he came to the swamp, he bid the Indian go [and]¹ see if he could find his father. He was no sooner gone, but Captain Church discovered a track coming down out of the woods; upon which he and his little company lay close, some on one side of the track, and some on the other. They heard the Indian soldier making a howling for his father, and at length somebody answered him; but while they were listening, they thought [that] they heard somebody coming towards them; presently [they] saw an old man coming up with a gun on his shoulder, and a young woman following in the track which they lay by. They let them come up between them, and then started up and laid hold of them both. Captain Church immediately examined them apart, telling them what they must trust to, if they told false stories. He asked the young woman, what company they came from last? She said, "From Captain Annawon's." He asked her how many were in company with him when she left him? She said, "Fifty or sixty." He asked her how many miles it was to the place where she left him? She said, [that] she did not understand miles, but he was up in Squannaconk swamp.*

The old man, who had been one of Philip's council, upon examination, gave exactly the same account. Captain Church asked him if they could get there that night? He said, [that] if they went presently, and travelled stoutly, they might get there by sunset. He asked whither he was going? He answered, that Annawon had sent him down to look [for] some Indians, that were gone down into Mounthope neck to kill provisions. Captain Church let him know that those Indians were all his prisoners.

¹ [to] ² [but]

---

* (Southeasterly part of Rehoboth)

By this time came the Indian soldier and brought his father and one Indian more. The Captain was now in a great strait of mind what to do next; he had a mind to give Annawon a visit, now he knew where to find him. But his company was very small, [only]¹ half a dozen men beside himself, and was under a necessity to send some body back to acquaint his Lieutenant and company with his proceedings. However, he asked his small company that were with him, whether they would willingly go with him and give Annawon a visit? They told him, [that] they were always ready to obey his commands, &c.; but withal told him, that they knew this Captain Annawon was a great soldier; that he had been a valiant Captain under Asuhmequin,* Philip's father; and

¹ [but]

---

* Morton, 122, calls him Woosamequen. This was the last name by which the "good old Massassoit" was known. This name he took about the time of the Pequot war as was mentioned in note 1, on page 17. Allen in his Biographical Dictionary, has given a short sketch of him, which is very deficient. Not even informing us that he was ever known by any other name than Massassoit. This celebrated chief entered into a league of friendship with the Plymouth Pilgrims, the next spring after their arrival, which was kept until his death. Some of the other tribes insultingly told him, that through his cowardice he had treated with the English. However this might be, he is said always to have advised his sons against engaging in a war with them, for he believed that in time the Indians would be annihilated. He was remarkable for his aversion to the English religion. Hutchinson, I, 252, says that "when he was treating for the sale of some of his lands at Swanzey, insisted upon it as a condition, that the English should never attempt to draw off any of his people from their religion to christianity, and would not recede until he found the treaty would break off if he urged it any further." He was personally several times at Plymouth. On his first arrival there, in March, 1620-21, he made his appearance on the hill, the south side of Town brook, with several of his principal men with him. Here he made a stop and Mr. Edward Winslow was sent to him with a present, and the Governour's (Carver) compliments that he desired to see him, and treat with him. He left Mr. Winslow

that he had been Philip's chieftain all this war. A very subtle man, of great resolution, and had often said, that he would never be taken alive by the English.

---

as a hostage with his men, and with about twenty of his soldiers went down to the brook, where Captain Standish met him with a file of six men, and conducted him to a new house. A green rug was spread over the floor, and three or four cushions laid upon it. The Governour then came, preceded by a drum and trumpet, at the sound of which they appeared much delighted. After some introduction, the above mentioned league or treaty was entered upon and concluded as follows:

Article I. That neither he, nor any of his, should injure or do hurt to any of their people. *Art.* II. That if any of his did any hurt to any of theirs, he should send the offender that they might punish him. *Art.* III. That if any thing were taken away from any of theirs, he should cause it to be restored ; and they should do the like to his. *Art.* IV. That if any did unjustly war against him, they would aid him; and if any did war against them, he should aid them. *Art.* V. That he should send to his neighbour confederates, to inform them of this, that they might not wrong them, but might be likewise comprised in these conditions of peace. *Art.* VI. That when his men came to them upon any occasion, they should leave their arms (which were then bows and arrows) behind them. *Art.* VII. Lastly, that so doing, their sovereign Lord, King James would esteem him as his friend and ally.

Two years after (in 1623) Massassoit fell sick, and Mr. Winslow went to visit him. He found the house crowded with men who were using their rude exertions to restore him to health. Being informed that his friends were come to see him, he desired to speak with them. (He was very sick and his sight had left him.) When Mr. Winslow went to him he took him by the hand and faintly said, "Keen Winsnow?" That is, "Art thou Winslow?" Being informed that he was, he then said, "*Matta neen wonckunet namen Winsnow!*" That is, "O Winslow I shall never see thee again!" He had not taken any thing for two days, but Mr. Winslow gave him something that he had prepared which he was able to swallow, and he immediately grew better, and soon entirely recovered. In 1639, this Indian King was at Plymouth with Mooanam or Wamsutta, his son, then or afterwards named Alexander, and renewed the former league. The precise time of his death is unknown. But from Hubbard, 59, it appears that it was about 1656. Morton, 26, and 122. Hutchinson, J 252, 253. Belknap, Amer. Biog. I, 212, 294.

And moreover they knew that the men that were with him were resolute fellows, some of Philip's chief soldiers; and therefore, feared whether it was practicable to make an attempt upon him with so small a handful of assailants as were now with him. Told him further, that it would be a pity, [—][1] after all the great things he had done, [that] he should throw away his life at last. Upon which he replied, that he doubted not Annawon was a subtle and valiant man; that he had a long time, but in vain, sought for him, and never till now could find his quarters and he was very loath to miss of the opportunity; and doubted not, [—][2] that if they would cheerfully go with him, the same Almighty Providence that had hitherto protected and befriended them, would do so still, &c.

Upon this with one consent they said, [that] they would go. Captain Church then turned to one Cook of Plymouth, (the only Englishman then with him) and asked him, what he thought of it? [He][3] replied, "Sir, I am never afraid of going any where when you are with me." Then Captain Church asked the old Indian, if he could carry his horse with him? (For he conveyed a horse thus far with him.) He replied that it was impossible for a horse to pass the swamps. Therefore, he sent away his new Indian soldier with his father, and the Captain's horse, to his Lieutenant, and orders for him to move to Taunton with the prisoners, to secure them there, and to come out in the morning in the Rehoboth road, in which he might expect to meet him, if he were alive and had success.

The Captain then asked the old fellow if he would pilot him [to][4] Annawon? He answered, that he hav-

[1] [that]   [2] [but]   [3] [who]   [4] [unto]

Holmes, I, 208. Prince, 185, &c. Whether he had more than two sons is uncertain; but it seems by a letter to London, written during this war, that there was another. See Hutchinson, I, 265

ing given him his life, he was obliged to serve him. He bid him move on then, and they followed. The old man would out travel them so far sometimes, that they were almost out of sight; [and] looking over his shoulder, and seeing them behind, he would halt.

Just as the sun was setting, the old man made a full stop and sat down; the company coming up, also sat down, being all weary. Captain Church asked, "What news?" He answered, that about that time in the evening, Captain Annawon sent out his scouts to see if the coast were clear, and as soon as it began to grow dark, the scouts returned; and then (said he) "we may move again securely." When it began to grow dark, the old man stood up again, [and] Captain Church asked him if he would take a gun and fight for him? He bowed very low, and prayed him not to impose such a thing upon him, as to fight against Captain Annawon his old friend. But says he, "I will go along with you, and be helpful to you, and will lay hands on any man that shall offer to hurt you."

It being now pretty dark, they moved close together;—anon they heard a noise. The Captain stayed the old man with his hand, and asked his own men what noise they thought it might be? They concluded it to be the pounding of a mortar. The old man had given Captain Church a description of the place* where Annawon now lay, and of the diffi-

---

* This solitary retreat is in the southeasterly part of the town of Rehoboth, but being near Taunton line, some, in relating the story, report it to be in this town. It is about 8 miles from Taunton green, and nearly in a direct line to Providence. The northwest corner of Dighton runs up between Taunton and Rehoboth, through which we pass in going from Taunton to ANNAWON'S ROCK. (By this name it is known throughout that part of the country.) It is in a great swamp, called Squannaconk, containing nearly 3000 acres, as 1 was informed by Mr. A. Bliss, the nearest inhabitant to it. The road passes round the northwesterly part of

culty of getting at him. Being sensible that they
were pretty near them, with two of his Indians he
creeps to the edge of the rocks, from whence he
could see their camps. He saw three companies of
Indians at a little distance from each other; being
easy to be discovered by the light of their fires. He
saw also the great ANNAWON and his company,
who had formed his camp or kenneling place by
falling a tree under the side of the great cliffs of
rocks, and setting a row of birch bushes up against
it; where he himself, his son, and some of his chiefs
had taken up their lodgings, and made great fires
without them, and had their pots and kettles boiling,
and spits roasting. Their arms also he discovered,
all set together, in a place fitted for the purpose,
standing up an end against a stick lodged in two
crotches, and a mat placed over them, to keep them
from the wet or dew. The old Annawon's feet and
his son's head were so near the arms, as almost to
touch them. [—][1]

The rocks were so steep that it was impossible to
get down, [only][2] as they lowered themselves by the

[1] [but]   [2] [but]

---

the swamp, and within 6 or 8 rods of the rock. This immense rock extends northeast and southwest 70 or 80 feet,
and to this day the camp of Annawon is approached with
difficulty. A part of its southeast side hangs over a little,
and the other, on the northeast part, seems in no very distant period, to have tumbled down in large clefts. Its height
may be 30 feet. It is composed of sand and pebbles. A few
scattering maple, beech, birch, &c., grow about it; as also
briars and water bushes, so thick as almost to forbid approach. Formerly, it was, no doubt, entirely surrounded by
water, as it is to this time in wet seasons. The northwest
side of the rock is easily ascended, as it gradually slopes away
from its summit to its base, and at an angle, perhaps, not exceeding 35°. Small bushes grow from the seams in its steep
side, as in the days of Church. Near the southwest extremity is an opening of an angular form, in which, it is said,
Annawon and the other chiefs were encamped. This opening now contains the stump of a large tree, which must have
grown since those days, as it nearly fills it up.

boughs, and the bushes that grew in the cracks of the rocks. Captain Church creeping back again to the old man, asked him, if there were no possibility of getting at them some other way? He answered, "No." That he and all that belonged to Annawon, were ordered to come that way, and none could come any other way without difficulty, or danger of being shot.

Captain Church then ordered the old man and his daughter to go down foremost with their baskets at their backs, that when Annawon saw them with their baskets he should not mistrust the intrigue. Captain Church and his handful of soldiers crept down also, under the shadow of those two and their baskets. The Captain himself crept close behind the old man, with his hatchet in his hand, and stepped over the young man's head to the arms. The young Annawon discovering of him, whipped his blanket over his head, and shrunk up in a heap. The old Captain Annawon started up on his breech, and cried out "Howoh."* And despairing of escape, threw himself back again, and lay silent until Captain Church had secured all the arms, &c. And having secured that company, he sent his Indian soldiers to the other fires and companies, giving them instructions, what to do and say. Accordingly they went into the midst of them. When they [had] discover-

---

* This word according to the tradition of aged people, signified, "I am taken." Dr. Morse has thought fit to alter the spelling of this word to Howah. It is very evident that the writer of this history, intended in the termination of this word to convey the sound of *oh*, and not *ah*. Were this not the case, it is certainly better to give it to posterity as we find it. Such alterations, however small and unimportant they may seem to some readers, have a very bad tendency; they tend to cause us to doubt of the authenticity of any accounts that are handed down to us. It may be said that an alteration of this kind is of no consequence, because it does not alter the sense. But it should be recollected, that the authority is as good for any other alteration; for to alter letters is to alter words; to alter words is to change the sense.

ed themselves [to the enemy, they][1] told them that, their Captain Annawon was taken, and [that] it would be best for them, quietly and peaceably to surrender themselves, which would procure good quarter for them; otherwise, if they should pretend to resist or make their escape, it would be in vain, and they could expect no other but that Captain Church, with his great army, who had now entrapped them, would cut them to pieces. Told them also, [that] if they would submit themselves, and deliver up all their arms unto them, and keep every man in his place until it was day, they would assure them that their Captain Church, who had been so kind to themselves when they surrendered to him, should be as kind to them. Now they being old acquaintance, and many of them relations, did much the readier give heed to what they said; [so] complied, and surrendered up their arms unto them, both their guns and hatchets, &c., and were forthwith carried to Captain Church.*

Things being so far settled, Captain Church asked Annawon, " what he had for supper?" " for (said he) I am come to sup with you." " *Taubut*," (said Annawon) with a big voice, and looking about upon his women, bid them hasten and get Captain Church and his company some supper. [He] then turned to Captain Church and asked him whether he would eat cow beef or horse beef? The Captain told him cow beef would be most acceptable. It was soon got ready, and pulling his little bag of salt out of his pocket, which was all the provision he brought with him. This seasoned his cow beef. So that with it and the dried green corn, which the old squaw was pounding in the mortar, while they were sliding

[1] [who they were]

---

* Mr. Hubbard differs considerably in his relation of the taking of Annawon, from our author, and is much shorter. Nothing very important seems to be omitted in this account, excepting the date, and that Mr. Hubbard omits also.

down the rocks, he made a very hearty supper. And this pounding in the mortar, proved lucky for Captain Church's getting down the rocks; for when the old squaw pounded, they moved, and when she ceased, to turn the corn, they ceased creeping. The noise of the mortar prevented the enemy's hearing their creeping, and the corn being now dressed, supplied the want of bread, and gave a fine relish with the cow beef.

Supper being over, Captain Church sent two of his men to inform the other companies, that he had killed Philip, and taken their friends in Mounthope neck, but had spared their lives, and that he had subdued now all the enemy, (he supposed) except this company of Annawon; and now if they would be orderly and keep their places until morning, they should have good quarter, and that he would carry them to Taunton, where they might see their friends again, &c.

The messengers returned, [and informed] that the Indians yielded to his proposals.

Captain Church thought it was now time for him to take a nap, having had no sleep in two days and one night before. [So he] told his men, that if they would let him sleep two hours, they should sleep all the rest of the night. He laid himself down and endeavoured to sleep, but all disposition to sleep departed from him.

After he had lain a little while, he looked up to see how his watch managed, but found them all fast asleep. Now Captain Church had told Captain Annawon's company, as he had ordered his Indians to tell the others; [namely] that their lives should all be spared, excepting Captain Annawon's, and it was not in his power to promise him his life, but he must carry him to his masters at Plymouth, and he would entreat them for his life.

Now when Captain Church found not only his own men, but all the Indians fast asleep, Annawon only excepted, who, he perceived was as broad awake as himself; and so they lay looking one upon the other, perhaps an hour. Captain Church said nothing to him, for he could not speak Indian, and thought Annawon could not speak English.

At length Annawon raised himself up, cast off his blanket, and with no more clothes than his small breeches, walked a little way back from the company. Captain Church thought no other but that he had walked a little distance for some necessary errand, and would very soon return. But by and by he was gone out of sight and hearing, and then Captain Church began to suspect some ill design in him; and got all the guns close to him, and crowded himself close under young Annawon; that if he should anywhere get a gun, he should not make a shot at him, without endangering his son. Lying very still awhile, waiting for the event, at length, he heard somebody coming the same way that Annawon went. The moon now shining bright, he saw him at a distance coming with something in his hands, and coming up to Captain Church, he fell upon his knees before him, and offered him what he had brought, and speaking in plain English, said, " Great Captain, you have killed Philip, and conquered his country; for I believe that I and my company are the last that war against the English, so suppose the war is ended by your means; and therefore these things belong unto you." Then opening his pack, he pulled out Philip's belt,* curiously wrought with wompom,† being nine inches broad,

---

* This belt and some other of Philip's ornaments are now owned in a family at Swanzey, as I was informed by an inhabitant of the place.

† Wampum, or wampom, called also wampampeag; a kind of money in use among the Indians. It was a kind of bead made of shells of the great conch, muscles, &c., and curiously wrought and polished, with a hole through them. They were of different colours, as black, blue, red, white and purple; the last of which were wrought by the Fivenations. Six of the white, and three of the black, or blue passed for a penny. Trumbull, Hist. U S. I, 23. In 1667 wampom

wrought with black and white wompom, in various figures, and flowers and pictures of many birds and beasts. This, when hanged upon Captain Church's shoulders, reached his ancles; and another belt of wompom he presented him with, wrought after the former manner, which Philip was wont to put upon his head. It had two flags on the back part, which hung down on his back, and another small belt with a star upon the end of it, which he used to hang on his breast, and they were all edged with red hair, which Annawon said they got in the Mohog's* country. Then he pulled out two horns of glazed powder, and a red cloth blanket. He told Captain Church [that] these were Philip's royalties, which he was wont to adorn himself with, when he sat in state; that he thought himself happy that he had an opportunity to present them to Captain Church, who had won them, &c. [They] spent the remainder of the night in discourse. And [Captain Annawon] gave an account of what mighty success he had [had] formerly in wars against many nations of Indians,† when he served Asuhmequin, Philip's father, &c.‡

---

was made a tender by law for the payment of debts " not exceeding 40 shillings, at 8 white or 4 black a penny; this was repealed in 1671." Douglass, I, 437.

* Mohawk's. This word is spelt Moohag on page 68. See note 2, of page 68.

† How much it is to be lamented that Mr. Church did not preserve the conversation of Annawon at this time. Nothing could have added more value to his history.

‡ Thus ended Monday night 28 August. It is unaccountable that Mr. Hubbard fixes no date to this transaction, and the more so, as he wrote so near the time that it took place. It is not without some hesitation that the above is admitted, on account of the disagreements in the narratives. Hubbard, 230, says that Tispaquin came in, in September, and places it before the taking of Annawon, which if our author be correct is a gross mistake. Now it is evident that it was on Monday night from the text, and that there was a moon not long after dark, perhaps an hour or two. This ex-

In the morning, as soon as it was light, the Captain marched with his prisoners out of that swampy country towards Taunton. [He] met his Lieutenant and company about four miles out of town, who expressed a great deal of joy to see him again, and said, [that] it was more than ever they expected. They went into Taunton, were civilly and kindly treated by the inhabitants. [Here they] refreshed and rested themselves that night.

Early next morning, the Captain took old Annawon, and half a dozen of his Indian soldiers, and his own man, and went to Rhodeisland; sending the rest of his company, and his prisoners by his Lieutenant* to Plymouth. Tarrying two or three days upon the island, he then went to Plymouth, and carried his wife and his two children with him.

Captain Church had been but a little while at Plymouth, when he was informed of a parcel of Indians who had haunted the woods between Plymouth and Sippican; that did great damage to the English, in killing their cattle, horses, and swine. The Captain was soon in pursuit of them. [He] went out from Plymouth the next Monday in the afternoon, [and] next morning early they discovered a track. The Captain sent two Indians on the track to see what they could discover, whilst he and his company followed gently after. But the two Indians soon returned with tidings, that they discovered the enemy sitting round their fires, in a thick place of brush. When they came pretty near the place, the Captain ordered every man to creep as he did, and surround them by creeping as near as they could, till they should be discovered, and then

---

actly corresponds with the date given above, because the moon was at the full on the 26 August, and this being two nights after, they would of course have the moon a short time after dark.

* Mr. Jabez Howland.

to run [—]¹ upon them, and take them alive if possible, (for their prisoners were their pay.) They did so, [taking]² every one* that were at the fires, not one escaping.

Upon examination they agreed in their stories, that they belonged to Tispaquin, who was gone with John Bump,† and one more, to Agawam‡ and Sippican§ to kill horses, and were not expected back in two or three days.‖

This same Tispaquin had been a great Captain, and the Indians reported, that he was such a great *Pauwau*,¶ that no bullet could enter him, &c. Captain Church said, [that] he would not have him killed, for there was a war** broke out in the eastern part of the country, and he would have him saved to go with him to fight the eastern Indians. Agreeably he left two old squaws, of the prisoners, and bid them tarry there until their Captain, Tispaquin, returned, and to tell him that Church had been there, and had taken his wife and children, and company, and carried them down to Plymouth, and would spare all their lives, and his too, if he would come down to them, and bring the other two that were with him, and they should be his soldiers, &c.

Captain Church then returned to Plymouth, leaving the old squaws well provided for, and biscuit for Tispaquin when he returned; telling his soldiers, that he doubted not, but he had laid a trap that

¹[on]   ²[took]

---

* About 50, according to Hubbard, 231. "The place was near Lakenham upon Pocasset neck, so full of bushes that a man could not see a rod before him." Ibid.

† Nothing more is said of this Indian as I can find. There are respectable white people in Middleborough by this name, from the ancestors of whom he might have derived his name.

‡ (Wareham.)   § (Rochester.)

‖ This was in September.

¶ Wizard or conjurer. English writers denominate their priests by this name.

** An account of this war will be given in the Appendix. See No. V.

would take him. Captain Church two aays after went to Boston, (the commissioners* then sitting) and waited upon the honourable Governour Leverett,† who then lay sick. [He]¹ requested Captain Church to give him some account of the war, who readily obliged his honour therein, to his great satisfaction, as he was pleased to express himself; taking him by the hand, and telling him, [that] if it pleased God [that] he lived, he would make it a brace of a hundred pounds advantage to him out of the Massachusetts colony, and would endeavour that the rest of the colonies should do proportionably. But he died within a fortnight after, and so nothing was done of that nature.

¹[who]

* I find no mention of any other court in Massachusetts at this time, than that called together the 9 August, occasioned by a letter from the King, summoning the colony to appoint commissioners to answer to the complaints of Gorges and Mason, concerning boundaries, &c. See Hist. Mass, I, 280, 281. This and other business, it is probable, kept them together until the time alluded to in our text.

† Governour John Leverett came to America with his father in 1633, from Boston in Lincolnshire, England. He was made deputy Governour in 1671, and in 1673, Governour. He continued in the office until his death, which, according to our author, was in 1676. Dr. Douglass also, in his Summary, I, 429, says that it was " in the autumn of 1676." It is remarkable, that most, if not all, later historians place his death in 1678, on the authority of Mather, I conclude. In my first edition of this work I followed the Biographical Dictionaries without scruple, but soon discovered the errour. Eliot and Allen, perhaps, followed Mather without hesitation, because Hutchinson did not differ from him.

The former part of this note was written previous to the appearance of Mr. Savage's edition of Winthrop's History of Newengland. It there appears, II, 245, note 2, that a letter was received 1677, from the court of England, creating him Knight. This title was never used, which Mr. Savage conjectures various reasons for. But if he were dead before his appointment arrived, that is a sufficient reason. In Snow's Hist. Boston, some account of his funeral is given, but under the same date.

The same day* Tispaquin came in, and those that were with him. But when Captain Church returned from Boston, he found, to his grief, the heads of Annawon, Tispaquin, &c.,† cut off which were the last of Philip's friends.‡

---

* The same day that the *trap* was set.

† The full import of this &c. is not known. We can only observe, that a great many others at different times were executed, much to the dishonour of those concerned. Of the numbers of those poor natives that were thus murdered, we must remain ignorant.

‡ Melancholy indeed is the reflection, a nation is no more! Thus we behold the instability of all things, acted upon by the exterminating hand of time. The rude government of the natives could not protect them against treachery in an uncommon degree. Their means of support being often scant, and many times nearly cut off, was a great inducement to desertion to the English, where they always fared much better. Hence their first great disaster, at the swamp fight in Narraganset, was owing to a fugitive's leading the English to the only assailable part of the fort; Philip fell by the same foul treachery; and, lastly, Annawon, who, had he been a Roman, would have been called the great. The following lines admirably portray the frailty of man.

> " Like leaves on trees the race of man is found;
> Now green in youth, now with'ring on the ground;
> Another race the following spring supplies;
> They fall successive, and successive rise:
> So generations, in their course, decay;
> So flourish these, when those are past away." POPE'S HOMER.

The conduct of the government in putting to death " Annawon, Tispaquin, &c.," has ever been viewed as barbarous; no circumstance now made it necessary. The Indians were subdued, therefore no example was wanting to deter others. It is true, some were mentioned by the government as unmeriting mercy; but humanity forbade the execution of laws formed only for the emergencies of the moment. Governour Hutchinson observes, " Every person, almost, in the two colonies, [Massachusetts and Plymouth] had lost a relation or near friend, and the people in general were exasperated: but all does not sufficiently excuse this great severity." Hist. Mass. I, 277.

Mr. Hubbard, who wrote at the time does not fail to justify all the measures of government. He says that Church promised Tispaquin an office under him, if what he had made

PHILIP'S WAR. 147

The general court of Plymouth then sitting, sent for Captain Church, who waited upon them accordingly, and received their thanks for his good service, which they unanimously voted, [and] which was all that Captain Church had for his aforesaid service.

Afterwards, in the year 1676,* in the month of January, Captain Church received a commission from Governour Winslow,† to scour the woods of some of the lurking enemy, which they were well informed were there.

[Here followed the commission which is omitted as it is very similar to that at page 93. It bears date 15 Jan. 1676, but should be taken 1676-7.]

---

his followers believe were true, that a bullet could not kill him. When he delivered himself up, the government thought proper to see if it were the case; so shot at him, and he fell dead the first fire! Annawon was accused of torturing and murdering many English prisoners, "which he could not deny," therefore he was put to death in the same manner. Mr. Hubbard, though an eminent historian, was not free from the prejudices of the times. As for us, we can only lament the end of those heroes, and in no better language, than that of our eminent native poet.

> "Indulge, our native land, indulge the tear
> That steals impassioned o'er a nation's doom;
> To us each twig from Adam's stock is dear,
> And tears of sorrow deck an Indian's tomb."
>
> Dwight's Greenfield Hill.

* This was according to the old method of dating, when the new year did not begin until the 25 March; therefore, this must be understood 1677. Under the old supputation, the year was often written with an additional figure, from 1 Jan. to 25 March, to represent both the old and new method; thus, at that time the above date would have been properly written 1676-7. By the inattention of authors, sometimes using the additional figure, and sometimes omitting it, many anachronisms have been committed. Another method, which signifies the same was often used; thus, $167\frac{6}{7}$ express the same as 1676-7. But writers frequently fell into mistakes by taking the wrong figure of the fraction.

† This Gentleman having managed the affairs of Plymouth colony during this troublesome war, it will be proper to give some account of him at its close. He was a son of the distinguished Edward Winslow whose name is the third to that

Accordingly Captain Church accompanied with several gentlemen and others, went out and took

celebrated "combination," or "first foundation of the government of New Plymouth." In 1656, Alexander was mistrusted of plotting against the English, as has been mentioned in note 1, on page 17. Mr. Winslow with eight or ten men surprised him at a hunting house where he had just arrived with about 80 men. These having left their guns without their house, were seized by Winslow, who then induced Alexander to go with him to Plymouth. A short time after this, Alexander was taken sick and died.

When Philip's war commenced, Mr. Winslow wrote to the Governour of Massachusetts as follows: "July 4, 1675. I do solemnly profess we know not any thing from us that might put Philip upon these motions, nor have heard that he pretends to have suffered any wrong from us, save only that we had killed some Indians and intended to send for himself for the murder of John Sausaman [Sassamon.] The last that was executed this week confessed that he saw the other two do the murder. Neither had we any thoughts to command him in about it." See note 1, on page 26.

Again he writes, "I think I can clearly say, that before these present troubles broke out, the English did not possess one foot of land in this colony, but what was fairly obtained by honest purchase of the Indian proprietors: Nay, because some of our people are of a covetous disposition, and the Indians are in their straits easily prevailed with to part with their lands, we first made a law that none should purchase or receive by gift, any land of the Indians without the knowledge and allowance of our court," &c. Hubbard, 66. Thus justice appears to have been aimed at by the leaders in government, from its beginning, but does not appear to have effectually prevented the private abuses of individuals, which was, no doubt, impossible. The remark of Mr. Makin I will lay before the reader that he may judge how far it is correct, and whether the contrast be so great between the treatment of the Indians in Newengland and Pennsylvania, as to deserve what follows. (See Appendix, XIII.)

> "On just and equal terms the land was gain'd,*
> No force of arms has any right obtain'd;
> 'Tis here without the use of arms, alone,
> The bless'd inhabitant enjoys his own;
> Here many, to their wish, in peace enjoy
> Their happy lots, and nothing doth annoy.
> But sad *New England's* diff'rent conduct show'd
> What dire effects from injur'd *Indians* flow'd."
> * *In Pennsylvania.* Makin in Proud, II, 963.

divers parties of Indians. In one of which there was a certain old man, whom Captain Church seemed to take particular notice of, and asking him where he belonged, he told him at Swanzey. The Captain asked his name, he replied, Conscience. Conscience, said the Captain, smiling, then the war is over; for that was what they were searching for, it being much wanted, and returned the said Conscience to his post again at Swanzey, to a certain person [that] the said Indian desired to be sold to, and then returned home.*

---

*Nothing very brilliant, to be sure, occurred in those expeditions, if the author has given us the chief exploit of them all, and we may be satisfied that we have no more of them. Mr. Hubbard takes no notice of any actions of Church after the taking of Annawon, which had they been very important would not have escaped his attention. He closes the war in this quarter with a few interesting exploits, the chief of which it will be proper to notice. In October one Mr. Stanton with three Indians came from Seconet and on the way heared by a captive, that there were a number of the enemy not far off. The Indians leaving Mr. Stanton pursued and took them all. Among them was an old man not able to go their pace, and they spared his life by his promising to come after. It appears that those taken, were mostly women and children, whose men were out a hunting. They soon returned, and the old man informed them of what had befel their friends, and they set out in pursuit of them, overtook them, and retook the prisoners. One friendly Indian was killed in the skirmish, and the other two hardly escaped. One of these was called Major Symon, part Pequot and part Narraganset. He was remarkable for his strength and courage, and at the first, offered to fight any five of the enemy hand to hand with their hatchets, but they declined; upon which he discharged his gun among them, and then rushed upon them with great fury, broke through them and escaped with the other, without injury. Hubbard, 237, 238.

THE
FRENCH AND INDIAN
WARS IN NEWENGLAND,

BETWEEN THE YEARS 1689, AND 1704;

[BEING] A FURTHER ACCOUNT OF THE ACTIONS IN THE MORE LATE WARS AGAINST THE COMMON ENEMY AND INDIAN REBELS, IN THE EASTERN PARTS, UNDER THE COMMAND OF THE AFORESAID

CAPTAIN BENJAMIN CHURCH.

In the time of Sir Edmund Andross'* government, began that bloody war in the eastern parts of Newengland; so that immediadely Sir Edmund sent an

---

* Andross was sent over as Governour of the province of Newyork, in 1674, by the Duke of York. Was appointed Governour of Newengland, and arrived in Boston, 20 December 1684. Smith, Hist. N. Y., 63, gives a very just idea of his character in a very few words. "He knew no law, but the will of his master, and Kirk and Jefferies were not fitter instruments than he to execute the despotick projects of James II." And that "the historians of Newengland justly transmit him to posterity, under the odious character of a sycophantick tool to the Duke, and an arbitrary tyrant over the people committed to his care." He was checked in the midst of his oppressive measures by the abdication of King James. This had been expected by the colonies, and eagerly wished for. The people of Boston on a report of the change in England, and without waiting for its confirmation, daringly began the revolution in Newengland. Andross and about 50 other obnoxious persons were seized, and the old government reassumed. He was afterwards Governour of Virginia, and we hear but little more about him. He died in London, Feb. 24, 1713. Holmes,' I, 475. His life is more particularly given by Eliot, but larger and better by Allen.

express for Captain Church, who then being at Littlecompton, received it on a Lord's day, in the afternoon meeting. Going home after meeting, [he] took his horse and set out for Boston, as ordered; and by sunrise next morning, got to Braintree,* where he met with Colonel Page on horseback going to Weymouth and Hingham to raise forces to go east. [He]¹ said [that] he was glad to see him, and that his excellency would be as glad to see him in Boston so early. So parting he soon got to Boston, and waited upon his excellency, who informed him of an unhappy war, broken out in the eastern parts; and said, [that] he was going himself in person, and that he wanted his company with him. But Captain Church not finding himself in the same spirit he used to have, said, [that] he hoped his excellency would give him time to consider of it. He told him he might; and also said that he must come and dine with him. Captain Church having many acquaintance in Boston, who made it their business, some to encourage, and others to discourage him from going with his excellency. So after dinner his excellency took him into his room, and discoursed freely; saying, that he having knowledge of his former actions and successes, and that he must go with him, and be his second, with other encouragements. But in short, the said Captain Church did not accept, so was dismissed and went home.†

¹[who]

---

* Formerly mount Wollaston. Its Indian name was Wessagusset. It is about 10 miles from Boston, and is renowned as the birth place of JOHN ADAMS, second President of the U. STATES, whose life and death add so much veneration to the auspicious FOURTH OF JULY.

Though the residence of the President is nearly 4 miles from what was mount Wollaston, and in the present town of Quincy, yet it is believed, that it was anciently included in it.

† Notwithstanding, Andross undertook an eastern expedition at the head of 7 or 800 men, and the enemy fled before

FRENCH AND INDIAN WARS.

Soon after this, was the revolution,* and the other government reassumed, and then Governour Bradstreet† sent for Captain Church to come to Boston, as soon as his business would permit; whereupon he went to Boston and waited upon his honour, who told him [that] he was requested by the council to send for him, to see if he could be prevailed with to raise volunteers, both English and Indians to go east; for

him. "But, by establishing garrisons, by detaching numerous parties, to attack their settlements, and destroy their scanty provisions, he reduced them to the greatest distress, and secured the country from their incursions." Holmes, I, 474. But he did as much mischief, or perhaps more than he did good. He plundered Castine's house, a Frenchman, who had great influence among the Indians, which caused him to stir them up anew. Belknap, I, 196.

* The change of government at home being mentioned in a preceding note, it will be necessary here to take notice only of its origin. King James II, in his efforts to establish popery overthrew himself. He published certain declarations, with injunctions upon the clergy to read them to the people after service, which they refused. The Bishops in an address to the King, remonstrated that they could not read his declarations consistent with their consciencies; and they were immediately prosecuted for a seditious libel. The people took great interest in their trial, and when they were acquitted the rejoicing was almost universal. At this very juncture, while the people were enraged against the King, William, Prince of Orange, who had married Mary, eldest daughter of King James, landed in England with an immense army from Holland, and were proclaimed without opposition. The old King with much difficulty effected his escape to France. Goldsmith's Hist. England.

† Simon Bradstreet was born in Lincolnshire, England, in March, 1603, and lived to be the oldest man in Newengland. After marrying a daughter of Thomas Dudley, he was persuaded to make a settlement in Massachusetts. In 1630 he was chosen assistant of the colony, and arrived at Salem the same year. He was in several important offices, and at length succeeded Governour Leverett in the chief magistracy of Massachusetts, in which office he continued until the arrival of Andross, when he was superseded; but Andross, in 1689, being put down, Mr. Bradstreet again assumed the government, and continued in it until the arrival of Sir William Phips, in 1692. He died in Salem, March, 1697, aged 94 years. Allen, and Eliot.

the eastward Indians had done great spoil upon the English in those parts; giving him an account of the miseries and sufferings of the people there. Captain Church's spirits being affected, said, if he could do any service for his honour, the country, and their relief, he was ready and willing. He was asked how he would act? He said [that] he would take with him as many of his old soldiers as he could get, both English and Indians, &c. The gentlemen of Boston requested him to go to Rhodeisland government to ask their assistance. So giving him their letter, and about forty shillings in money, he took leave and went home to Bristol* on a Saturday; and the next Monday morning he went over to Rhodeisland, and waited upon their Governour,† delivering the letter as ordered, [and] prayed his honour for a speedy answer, who said, they could not give an answer presently; so he waited on them till he had their answer. And when he had obtained it, he carried it to the Boston gentlemen, who desired him to raise what volunteers he could in Plymouth colony, and Rhodeisland government, and what was wanting they would make up out of theirs that were already out in the eastern parts.

The summer being far spent, Captain Church made what despatch he could, and raised about two hundred and fifty men, volunteers, and received his commission from Governour Hinkley‡ which is as followeth, viz:

---

* He settled at Bristol soon after Philip's war. See his life page xv.

† We may infer from Judge Sewall's diary, in Holmes, I, 468, that one Clark was the Governour of Rhodeisland in 1686, on the arrival of Andross, who of course was displaced. But in May of this year, 1689, it was resumed, and *all* the general officers replaced. Ibid. 476. I have not even learned his baptismal name. A good history of Rhodeisland is a very desirable work.

‡ Thomas Hinkley was born about the year 1632. I find no mention of him, until he assumed the government, or rather

G

"*The council of War of their Majesties' colony of New Plymouth in Newengland: To Major Benjamin Church, Commander in Chief.*

Whereas the Kennebeck and eastern Indians with their confederates, have openly made war upon their Majesties' subjects of the province of Maine, Newhampshire, and of the Massachusetts colony, having committed many barbarous murders, spoils and rapines upon their persons and estates. And whereas there are some forces of soldiers, English and Indians, now raised and detached out of the several regiments and places within this colony of New Plymouth, to go forth to the assistance of our neighbours and friends, of the aforesaid provinces and colony of the Massachusetts, subjects of one and the same crown; and to join with their forces for the repelling and destruction of the common enemy. And whereas, you Benjamin Church, are appointed to be Major, and commander in chief of all the forces, English and Indians, detached within this colony for the service of their Majesties aforesaid. THESE are in their Majesties' name to authorize and require you to take into your care and conduct all the said forces, English and Indians, and diligently to attend that service, by leading and exercising of your inferiour officers and soldiers, commanding them to obey you as their chief commander; and to pursue, fight, take, kill, or destroy the said enemies, their aiders and abettors, by all the ways and means you can, as you shall have opportunity. And you are to observe and obey all such orders and instructions as from time to time you shall receive from the commissioners of the colonies, the council of war of this colony, or the Governour and council of the Massachusetts

---

the presidency of Plymouth colony after the fall of Andross, the Caligula of Newengland, in 1689. He continued in this office until 1692, when Sir William Phips arrived. He died at Barnstable, in 1706, aged about 74 years. Morton, 208. Hutchinson, II, 141.

colony. In testimony whereof the publick seal of the said colony of New Plymouth is hereunto affixed. Dated in Plymouth, the sixth day of September, Anno Domini, 1689. *Annoque Regni Regis at Reginæ Willielmi et Mariæ Angliæ, &c., Primo.**

THOMAS HINKLEY, *President.*

And now marching them all down to Boston, then received his further orders and instructions, which are as followeth.

"*Boston, September* 16*th,* 1689.
To all Sheriffs, Marshals, Constables, and other officers, military and civil, in their Majesties' province of Maine.

Whereas pursuant to an agreement of the commissioners of the United Colonies, Major Benjamin Church is commissionated commander in chief over that part of their Majesties' forces, (levied for the present expedition against the common enemy) whose head quarters are appointed to be at Falmouth, in Casco bay. In their Majesties' names, you, and every of you, are required to be aiding and assisting to the said Major Church in his pursuit of the enemy, as any emergency shall require; and so impress boats or other vessels, carts, carriages, horses, oxen, provision and ammunition, and men for guides, &c., as you shall receive warrants from the said Commander in chief, or his Lieutenant so to do. You may not fail to do the same speedily and effectually, as you will answer your neglect and contempt of their Majesties' authority and service at your uttermost peril. Given under my hand and seal the day

---

† That is. *And of the reign of the King and Queen, William and Mary of England, &c., the first.*

and year above written. *Annoque Regni Regis et Reginæ Williemi et Mariæ Primo.*
By THOMAS DANFORTH.*
President of the province of Maine."

" By the Governour and Council of Massachusetts. To Major Benjamin Church.

Whereas you are appointed and commissioned by the council of war, of the colony of New Plymouth, commander in chief of the forces raised within the said colony, against the common Indian enemy, now ordered into the eastern parts to join with some of the forces of this colony; for the prosecution, repelling and subduing of the said enemy. It is therefore ordered that Captain Simon Willard, and Captain Nathaniel Hall, with the two companies of soldiers under their several commands, belonging to this colony, now in or about Casco bay, be, and are hereby put under you, as their commander in chief for this present expedition.—And of the commissions severally given to either of them, they are ordered to observe and obey your orders and directions as their commander in chief until further order from the Governour and council, or the commissioners of the colonies. Dated in Boston the 17th day of September, *Anno Domini,* 1698. *Annoque Regni*

---

*This gentleman was born in England 1622. He was a man of influence, which he employed to good account in the difficult days of Newengland. In 1679, he was elected deputy Governour, and the same year, the inhabitants of the province of Maine, chose him their President. On the arrival of the tyrant, Andross, he was suspended from office.— He died in 1699, aged 77 years. Nothing more honourable, perhaps, can be said of him, considering the age in which he lived, than, that he opposed with firmness the proceedings of those courts, which caused such a foul page in our history by their detestable prosecutions and persecutions for *witchcraft.* See Allen, Biog. 240.

Regis et Reginæ Guilielmi et Mariæ, Angliæ, &c. Primo.

S. BRADSTREET, *Gov.*
Past in Council. Attest, Isaac Addington,* Secr."

"*By the Commissioners of the Colonies of the Massachusetts, Plymouth and Connecticut, for managing the present war against the common enemy.*
Instructions *for* Major BENJAMIN CHURCH, *Commander in Chief of the Plymouth forces, with others of the Massachusetts, put under his command.*
In pursuance of the commission given you, for their Majesties' service in the present expedition against the common Indian enemy, their aiders and abettors; reposing confidence in your wisdom, prudence and fidelity in the trust committed to you for the honour of God, good of his people, and the security of the interest of Christ in his churches, expecting and praying that in your dependence upon him, you may be helped and assisted with all that grace and wisdom which is requisite for carrying you on with success in this difficult service; and though much is and must be left to your discretion, as providence and opportunity may present from time to time in places of attendance; yet the following instructions are commended unto your observation, and to be attended to so far as the state of matters with you in such a transaction will admit. You are with all possible speed to take care that the

---

* Mr. Addington was one of those who took a very active part in opposition to the tyrannical measures of Andross. On the accession of William and Mary he was appointed Secretary, which office he discharged with integrity for some time. It seems that in those days, as well as at the present, *office seekers* were not entirely unknown, but, "the emoluments of that office were small, compared with the duty, and so he was in less danger of a competitor." He belonged to the council for many years, and was respected as a justice of the peace for wisdom and industry. He died in 1714.

Plymouth forces, both English and Indians under your command, be fixed, and ready, and the first opportunity of wind and weather, to go on board such vessels as are provided to transport you and them to Casco, where, if it shall please God you arrive, you are to take under your care and command, the companies of Captain Nathaniel Hall, and Captain Simon Willard, who are ordered to attend your command, whom, together with the Plymouth forces, and such as from time to time may be added unto you, you are to improve in such way as you shall see meet, for the discovering, pursuing, subduing and destroying the said common enemy, by all opportunities you are capable of; always intending the preserving of any of the near towns from incursions, and destruction of the enemy; yet chiefly improving your men for the finding and following the said enemy abroad, and if possible to find out and attack their head quarters and principal rendezvous, if you find you are in a rational capacity for so doing. The better to enable you thereto, we have ordered two men of war sloops, and other small vessels for transportation to attend you for some considerable time. You are to see that your soldiers' arms be always fixed, and that they be furnished with ammunition, provisions and other necessaries, that so they may be in readiness to repel and attack the enemy. In your pursuit you are to take special care to avoid danger by ambushments, or being drawn under any disadvantage by the enemy in your marches, keeping out scouts and a forlorn hope before your main body, and by all possible means endeavouring to surprise some of the enemy, that so you may gain intelligence. You are to suppress all mutinies and disorders among your soldiers, as much as in you lies, and to punish such as disobey your officers, according to the rules of war herewith given you.

You are according to your opportunity, or any occasion more than ordinary occurring, to hold correspondence with Major Swaine, and to yield mutual assistance when, and as you are capable of it, and you may have reason to judge it will be of most publick service, and it will be meet, [that] you and he should agree of some signal, whereby your Indians may be known from the enemy. You are to encourage your soldiers to be industrious, vigorous, and venturous in their service, to search out and destroy the enemy, acquainting them, it is agreed by the several colonies, that they shall have the benefit of the captives, and all lawful plunder, and the reward of *eight pounds* per head, for every fighting Indian man slain by them, over and above their stated wages; the same being made appear to the commander in chief, or such as shall be appointed to take care therein. If your commission officers, or any of them should be slain, or otherwise incapable of service, and for such reason dismissed, you are to appoint others in their room, who shall have the like wages, and a commission sent upon notice given; you [are] to give them commissions in the mean time. You are to take effectual care that the worship of God be kept up in the army; morning and evening prayer attended as far as may be, and as the emergencies of your affairs will admit; to see that the holy Sabbath be duly sanctified. You are to take care as much as may be, to prevent or punish drunkenness, swearing, cursing or such other sins as do provoke the anger of God. You are to advise with your chief officers in any matters of moment, as you shall have opportunity. You are from time to time to give intelligence and advice to the Governour and council of the Massachusetts, or commissioners of the colonies, of your proceedings and occurrences that may happen, and how it shall please the Lord to deal with you in this present expedition. If you find the vessels are not likely to be serviceable to you, dismiss them as soon as you may.

Captain Sylvanus Davis is a prudent man and well acquainted with the affairs of those parts, and is written unto to advise and inform you all he can.

Such further instructions as we shall see reason to send unto you, you are carefully to attend and observe; and in the absence of the commissioners, you shall observe the orders and instructions directed unto you from the Governour and council of the Massachusetts.

Given under our hands in Boston, Sept. 18, 1689.

THOMAS DANFORTH, *President.*
ELISHA COOKE,
SAMUEL MASON,
WILLIAM PITKIN,
THO. HINKLEY,
JOHN WALLEY.

THE FIRST EXPEDITION EAST.

BEING ready, Major Church embarked with his forces on board the vessels provided to transport them for Casco.* Having a brave gale at southwest, and on Friday about three o'clock, they got in sight of Casco harbour. And discovering two or three small ships there, [and] not knowing whether they were friends or enemies, whereupon the said commander, Major Church, gave orders that every man that was able should make ready, and all lie close; giving orders how they should act in case they were enemies. He, going in the Mary sloop, together with the Resolution, went in first, being both well fitted with guns and men. Coming to the first, hailed them, who said they were friends; presently manned their boat, brought to, and so came along the

---

* What was since included in the towns of Falmouth, Cape Elizabeth and Portland, was called Casco. It is situated on Casco bay. This bay at its entrance between Cape Porpoise and Cape Elizabeth, is about 40 miles wide. Sullivan's Hist. Maine, 13. In Philip's war depredations were committed here by the savages and many were killed. Ib. 198, &c.

side of [him.][1] [They][2] gave the said Church an account, that yesterday there was a very great army of Indians, and French with them upon the island,* at the going out of the harbour, and that they were come on purpose to take Casco fort and town;† likewise informed him that they had got a captive woman aboard, (Major Walden's‡ daughter, of Piscata-

[1] [them.]   [2] [who]

---

* There are about 300 islands in Casco bay. What the name of this was I have not learned.

† Is this the "body of 600 Indians," mentioned by Belknap, N. H. I, 267, that were going to attack Casco? I do not find any thing like it in the place it should be. He cites "Church's memoirs, 104," perhaps he used the first edition of this history, as no mention of any thing of the kind is seen in the second. In touching upon the operations under Church in 1704, he says, "while they were at Mountdesert Church learned from 9 of his prisoners" of the body of Indians just named. It will be seen in the *Fifth Expedition*, that Lafaure's son informed Church at Montinicus, of some French and Indians "that were to go westward to fight the English," but nothing of the kind took place at Mountdesert, nor any information from "9 prisoners," or that the expedition was to attack Casco.

‡ Waldron is now the correct way of writing this name. Hubbard wrote it as our author does, but more frequently with an *r* after the *e*. Some other historians put the *r* before the *e*, so we are at a loss how the name was originally spelt.

Major Richard Waldron was a native of Somersetshire, England, and was one of the first settlers at Cochecho, now Dover, Newhampshire. The tragical death of this noted man is given by Dr. Belknap, Hist. N. H. I, 197, 198; but as that excellent work is not in the hands of many, it may be proper to give the particulars in this place. At the close of Philip's war, many of the western Indians fled to the eastward. Some of them, with others of Pannacook and Pigwocket, had assembled at Major Waldron's with whom they had lately treated. Captains Syll and Hawthorne, being despatched by the Massachusetts' government against the Indians on the Kennebeck, arrived there with their men, under orders to seize all Indians that had been concerned in the war. They were about to execute their orders by seizing these Indians, but Maj. Waldron formed the design of taking them in a sham training, which he had invited them

qua) that could give him a full account of their numbers and intentions. He bid them give his ser-

to join in. Accordingly all were taken, in number about 400. Those that were not found to have been in the former war were dismissed, and the rest were sent to Boston. About 8 or 10 were hanged as murderers, and the rest sold into slavery. This was the latter part of 1676. Now 13 years had expired, but revenge remained in the breasts of those tribes whose friends had been so cruelly treated. They therefore formed the design to destroy all the garrisons at Cochecho, which was thus artfully concerted. Two squaws were to get permission to lodge in each, and after all was still in the dead of night, they were to open the doors for their friends. No fear was discovered among the English, and the squaws were admitted. One of those admitted into Waldron's garrison, reflecting, perhaps, on the ingratitude she was about to be guilty of, thought to warn the Major of his danger. She pretended to be ill, and as she lie on the floor would turn herself from side to side, as though to ease herself of pain that she pretended to have. While in this exercise she began to sing and repeat the following verse.

> "O Major Waldo,
> You great Sagamore,
> O what will you do,
> Indians at your door!"

No alarm was taken at this, and the doors were opened according to their plan, and the enemy rushed in with great fury. They found the Major's room as he leaped out of bed, but with his sword he drove them through two or three rooms, and as he turned to get some other arms, he fell stunned by a blow with the hatchet. They dragged him into his hall and seated him on a table in a great chair, and then began to cut his flesh in a shocking manner. Some in turns gashed his naked breast, saying, "I cross out my account." Then cutting a joint from a finger, would say, "Will your fist weigh a pound now?"* His nose and ears were then cut off and forced into his mouth. He soon fainted, and fell from his seat, and one held his own sword under him, which passed through his body, and he expired. The family were forced to provide them a supper while they were murdering the

---

* It is a tradition concerning Major Waldron, that he used in trading with the Indians, to count his fist as weighing a pound, also that his accounts were false and not crossed out according to agreement. But in justice to the Major, it should be remembered, that strange Indians, who thought themselves injured by one Englishman, would take revenge on the first that fell into their hands.

vice to their captain, and tell him, [that] he would wait upon him after he had been on shore and given some orders and directions. Being come pretty near, he ordered all the men still to keep close; giving an account of the news [which] he had received, and then went ashore; where were several of the chief men of the town, who met him, being glad that he came so happily to their relief; told him the news [that] Mrs. Lee* had given them, being the woman aforesaid.

He [went][1] to Captain Davis,† to get some refreshment, having not eaten a morsel since he came by Boston castle. And now having inquired into the state of the town, found them in a poor condition to defend themselves against such a number of enemies. He gave them an account of his orders and instructions, and told them what forces he had brought, and

[1] [going]

---

the Major. This was on Thursday 27 June, 1689. Major Waldron was 80 years old when killed. Fifty two persons were killed, and taken captive, of the former were 23. MS. Recollections.

*Daughter of Major Waldron, as mentioned above. She was taken the same time her father was killed, as related in the last note. Her husband's name was Abraham Lee, who was killed when the garrison was taken.

† Captain Sylvanus Davis, the same mentioned in the preceding instructions. By Hutchinson, II, 21, it appears that he was once taken prisoner and carried to Canada, and that he commanded the fort at Casco from which he was taken, which, I suppose, was in 1690; for in that year the country upon the bay was desolated. There were a number of garrisons, and a fort, but were all taken. Captain Davis with one Captain Lake were besieged on Arrowsike island in 1676, but effected their escape out of the back door of a house, and ran to the water's edge, and in a boat fled to the nearest land. Capt. Lake was shot down as he landed, but Davis escaped with a wound. The body of Lake was afterward found, and conveyed away by Major Waldron, Davis, on the arrival of Gov. Phips, in 1692, was appointed one of the counsellors for the eastern country. How long he continued in that office is not known to me, but by Sullivan, 167, it appears that he sustained it in 1701.

that when it was dark they should all land, and not before, lest the enemy should discover them. And then he went on board the privateer [which was a Dutchman.]¹ But as he went, called on board every vessel, and ordered the officers to take care that their men might be all fitted and provided to fight; for the people of the town expected the enemy to fall upon them every minute. But withal, charging them to keep undiscovered.

And coming on board said privateer, was kindly treated. [He] discoursed [with] Mrs. Lee, who informed him, that the company she came with, had four score canoes, and that there were more of them, whom she had not seen, which came from other places, and that they told her, when they come all together should make up seven hundred men. He asked her whether Casteen* was with them? She answered, that there were several French men with

¹ [who were Dutchmen]

---

*Baron De St. Castine, a very extraordinary character. According to Voltaire and the Abbe Raynal he had been Colonel of the regiment of Corignon, in France, and was a man of family and fortune. He came to America in 1670, and settled among the Penobscot Indians; married a daughter of the chief, and had several other wives. By the treaty of Breda, the territory beyond the Penobscot was ceded to France, and Castine lived within that country. Some difficulty arose about a cargo of wine, which was landed in the country, and a new line was run by the English, by which the place of landing, together with Castine's lands, was taken within the English claim. Andross, in his expedition before named, plundered Castine's house of every thing valuable in his absence. This base act so exasperated him, that he used his exertions to inflame the Indians against the English, which he effectually did, and their chief supplies of arms and ammunition were furnished by him. He had an estate in France, to which he retired when the French lost their possessions in that part of the country. See Sullivan's Hist. 93, 158, 226. Hist. N. H. I, 195, 196. If we name this war from those that occasioned it, we may call it Castine's war. But the French, perhaps, would call it Andross' war.

them, but did not know whether Casteen was there or not. He then having got what intelligence she could give him, went ashore and viewed the fort and town; discoursing with the gentlemen there according to his instructions.

And when it began to grow dark, he ordered the vessels to come as near the fort as might be, and land the soldiers with as little noise as possible; ordering them as they landed to go into the fort and houses, that stood near, that so they might be ready upon occasion. Having ordered provisions for them, [he] went to every company and ordering them to get every thing ready; they that had no powderhorns or shotbags, should immediately make them; ordering the officers to take special care that they were ready to march into the woods an hour before day; and also directing the watch to call him two hours before day. So he hastened to bed to get some rest.

At the time prefixed he was called and presently ordering the companies to make ready, and about half an hour before day they moved. Several of the town's people went with them into a thick place of brush about half a mile from the town. Now ordering them to send out their scouts as they used to do, and seeing them all settled at their work, he went into town by sunrise again, and desired the inhabitants to take care of themselves, till his men had fitted themselves with some necessaries; for his Indians, most of them, wanted both bags and horns. So he ordered them to make bags like wallets, to put powder in one end, and shot in the other.

So most of them were ready for action, viz., the Seconet Indians, but the Cape Indians were very bare, lying so long at Boston before they embarked, that they had sold every thing [that] they could make a penny of; some tying shot and powder in the corners of their blankets.

He being in town, just going to breakfast, there was an alarm; so he ordered all the soldiers in town to move away as fast they could, where the firing was. And he, with what men more were with him of his soldiers, moved immediately. [They met]¹ with Captain Bracket's* sons, who told [them that,]² their father was taken; and that they saw a great army of Indians in their father's orchard, &c. By this time our Indians that wanted bags and horns were fitted, but wanted more ammunition. Presently came a messenger to him from the town, and informed him, that they had knocked out the heads of several casks of bullets, and they were all too big, being musket bullets, and would not fit their guns, and that if he did not go back himself, a great part of the army would be kept back from service for want of suitable bullets.

He ran back and ordered every vessel to send ashore all their casks of bullets; being brought, [they] knocked out their heads, and turned them all out upon the green by the fort, and set all the people in the town, that were able, to make slugs; being

¹ [and meeting]   ² [him]

---

*Captain Anthony Bracket, an early settler on Casco bay, where his posterity yet remain. Notice is taken by Sullivan, 116, that the family were considerable landholders in Falmouth, between the 1680, and 1690, under a title of the government, signed by president Danforth. Ib. 196, 197. When Casco was destroyed in 1676, Captain Bracket with his wife and one child was taken by the savages. This was on the 11 August, and the November following they made their escape. Those that had them prisoners, landed them on the north shore of the bay, and here their keepers had intelligence of a valuable house, taken by another party, the spoils of which they were eager to share; therefore, leaving Bracket, his wife and child, and a negro, with some provisions, who promised that they would come after, and departed. They found an old birch canoe, in which they escaped to the other side of the bay, where, only the day before the enemy had left. Here they got on board a vessel bound to Pascataqua, were they arrived safe. Hubbard, 293 to 296. What time Bracket returned to his lands does not appear. When Andross erected forts there in 1688, Captain Bracket was put in command of three. Sullivan, 260.

most of them too large for their use, which had like to have been the overthrow of their whole army. He finding some small bullets, and what slugs were made, and three knapsacks of powder, went immediately to the army, which was very hotly engaged. But coming to the river the tide was up; he called to his men that were engaged, encouraging them, and told them [that] he had brought more ammunition for them. An Indian, called Captain Lightfoot,* laid down his gun, and came over the river, taking the powder upon his head, and a kettle of bullets in each hand, and got safe to his fellow soldiers.

He perceiving great firing upon that side he was of, went to see who they were, and found them to be two of Major Church's companies, one of English and the other of Indians, being in all about four score men, that had not got over the river, but lay firing over our men's heads at the enemy. He presently ordered them to rally, and come all together, and gave the word for a Casco man. So one Swarton, a Jersey man,† appearing, whom he could hardly understand. He asked him how far it was to the head of the river, or whether there were any place to get over? He said [that] there was a bridge about three quarters of a mile up, where they might get over. So he calling to his soldiers, engaged on the other side, that he would soon be with them over the bridge, and come upon the backs of the enemy, which put new courage into them. So they immediately moved up towards the bridge, marching very thin; being willing to make what show they could; shouting as they marched. They saw the enemy running from the river side, where they had made stands with wood to prevent any body from coming over the river; and coming to the bridge, they saw on the other side, that the enemy had laid logs, and

---

* See note 2 on page 100.
† An Irishman.

stuck birch brush along to hide themselves from our view.

He ordered the company to come altogether, bidding them all to run after him, who would go first; and that as soon as they got over the bridge, to scatter; that so they might not all be shot down together; expecting the enemy to be at their stands. So running up to the stands, found none there, but were just gone; the ground being much tumbled with them behind the said stands. He ordered the Captain with his company of English to march down to our men, engaged, and that they should keep along upon the edge of the marsh, and himself, with his Indian soldiers would march down through the brush. And coming to a parcel of low ground, which had been formerly burnt, the old brush being fallen down, lay very thick, and the young brush being grown up, made it bad travelling. But coming near the back of the enemy, one of his men called unto him, (their commander) and said, "The enemy run westward to get between us and the bridge." And he looking that way, saw men running; and making a small stop, heard no firing, but a great chopping with hatchets; so concluding the fight was over, made the best of their way to the bridge again; lest the enemy should get over the bridge into the town.

The men being most of them out, (our ammunition lay exposed) [and] coming to the bridge where he left six Indians for an ambuscade on the other side of the river, that if any enemy offered to come over, they should fire at them, which would give him notice; so would come to their assistance. (But in the way, having heard no firing, nor shouting, concluded the enemy were drawn off.) He asked the ambuscade whether they saw any Indians? they said "Yes, abundance." He asked them where? They answered, that they ran over the head of the river by the cedar swamp, and were running into the neck towards the town.

There being but one Englishman with him, he bid his Indian soldiers scatter, [and] run very thin, to preserve themselves and be the better able to make a discovery of the enemy. And soon coming to Lieutenant Clark's* field, on the south side of the neck, and seeing the cattle feeding quietly, and perceiving no track, concluded the ambuscade had told them a falsehood. They hastily returned back to the said bridge, perceiving [that] there was no noise of the enemy.

He hearing several great guns fire at the town concluded that they were either assaulted, or that they had discovered the enemy; [—][1] having ordered that in case such should be, that they should fire some of their great guns to give him notice. He being a stranger to the country, concluded [that] the enemy had, by some other way, got to the town; whereupon he sent his men to the town, and himself going to the river, near where the fight had been, asked them how they did, and what was become of the enemy? [They][2] informed him that the enemy drew off in less than an hour after he left them, and had not fired a gun at them since. He told them [that] he had been within little more than a gun shot of the back of the enemy, and had been upon them, had it not been for thick brushy ground, &c.

Now some of his men returning from the town, gave him the account, that they went while they saw

[1] [He]   [2] [Who]

---

* The name of Clark occurs early among the first claimers of the soil in this part of the country. To Thomas Clark and Roger Spencer, was sold the island of Arrowseag, as the Indians called it, but the English, Arrowsike. It appears also that Clark possessed lands on the main, from whence he was driven in 1675. Sullivan, 145, 169, 173. This if not the same may be a relative. Mather, Mag., 524, informs us, that one Lieut. Clark was killed here in a sally in May, 1690.

the colours standing, and men walking about as not molested. He presently ordered that all his army* should pursue the enemy, but they told him that most of them had spent their ammunition; and that if the enemy had engaged them a little longer, they might have come and knocked them on the head; and that some of their bullets were so unsizeable, that some of them were forced to make slugs while they were engaged.

He then ordered them to get over all the wounded and dead men, and to leave none behind, which was done by some canoes they had got. Captain Hall† and his men being first engaged, did great damage, and suffered the greatest loss in his men. But Captain Southworth,‡ with his company, and Captain Numposh with the Seconet Indians, and the most of the men belonging to the town all coming suddenly to his relief, prevented him and his whole company from being cut off, &c.

By this time the day was far spent, and marching into town about sunset, carrying in all their wounded and dead men; being all sensible of God's goodness to them, in giving them the victory, and causing the enemy to fly with shame; who never gave one shout at their drawing off. The poor inhabitants wonderfully rejoiced that the Almighty had favoured them so much; saying, that if Major Church with his forces had not come at that juncture, they had been all cut off; and said further, that it was the first time, that ever the eastward Indians had been put to flight.

---

* How numerous this army was is not told us, but it probably consisted of near 400 men, as his own volunteers numbered 250, and these men were joined by two other companies as mentioned in his commission from the Massachusetts government.

† Captain Nathaniel Hall was of the Massachusetts where the name is very common at this day. Mather, Mag. II, 515, says, "he had been a valiant captain in the former war."

‡ Captain Nathaniel Southworth of Plymouth colony. I find no particulars of him.

The said Church with his volunteers were wonderfully preserved, having never a man killed outright, and but one Indian mortally wounded, who died; several more being badly wounded, but recovered.*

After this engagement Major Church, with his forces, ranging all the country thereabout, in pursuit of the enemy, and visiting all the garrisons at Black point,† Spurwink,‡ and Blue point,§ and went up Kennebeck‖ river, but to little effect. And now winter drawing near, he received orders from the government of Massachusetts bay, to settle all the garrisons, and put in suitable officers according to his best discretion, and to send home all his soldiers, volunteers and transports, which orders he presently obeyed.¶ Being obliged to buy him a horse to go home by land, that so he might the better comply with his orders.

---

* The killed and wounded spoken of above as being brought over in canoes, were Captain Hall's men By this statement reference is only made to the Plymouth forces. Mather says, that 10 or 12 were killed. Magnalia, II, 515.

† A short distance to the west of Cape Elizabeth, in the town of Scarborough, and was called the east parish.

‡ "On the west line of Cape Elizabeth [town] or on the ast line of Scarborough." A small river meets the sea here of the same name. Sullivan, 26, 115.

§ A little to the west of Black point and was the west parish of Scarborough. Ib. 213.

‖ Sullivan, 31, tells us, that this name, "no doubt," is derived "from a race of Sagamores of the name of Kenebis." This noble and beautiful river enters the ocean to the east of Casco bay, in about 33 d. 42 min., north latitude. It is the ancient Sagadahock, and is celebrated as the place where the first settlement was made in Newengland. It was on an island at the mouth of said river, called Stage island, in 1607, by a colony of 100 persons in two ships under the direction of Sir John Popham. But the next year, their chief men being dead, the colony returned to England. An earlier date is assigned to the discovery of the river by the French, namely, in 1604. See an anecdote of this settlement in the Appendix, No. XII, 4.

¶ At this time, the whole eastern country was saved by this expedition. Sullivan. 202.

The poor people, the inhabitants of Casco, and places adjacent, when they saw [that] he was going away from them, lamented sadly, and begged earnestly that he would suffer them to come away in the transports; saying, that if he left them there, that in the spring of the year, the enemy would come and destroy them and their families, &c. So by their earnest request, the said Major Church promised them, that if the governments that had now sent him, would send him the next spring, he would certainly come with his volunteers and Indians to their relief; and, that as soon as he had been at home, and taken a little care of his own business, he would certainly wait upon the gentlemen of Boston, and inform them of the promise [that] he had made to them; and if they did not see cause to send them relief, to entreat their honours, seasonably to draw them off, that they might not be a prey to the barbarous enemy.

Taking his leave of those poor inhabitants, some of the chief men there, waited upon him to Black point, to Captain Scottaway's* garrison. Coming there, they prevailed with the said Captain Scottaway to go with him to Boston, which he readily complied with, provided the said Church would put another in to command the garrison; which being done, and taking their leave one of another, they set out and travelled through all the country, home to Boston; (having employed himself to the utmost to fulfil his instructions, last received from Boston; which cost him about a month's service over and above what he had pay for from the Plymouth gentlemen.) And in his travel homeward, several gentlemen waited upon the said Major Church, who was obliged to bear their expenses.†

---

* No more of this gentleman is found, than what is given in this place.

† Whether this was a general custom in those days, or not, I have taken no trouble to ascertain, but it would contribute very little to the dignity of an office now.

When he came to Boston gentlemen, he informed them of the miseries those poor people were in, by having their provisions taken from them by order of the president,* &c., then went home.

[He] staid not long there before he returned to Boston, where Captain Scottaway waited for his coming, that he might have the determination of the government of Boston to carry home with him. [—]¹ It being the time of the small pox there, ([—]² Major Church not having had it) [he took]³ up his lodging near the Court house, [and had]⁴ the first opportunity to inform those gentlemen of the Court [of] his business. [They]⁵ said [that] they were very busy in sending home Sir Edmund, the ship being ready to sail.

The said Major Church still waited upon them, and at every opportunity entreated those gentlemen in behalf of the poor people of Casco, informing the necessity of taking care of them, either by sending them relief early in the spring, or suffer them to draw off, otherwise they would certainly be destroyed, &c. Their answer was, that they could do nothing till Sir Edmund was gone. Waiting there three weeks upon great expenses, he concluded to draw up some of the circumstances of Casco, and places adjacent, and to leave it upon the council board, before the Governour and council. Having got it done, obtained liberty to go up where the Governour and council were sitting, he informed their honours, that he had waited till his patience was worn out, so had drawn up the matter to leave upon the board before them, which is as follows.

"*To the honoured Governour and council of the Massachusetts.*

Gentlemen,

Whereas by virtue of yours, with Plymouth's de-

¹ [and]   ² [and]   ³ [taking]   ⁴ [took]   ⁵ [who]

---

* Thomas Danforth.

sires and commands, I went eastward in the last expedition against the common Indian enemy, where providence so ordered that we attacked their greatest body of forces, coming then for the destruction of Falmouth, which we know marched off repulsed with considerable damage, leaving the ground, and have never since [been] seen there, or in any place adjacent. The time of the year being then too late to prosecute any further design, and other accidents falling out contrary to my expectation, impeded the desired success. Upon my then removal from the province of Maine, the inhabitants were very solicitous that this enemy might be further prosecuted, willing to venture their lives and fortunes, in the said enterprise, wherein they might serve God, their King, and country, and enjoy quiet and peaceable habitations. Upon which I promised to signify the same to yourselves, and willing to venture that little which providence hath betrusted me with, on the said account. The season of the year being such, if some speedy action be not performed in attacking them, they will certainly be upon us in our out towns, God knows where, and the inhabitants there, not being able to defend themselves, without doubt many souls may be cut off, as our last year's experience wofully hath declared. The inhabitants there, trust to your protection, having undertaken government and your propriety; if nothing be performed on the said account the best way, under correction, is to demolish the garrison, and draw off the inhabitants, that they may not be left to a merciless enemy; and that the arms and ammunition may not be there for the strengthening of the enemy, who without doubt have need enough, having exhausted their greatest store in this winter season. I have performed my promise to them, and acquitted myself in specifying the same to yourselves. Not that I desire to be in any action although willing to serve my King and country, and may pass under the censure of scandalous tongues

in the last expedition, which I hope they will amend on the first opportunity of service. I leave to mature consideration, the loss of trade and fishery; the war brought to the doors. What a triumph it will be to the enemy; derision to our neighbours, beside dishonour to God and our nation, and grounds of frown from our Prince; the frustration of those, whose eyes are upon you for help, who might have otherwise applied themselves to their King. Gentlemen, this I thought humbly to propose unto you, that I might discharge myself in my trust from yourselves, and promise to the inhabitants of the province, but especially my duty to God, her Majesty, and my nation, praying for your honours prosperity, subscribe,
Your servant,
BENJAMIN CHURCH.

A true copy given in at Boston, this 6*th of February,* 1689,* *at the Council Board.*
Attest. T. S."†

Major Church said, moreover, that in thus doing he had complied with his promise to those poor people of Casco, and should be quit from the guilt of their blood. The Governour was pleased to thank him for his care and pains taken, then taking his leave of them went home, and left Captain Scottaway in a very sorrowful condition, who returned home sometime after with only a copy of what was left on the board by the said Church. Major Church not hearing any thing till May following, and then was informed, that those poor people of Casco were cut off by the barbarous enemy;‡ and although they

---

* It should be 1690, or 1689-90. See note 1, on page 147.

† For whose name these initials stand I have not satisfactorily ascertained.

‡ In May, 1690. Some forces had just left Casco, and joined Sir Wm. Phips to go against Portroyal, when an army of four hundred, or more, French and Indians were discovered about the place. "There was a fort near the water, and

made their terms with Monsieur Casteen, who was commander of those enemies, yet he suffered those merciless savages to massacre and destroy the most of them.

To conclude this first expedition East, I shall just give you a hint how Major Church was treated, although he was commander in chief of all the forces out of Plymouth and Boston government. After he came home, Plymouth gentlemen paid him but *forty-two pounds*, telling him, he must go to Boston gentlemen for the rest, who were his employers as well as they. Of whom he never had *one penny*, for all travel and expenses in raising volunteers, and services done; except *forty shillings* or thereabout, for going from Boston to Rhodeisland on their business, and back to Boston again; also for sending a man to Providence for Captain Edmunds,* who raised a company in those parts, and went east with them.

---

another on the hill, near where the burying ground is, and another on the rocky ground, south from the place where the first meeting house stands," in what was the town of Falmouth. That near the burying ground was abandoned as untenable, and both of the others after some time were carried by assault. One hundred persons now fell into the hands of the enemy. The French commander promised the garrisons safety to their persons, and liberty to go to the next English town, but he kept his promise no longer than while he was in possession. The whole country hereabout was laid desolate, and presented a most dreadful scene of ruin. The ground was strewed with the bones of the dead, which Church, on his arrival afterward, gathered up and buried. Hist. Maine, 202. Magnalia, II, 524.

* The same who is mentioned in Philip's war, 52. I learn nothing of his eastern expedition.

FRENCH AND INDIAN WARS. 177

THE SECOND EXPEDITION EAST.

In the year 1690 was the expedition* to Canada,† and Major Walley‡ often requested Major Church

---

* Canada had long been considered the source of all the evils endured by the colonies. Hence the long train of wars at the expense of so much blood and treasure to " drive the French out of Canada." Sir William Phips was the chief mover and executor of this expedition. His fleet, retarded by unavoidable accidents, did not arrive before Quebeck until the 5 October. The next morning, he sent a summons on shore, but received an insolent answer from the Governour. The next day, he attempted to land his troops, but was prevented by the violence of the wind. On the 8, all the effective men (12 or 1300) landed on the island of Orleans, 4 miles below the town, and were fired on, from the woods, by the French and Indians. Having remained on shore until the 11, and then learning by a deserter, the strength of the place, they embarked with precipitation. In their way to Boston, the fleet was dispersed in a tempest. Some of the vessels were blown off to the West Indies, one was lost on an island near the mouth of the St. Lawrence, and two or three were never heard of. Holmes, I, 478, 479. No provisions at home had been made to pay the forces, relying on plunder; bills of credit, therefore, were resorted to, which were the first ever used in this country. Hutchinson, I, 356, 357.

† The derivation of the word *Canada*, being so curious it was thought that it would be pardonable to give it a place in this work. Mr. Bozman, in his excellent " Introduction to a History of Maryland," 34, says that it is a traditional report, that previous to the visiting of Newfoundland by Cartier, in 1534, some Spaniards visited that coast in search of gold, but its appearance discouraged them, and they quitted it in haste crying out as they went on board their vessel, " *Aca nada, Aca nada*," that is, in English, " *There is nothing here.*" The Indians retained these words in their memories, and afterward, when the French came to the country, they were saluted with the same words, and mistook them for the name of the country. And in time the first letter was lost, hence the name *Canada*. Something amounting to nearly the same thing may be seen in Mather's Magnalia, II, 522.

‡ John Walley, who had the command of the land forces, under Sir William Phips, against Canada. An entire journal, kept by Walley, of that expedition, is preserved in

H

that if he would not go himself in that expedition, that he would not hinder others. He answered the said Walley, that he should hinder none but his old soldiers, that used to go along with him, &c.

The said Church going down to Charlestown, to take his leave of some of his relations and friends, who were going into that expedition, promised his wife and family not to go into Boston, the small pox* being very rife there. Coming to Charlestown, several of his friends in Boston came over to see him. And the next day after the said Church came there, Major Walley came to him, and informed him that the Governour and council wanted to speak with him. He answered him, that he had promised his wife and family not to go into Boston; saying, [that] if they had any business, they could write to him, and that he would send them his answer.

Soon after came over two other gentlemen with a message, that the Governour and council wanted to have some discourse with him. The answer returned, was, that he intended to lodge that night at the Greyhound, in Roxbury, and that in the morning, would come to Pollard's† at the south end of Boston, which accordingly he did. Soon after he came

---

Hutchinson, Ap. I, 470. He was judge of the superiour court of Massachusetts, and a member of the council. The church of Bristol is indebted to him as one of its principal founders He is represented, as possessing sweetness of spirit, wisdom in council, and impartiality as a Judge. He died 11 January, 1712, aged 68 years.

* I find no mention of the Small Pox at this time in Boston by any author that I have consulted; but in the History of Dorchester it is noted, page 24, " that from the first of April, 1690, unto the first of July, 1691, there died in Dorchester 57 persons; 33 of them of the *small pox*, the rest of a fever." Hence from its near vicinity to Boston, no doubt it was very prevalent there. [Having since seen in Mr. Snow's History of Boston, that it did prevail there as mentioned in the text.]

† A publick house, under this name, is yet known in Boston, at the golden ball, Elm street.

thither, received a letter from the honourable Captain Sewall,* to request him to come to the council. The answer [that] he returned by the bearer was, that he thought there was no need of his hazarding himself so much as to come and speak with them; not that he was afraid of his life, but because he had no mind to be concerned; and further by reason [that] they would not hearken to him about the poor people of Casco. But immediately came Mr. Maxfield† to him, saying, that the council bid him tell the said Church, that if he would take his horse and ride along the middle of the street, there might be no danger. They were then sitting in council. He bid [him][1] go and tell his masters not to trouble themselves whether he came upon his head or his feet, he was coming. However, thinking the return was something rude, called him back to drink a glass of wine, and then he would go with him.

So coming to the council, they were very thankful to him for his coming, and told him, that the occasion of their sending for him was, that there was a captive come in, who gave them an account, that the Indians were come down, and had taken possession of the stone fort at Pejepscot,‡ so that they

[1] [them]

* Stephen Sewall, I conclude this must be, who was commander of the fort at Salem. He was a brother of Judge Sewall, and sustained several important offices. He married a daughter of the Rev. Mr. Mitchel of Cambridge, who had 17 children. He died about the 21 October, 1725, greatly respected and lamented. Eliot, N. E. Biog. 420.

† I learn nothing of this person. The name is common in Newhampshire.

‡ A fall of water in the Androscoggin. What the true orthography of this word is, is unknown to me. Sullivan ends it with a double *t*, and again alters to Pegypscott. Mather has it Pechypscot. Some authors write *u* instead of *o* in the termination. Thus the different ways are brought under the view of the reader, that he may employ which he chooses. The stone fort was near the falls on the north side of the ri-

wanted his advice and thoughts about the matter; whether they would tarry and keep in the fort or not? and whether it were not expedient to send some forces to do some spoil upon them? and further to know whether he could not be prevailed with to raise some volunteers, and go, to do some spoil upon them? He answered them, [that] he was unwilling to be concerned any more; it being very difficult and chargeable to raise volunteers, as he found by experience in the last expedition.

But they using many arguments prevailed so far with him, that if the government of Plymouth saw cause to send him, he would go; thinking the expedition would be short. [He then] took his leave of them and went home.

In a short time after, there came an express from Governour Hinkley, to request Major Church to come to Barnstable to him, he having received a letter from the government of Boston to raise some forces to go east. Whereupon the said Major Church went the next day to Barnstable, as ordered. Finding the Governour and some of the council of war there, [who] discoursed [with] him; [concluded][1] that he should take his Indian soldiers, and two English Captains, with what volunteers could be raised; and that one Captain should go out of Plymouth and Barnstable counties, and the other out of Bristol county, with what forces he could raise; concluding to have but few officers, to save charge.

The said Church was at great charge and expense in raising of forces. Governour Hinkley promised that he would take care to provide vessels to transport the said army, with ammunition and provisions, by the time prefixed by himself; for the government of Boston had obliged themselves by their let-

---
[1] [concluding]

---

ver, and was taken in the spring of this year, (1690) after the English had left it, (probably.) It was 4 miles from the waters of Casco bay. Sullivan, 178, 9.

ter, to provide any thing that was wanting. So at the time prefixed, Major Church marched down all his soldiers out of Bristol county to Plymouth, as ordered. And being come, found it not as he expected; for there were neither provisions, ammunition, or transports. So he immediately sent an express to the Governour, who was at Barnstable, to give him an account that he with the men were come to Plymouth, and found nothing ready. In his return to the said Church, [he] gave him an account of his disappointments, and sent John Lathrop* of Barnstable in a vessel, with some ammunition and provision on board, to him at Plymouth; also sent him word that there were more on board of Samuel Alling† of Barnstable, who was to go for a transport, and that he himself would be at Plymouth next day. But Alling never came near him, but went to Billingsgate,‡ at Cape Cod, as he was informed.

The Governour being come, said to Major Church, that he must take some of the open sloops, and make spar decks to them, and lay platforms for the soldiers to lie upon, which delays were very expensive to the said Church; his soldiers being all volunteers, daily expected to be treated by him, and the Indians always begging for money to get drink. But he using his utmost diligence, made what despatch he could to be gone. Being ready to embark, received his

---

* Probably, the ancestor of some eminent men of later times in Massachusetts. He perhaps was the son of John Lathrop, who fled from England in the days of persecution, and afterward settled in Barnstable. The first John died in 1653.

† It is thought that this name should have been written Allen. No pains have been taken to ascertain any thing concerning this person, but if what Dr. Mather says be correct, he is a descendant of one Thomas Allen, who came to this country in 1638, and was afterward a minister in Charlestown. Eliot, 20.

‡ In the town of Eastham.

commission, and instructions from Governour Hinkley, which are as follows.

[The commission being the same as that for the first expedition is here omitted. It was dated 2 September, 1690. The instructions, also, differing only in a few unimportant matters, are omitted to give place to more interesting information. It may be proper to notice the chief differences. No men of war vessels attended, nor was Church directed to confer with any persons except his officers. The *eight pounds* per head *over and above* is not mentioned, and are signed only by Governour Hinkley. Date, the same as that of the commission.]

Now having a fair wind, Major Church soon got to Piscataqua.* [He]¹ was to apply himself to Major Pike,† a worthy gentleman, who said, [that] he had advice of his coming from Boston gentlemen; also, [that] he had received directions, that what men the said Church should want, must be raised out of Hampshire, out of the several towns and garrisons. Major Pike asked him, how many men he should want? He said, enough to make up his forces that he brought with him, three hundred, at least, and not more than three hundred and fifty. And so in about nine days time, he was supplied with two companies of soldiers. He having been at about *twenty shillings* a day charge in expenses while there. Now

¹ [who]

---

* The country at the mouth of Pascataqua river went under the general name of Pascataqua, but since, the river only, is known by that name. The word was formerly, and sometimes latterly, spelt as in the text, but an *a* should take the place of *i*.

† Major Robert Pike was a person of distinction. He was among the first 28 counsellors appointed by charter, for the province of Massachusetts bay, who were to hold their offices until May 1693, or until others should be chosen in their stead. He might be the ancestor of the distinguished Nicholas Pike of Somersworth, to whom we are much indebted for the best system of Arithmetick that has appeared. An account might perhaps be found of the family in Newhampshire, for which I have not had an opportunity.

he received Major Pike's instructions, which are as followeth.

"Portsmouth, in Newhampshire, Sept. 9, 1690. To *Major Benjamin Church, Commander in Chief of their Majesties' forces, now designed upon the present expedition eastward, and now resident at Portsmouth.*

The Governour and council of the Massachusetts colony reposing great trust and confidence in your loyalty and valour, from experience of your former actions, and of God's presence with you in the same; in pursuance of an order, received from them commanding it; these are in their Majesties' names to empower and require you, as commander in chief, to take into your care and conduct these forces now here present at their rendezvous at Portsmouth; and they are alike required to obey you; and with them to sail eastward by the first opportunity to Casco, or places adjacent, that may be most commodious for landing with safety and secrecy; and to visit the French and Indians at their headquarters at Amerascogen, Pejepscot, or any other place, according as you may have hope or intelligence of the residence of the enemy; using always your utmost endeavour for the preservation of your own men, and the killing, destroying, and utterly rooting out of the enemy, wheresoever they may be found; and also, as much as may possibly be done, for the redeeming or recovering of our captives in any places.

You being there arrived, and understanding your way, to take your journey back again, either by land or water, as you shall judge most convenient for the accomplishing of the end intended; and to give intelligence always of your motions, whensoever you can with safety and convenience.

Lastly. In all to consult your council, the commanders or commission officers of your several companies, when it may be obtained, the greater part of whom to determine. And so the Lord of hosts, the God of armies, go along with you, and be your conduct. Given under my hand, the day and year above said,

Per ROBERT PIKE."

Being ready, they took the first opportunity, and made the best of their way to Pejepscot fort, where they found nothing. From thence they marched to Amerascogen,* and when they came near the fort, Major Church made a halt, ordering the Captains to draw out of their several companies sixty of their meanest men, to be a guard to the Doctor, and knapsacks, being not a mile from said fort. And then moving towards the fort, they saw young Doney† and his wife, with two English captives. The said Doney made his escape to the fort, his wife was shot down, and so the two poor captives were released out of their bondage.

The said Major Church and Captain Walton‡ made

---

* This river has its rise in Newhampshire and flowing eastward enters Maine in about 44 d. 20 min. N. Mather, says this place where they had now arrived at, was 40 miles up the river. Mag. 528. Perhaps few words have been written more different ways, than this. The authors of the Newhampshire Gazetteer prefer that as in the text, except, that they double the *g* and change the last *e* into *i*. But people in general, that live on said river, adopt the better method of Androscoggin.

† He was an Indian, and all we know of him is found in this history; except he be the one seized at Wells, mentioned by Mather, II, 545, and whose name is signed Robin Doney to the articles of peace at Pemmaquid in 1693. Ib. 543.

‡ Col. Shadrach Walton of Somersworth N. H. A brave and valuable officer. In the long wars that followed, he rendered important services. To recount his actions would be to write a narrative, much beyond the limits of a note. More particulars of him may be found in Penhallow's history, in I Newhampshire Hist. Soc. Collections, than in any other work extant. He was with Col. March, in 1707, in an unsuccessful attempt on Portroyal. Here he fought a body

no stop, making the best of their way to the fort, with some of the army, in hopes of getting to the fort before young Doney; but the river through which they must pass, being as deep as their armpits. However Major Church as soon as he was got over, stripped to his shirt and jacket, leaving his breeches behind, ran directly to the fort, having an eye to see if young Doney (who ran on the other side of the river,) should get there before him. The wind now blowing very hard in their faces, as they ran, was some help to them; for several of our men fired guns, which they in the fort did not hear, so that we had taken all in the fort, had it not been for young Doney, who got to the fort just before we did. [He][1] ran into the south gate, and out at the north, all the men following him, except one. [They][2] all ran directly down to the great river and falls.

The said Church and his forces being come pretty near, he ordered the said Walton to run directly with some forces into the fort, and himself with the rest, ran down to the river, after the enemy, who ran some of them into the river, and the rest under the great falls. Those who ran into the river were killed; for he saw but one man get over, and he only crept up the bank, and there lay in open sight. And those that ran under the falls, they made no discovery of, notwithstanding several of his men went in under the said falls, and were gone some considerable time, [but] could not find them. So leaving a watch there, returned up to the fort, where he found but one man

[1] [who]   [2] [who]

---

of the enemy and put them to flight, being the only field officer then on shore. Again in 1710, he rendered important service at the same place, when it was taken by the armament under Col. Nicholson. In a note to page 119, in Penhallow's history it is remarked that "He was dismissed from service" (in 1725) "and was succeeded by Col. Thomas Westbrook." But on what account he was dismissed, whether from age or misconduct is unknown to me. He is mentioned no more in Penhallow's history.

taken, and several women and children; amongst whom were Captain Hakins'* wife and Worumbos'† wife, the sachem of that fort, with their children. The said Hakins was sachem of Pennacook,‡ who de-

---

* Hawkins or Hogkins. This sachem had been treated with neglect by Governour Cranfield, which in part may account for his enmity to the English. He made a treaty with them in 1685, which perhaps, was broken more through the negligence of the English than the wish of Hogkins. He appears to have learned so much of the English language as to pretend to write and read. Four letters from under his hand are preserved in Belknap, I, Appendix, No. XLII, &c. One of which, as a curiosity, is here printed.

"*May* 15, 1685.
Honour Mr. Governor,
Now this day I com your house, I want se you, and I bring my hand at before you I want shake hand to you if your worship when please then you receve my hand then shake your hand and my hand. You my friend because I remember at old time when live my grant father and grant mother then Englishmen com this country, then my grant father and Englishmen they make a good govenant, they friend allways, my grant father leving at place called Malamake rever, other name chef Natukkog and Panukkog, that one rever great many names, and I bring you this few skins at this first time I will give you my friend. This all Indian hand.
JOHN × HAWKINS, Sagamore."

This letter is the best written of the four, and are all very similar. I copy it precisely as I find it in Belknap. Two of the others are signed *John Hogkins*, and one, *Mr. John Hogkins*, the last has no date, and one is dated 16 May, and the other two the 15, both having 14 signers beside *Hogkins*, who, it is probable, were his principal men. The name of Hogkins or rather Hawkins he received from some Englishman. His Indian name was Hancamagus. See N. H. Hist. Soc. Col. I, 221.

† A sachem of the Androscoggins. He was with Madokawando in the celebrated attack on Storer's garrison at Wells, an account of which may be seen in a succeeding note.

‡ The country on the Merrimake river, including the present town of Concord, and the lands above and below, but how far, cannot be told; as those people never set any particular bounds to their country, that we know of. See Farmer's account of the Pennacook Indians, in N. H. Hist. Soc. Col I, 218. The word should be spelt as in the text, but

stroyed Major Walden and his family, some time before, &c.

The said two women, viz. Hakins' and Worumbos' wives requested the said Church, that he would spare them and their children's lives; promising upon that condition, [that] he should have all the captives that were taken, and in the Indians' hands. He asked them how many? They said, about four score. So, upon that condition, he promised them their lives, &c. In the said fort there were several English captives, who were in a miserable condition. Amongst them was Captain Hucking's* wife, of Oyster river.†

Major Church proceeded to examine the man, taken, who gave him an account, that most of the fighting men were gone to Winterharbour,‡ to provide provisions for the bay of Fundy§ Indians, who

---

the author just cited, leaves out one *n*. Sullivan writes Pennycook. Belknap, whom many, justly in most respects, follow, writes it as in the text, with the omission of one *n*, as does Mather, whom he follows.

* Hucking's garrison was taken, about the last of August, 1689, in which were a few women and boys. The Indians had been in ambush for a number of days, until they had ascertained how many men belonged to the garrison, then as they all went out into the field one day, the Indians cut off their retreat, and killed them all excepting one, who escaped, being 18 in all. They then went to the garrison and demanded a surrender, but the boys at first refused, and some fighting was done; at length they surrendered on terms of life, &c. The assailants found means to fire the garrison, which hastened the surrender. Mather, Mag. II, 515. This woman is supposed to be the wife of the owner of the garrison.

† Now Durham. The country thereabout, was formerly known by this name.

‡ At the mouth of Saco river in Maine.

§ A large bay, sometimes called Frenchman's bay, containing the island Mountdesert, 8 or 10 miles to the eastward of the mouth of Penobscot river. Sullivan, 57, informs us, that it took the name of Frenchman's bay, from this circumstance. That with Demotte came over to America one Nicholas D'Aubri, a French ecclesiastic of respectability, who went on shore on the west side of the bay, and wandering into the

were to come and join with them to fight the English. The soldiers being very rude, would hardly spare the Indian's life, while in examination; intending when he had done, that he should be executed. But Captain Hucking's wife, and another woman, down on their knees, and begged for him, saying, that he had been a means to save their lives, and a great many more; and had helped several to opportunities to run away, and make their escape; and that never, since he came amongst them, had fought against the English, but being related to Hakins' wife, kept at the fort with them, having been there two years; but his living was to the westward of Boston. So, upon their request, his life was spared, &c.

Next day the said Church ordered that all their corn should be destroyed, being a great quantity; saving a little for the two old squaws, which he designed to leave at the fort, to give an account who he was, and from whence he came. The rest being knocked on the head, except the aforementioned, for an example; ordering them all to be buried. Having inquired where all their best beaver was? they said [that] it was carried away to make a present to the bay of Fundy Indians, who were coming to their assistance.

Now being ready to draw off from thence, he called the two old squaws to him, and gave each of them a kettle, and some biscuit, bidding them to tell the Indians, when they came home, that he was known by the name of Captain Church, and lived in the westerly part of Plymouth government; and that those Indians that came with him were formerly King Philip's men, and that he had met with them in Philip's war, and drawn them off from him, to

---

woods in search of curiosities, was left by the boat to his fate. After three weeks he was found by a boat from the same vessel, almost emaciated. From which circumstance it received the above appellation. But the waters between Novascotia and the main are generally understood to make the bay of Fundy.

fight for the English, against the said Philip, and his associates, who then promised him to fight for the English, as long as they had one enemy left. And said, that 'they did not question, but before Indian corn was ripe to have Philip's head;'* notwithstanding [Philip]¹ had twice as many men as were in their country; and that they† had killed and taken one thousand three hundred and odd of Philip's men, women and children, and Philip himself, with several other sachems, &c.; and that they should tell Hakins and Worumbos, that if they had a mind to see their wives and children, they should come to Wells‡ garrison, and that there they might hear of them, &c.

Major Church having done, moved with all his forces down to Mequait,§ where the transports were, (but in the way some of his soldiers threatened the Indian man prisoner very much, so that in a thick swamp, he gave them the slip and got away) and

¹ [he]

---

* See Philip's war, page 82.

† The English.

‡ Webhannet was the Indian name of Wells. This town is on the sea board about half way between York and Saco, being 13 miles from the former. Storer's garrison was in this town, which was near where the old meeting house stood, and nearly half a mile south of the present place of publick worship, and was standing since the year 1760. Sullivan, 236. The town suffered greatly by the savages. About 500 French and Indians made a desperate attempt on the garrison, in May, 1691, and though it had but 15 men, by the valour of the commander, Captain Converse, and this few, they were repulsed. A sloop happened to arrive just before the engagement, which was a help to them, although they fought on board their vessels. A flag was sent to Capt. Converse, to persuade him to surrender; at his refusing, the officer said, "We will cut you up as fine as tobacco before to-morrow morning." He bid them "come on for he wanted work." Magnalia, II, 532.

§ A small bay or cove in Casco bay. It is generally written Maquoit. Mather, and after him Belknap wrote Macquoit.

when they all got on board the transports, the wind being fair, made the best of their way for Winterharbour; and the next morning before day, and as soon as the day appeared, they discovered some smokes, rising towards Skaman's* garrison. He immediately sent away a scout of sixty men, and followed presently with the whole body. The scout coming near a river discovered the enemy to be on the other side of the river. But three of the enemy were come over the river, to the same side, [—][1] which the scout was of, [but discovering the scout,] ran hastily down to their canoe. One of which lay at each end, [—][2] and the third stood up to paddle over. The scout fired at them, and he that paddled, fell down upon the canoe, and broke it to pieces, so that all three perished.

The firing put the enemy to the run, who left their canoes and provisions to ours. And old Doney,† and one Thomas Baker, an Englishman, who was a prisoner amongst them, were up at the falls,‡ and heard the guns fire, expected the other Indians were come to their assistance, so came down the river in a canoe. But when they perceived that there were English as well as Indians, old Doney ran the canoe ashore, and ran over Baker's head, and followed the rest; and then Baker came to ours, and gave an account of the beaver, hid at Pejepscot plain.§ And coming to the place where the plunder was, the Major sent a scout to Pejepscot fort, to see if they could make any discovery of the enemy's tracks, or could discover any coming up the river.

¹ [of the river]   ² [of the canoe]

---

* This was on the east side of Saco river, about two miles below the falls. Sullivan, 180. The name should be spelt Scammon. Ib.

† Father of young Doney.   ‡ The falls in the Saco.

§ In Brunswick.

[They]¹ returned, and said [that] they saw nothing but our old tracks at the said fort, &c.

Now having got some plunder, one of the Captains* said [that] it was time to go home, and several others were of the same mind. The Major being much disturbed at this motion of theirs, expecting the enemy would come in a very short time, where they might have a great advantage of them, &c.

Notwithstanding all he could say, or do, he was obliged to call a council, according to his instructions, wherein he was outvoted. The said commander seeing [that] he was put by of his intentions, proffered, [that] if sixty men would stay with him, he would not embark as yet; but all he could say or do, could not prevail. Then they moved to the vessels, and embarked, and as they were going in the vessels, on the back side of Mayr point,† they discovered eight or nine canoes, who turned short about, and went up the river; being the same Indians that the Major expected, and would have waited for. The aforesaid Captain being much disturbed at what the Major had said to him, drew off from the fleet, and in the night ran aground.

In the morning Anthony Bracket, having been advised and directed by the Indian that had made his escape from our forces, came down near where the aforesaid vessel lay aground, and got aboard. [He]² has proved a good pilot and Captain for his country. The next day being very calm and misty,

¹ [who] ² [who]

---

* From what follows we may suppose this to be one of the Captains from Plymouth government. But as there were two, we cannot be positive which was meant, and but one is named; yet, another circumstance might induce us to suppose a Newhampshire Captain is meant, were it not said that the Plymouth forces sailed first.

† What, in Sullivan's history, it is thought, is called Merryconeag. It is a point in the east part of Casco bay. Mather calls it Mares point, II, 557.

so that they were all day getting down from Maquait to Perpodack,* and the masters of the vessels thinking it not safe putting out in the night, so late in the year, anchored there. [—]¹ The vessels being much crowded, the Major ordered that three companies should go on shore, and no more. Himself with Captain Converse† went with them to order their lodging. And finding just houses convenient for them, viz., two barns and one house; [and]² seeing them all settled, and their watches out, the Major and Captain Converse returned to go on board. And coming near where the boat was, it was pretty dark, they discovered some men, but did not know what or who they were. The Major ordered those that were with him, all to clap down and cock their guns, and he called out, and asked them who they were? And they said, "Indians." He asked them whose men they were? They said, "Captain Southworth's." He asked them where they intended to lodge? They said, "In those little huts that the enemy had made when they took that garrison."‡

The Major told them [that] they must not make any fires, for if they did, the enemy would be upon them before day. They laughed, and said, "Our Major is afraid." Having given them their directions, he, with Captain Converse, went on board the

---

¹ [at Perpodack]   ² [so]

---

* In the town of Cape Elizabeth, 6 or 8 miles from Portland. It is also known by the name of Spring point

† Captain James Converse. A distinguished partizan. No commander deserved better of their country than he. Beside his singular bravery in defending the garrison at Wells, mentioned in note 3, on page 189, the history of this war abounds with his exploits; to enumerate which would far exceed the limits of this note. See Magnalia, II, 529, &c.

‡ I can find no account of the Indians taking a garrison here until after this. In Queen Ann's or Villebon's war several persons were killed and some families carried into captivity. Sullivan, 195.

Mary sloop, designing to write home, and send away in the morning the two sloops which had the small pox on board, &c.

But before day our Indians began to make fires, and to sing and dance. So the Major called to Captain Southworth to go ashore and look after his men, for the enemy would be upon them by and by. He ordered the boat to be hauled up, to carry him ashore, and called Captain Converse to go with him; and just as the day began to appear, as the Major was getting into the boat to go ashore, the enemy fired upon our men, (the Indians) notwithstanding that one Philip, an Indian of ours, who was out upon the watch, heard a man cough, and the sticks crack, [and][1] gave the rest an account, that he saw Indians, which they would not believe; but said to him, "You are afraid." His answer was, that they might see them come creeping. They laughed and said, [that] they were hogs. "Ah," said he, "and they will bite you by and by." So presently they did fire upon our men. But the morning being misty, their guns did not go off quick, so that our men had all time to fall down before their guns went off, and saved themselves from that volley, except one man, who was killed.

This sudden firing upon our Indian soldiers, surprised them [so,] that they left their arms, but soon recovered them again, and got down the bank, which was but low. The Major, with all the forces on board landed as fast as they could, the enemy firing smartly at them; however all got safe ashore. The enemy had a great advantage of our forces, who were between the sun's rising and the enemy, so that if a man put up his head or hand they could see it, and would fire at it. However, some, with the Major, got up the bank, behind stumps and rocks, to have the advantage of firing at the enemy But when the sun was risen, the Major slipped

[1] [who]

down the bank again, where all the forces were ordered to observe his motion, viz., that he would give three shouts, and then all of them should run with him up the bank.

So, when he had given the third shout, [he] ran up the bank, and Captain Converse with him, but when the said Converse perceived that the forces did not follow, as commanded, called to the Major, and told him [that] the forces did not follow. [He,]¹ notwithstanding the enemy fired smartly at him, got safe down the bank again; and rallying the forces up the bank, soon put the enemy to flight. And following them so close, that they took thirteen canoes, and one lusty man, who had Joseph Ramsdel's scalp by his side. [He]² was taken by two of our Indians, and having his deserts, was himself scalped.

This being a short and smart fight, some of our men were killed and several wounded. Sometime after, an Englishman, who was prisoner amongst them, gave an account, that our forces had killed and wounded several of the enemy, for they killed several prisoners according to custom,* &c.

After this action was over, our forces embarked for Piscataqua. The Major went to Wells, and removed the Captain there, and put in Captain Andros, who had been with him; and knew the discourse left with the two old squaws at Amerascogen, for Hakins and Worumbos to come there in fourteen days, if they had a mind to hear of their wives and children; who did then, or soon after come with a flag of truce to said Wells garrison, and had leave to come in, and more appearing came in, to the number of eight, (without any terms) being all chief Sachems. [They]³ were very glad to hear of the women and children, viz., Hakins and Worumbos' wives and children. [They]⁴ all said three several times that they would

¹ [who]   ² [who]   ³ [and]   ⁴ [who]

---

* It was said to be a custom among most of the Indian nations, to kill as many prisoners as they lost in battle.

never fight against the English any more, for the
French made fools of them, &c. They saying as they
did, the said Andros let them go.

Major Church being come to Piscataqua, and two
of his transports having the small pox on board, and
several of his men having got great colds by their
hard service, pretended [that] they were going to
have the small pox; thinking by that means to be
sent home speedily. The Major being willing to try
them, went to the gentlemen there, and desired them
to provide a house; for some of his men expected
[that] they should have the small pox; which [they]
readily did, and told him, that the people belonging
to it were just recovered of the small pox, and had
been all at meeting, &c.

The Major returning to his officers, ordered them
to draw out all their men that were going to have the
small pox, for he had provided an hospital for them.
So they drew out seventeen men, that had as they
said all the symptoms of the small pox. He ordered
them all to follow him, and coming to the house, he
asked them how they liked it? They said, "Very
well." Then he told them that the people in the
said house, had all had the small pox, and were recovered; and that if they went in, they must not
come out till they [had] all had it. Whereupon
they all presently began to grow better, and to make
excuses, except one man who desired to stay out till
night before he went in, &c.

The Major going to the gentlemen, told them, that
one thing more would work a perfect cure upon his
men, which was to let them go home; which did
work a cure upon all, except one, and he had not the
small pox. So he ordered the plunder to be divided
forthwith, and sent away all the Plymouth forces.
But the gentlemen there desired him to stay, and
they would be assisting to him in raising new forces,
to the number of what was sent away; and that they
would send to Boston for provisions, which they did

and sent Captain Plaisted* to the Governour and council at Boston, &c.

And in the mean time, the Major with those gentlemen went into all those parts, and raised a sufficient number of men, both officers and soldiers. [They]¹ all met at the bank† on the same day that Captain Plaisted returned from Boston. [The]² return from the Boston gentlemen was, that the Canada expedition had drained them so that they could do no more. So that Major Church, notwithstanding he had been at considerable expenses in raising said forces to serve his King and country, was obliged to give them a treat and dismiss them. Taking his leave of them, [he] came home to Boston in the Mary sloop, Mr. Alden‡ master, and Captain Converse with him, on a Saturday. And waiting upon the Governour, and some of the gentlemen in Boston, they looked very strange upon them, which not only troubled them, but put them in some consternation; [wondering] what the matter should be, that after so much toil and hard service, [they] could not have

¹ [who]   ² [whose]

---

* The name of Plaisted is found in the earlier and later wars as well as in this. A letter from Roger Plaisted to Maj. Waldron, who was killed at Salmon fal's, 1675, showing his desperate situation, is printed in Hubbard, 281. Whether this was a son or not is not known to me, but from the author just cited should conclude that it was not. Perhaps he was a near connexion. In 1712, a Mr. Plaisted was taken at Wells, and ransomed for 300 pounds.

† By the *bank* I suppose is meant, that part of the town of Portsmouth, including Church hill, formerly called Strawberry bank, and was a general appellation for the town.

‡ The same mentioned further on, as old Mr. Alden, and Capt. Alden. He lived at Boston, and was one of the accused in the celebrated *witch age*, and was committed to prison by Hawthorn and Gidney, 31 May, 1692, where he remained 15 weeks; at the end of which time he made his escape. He afterwards returned, and none appearing against him, was cleared. See Calef's " More Wonders of the Invisible World," 210 to 214.

so much as one pleasant word, nor any money in their pockets; for Major Church had but *eight pence* left, and Captain Converse none, as he said afterwards.

Major Church seeing two gentlemen, which he knew had money, asked them to lend him *forty shillings*, telling them his necessity, yet they refused. So being bare of money, was obliged to lodge at Mr. Alden's three nights. The next Tuesday morning Captain Converse came to him, (not knowing each others circumstances as yet) and said, [that] he would walk with him out of town. So coming near Pollard's at the south end, they had some discourse. [Observed,] that it was very hard that they should part with dry lips. Major Church told Captain Converse that he had but *eight pence* left, and could not borrow any money to carry him home, and the said Converse said, that he had not a *penny* left; so they were obliged to part without going to Pollard's, &c.

The said Captain Converse returned back into town, and the said Church went over to Roxbury; and at the tavern he met with Stephen Braton of Rhodeisland, a drover, who was glad to see him, (the said Church) and he as glad to see his neighbour. Whereupon Major Church called for an *eight penny* tankard of drink, and let the said Braton know his circumstances, [and] asked him whether he would lend him *forty shillings?* He answered, " Yes, *forty pounds* if he wanted it." So he thanked him, and said [that] he would have but *forty shillings*, which he freely lent him.

Presently after Mr. Church was told that his brother, Caleb Church of Watertown, was coming with a spare horse for him, (having heard the night before that his brother was come in.) By which means the said Major Church got home. And for all his travel and expenses in raising soldiers, and service done, never had but *fourteen pounds* of Plymouth gentlemen, and not a *penny* of Boston; notwithstanding he had worn out all [of] his clothes, and run himself in debt, so that he was obliged to sell half a share of land in Tiverton, for about *sixty pounds*, which is now* worth *three hundred. pounds* more and above what he had.

Having not been at home long before he found out the reason why Boston gentlemen looked so disaffected on him. As you may see by the sequel of two letters, [which] Major Church sent to the gentlemen in the eastward parts, which are as followeth.

"*Bristol, November* 27, 1690.

Worthy Gentlemen,

According to my promise when with you last, I waited upon the Governour at Boston on Saturday, Captain Converse being with me. The Governour informed us that the council were to meet on the Monday following in the afternoon, at which time we both there waited upon them, and gave them an account of the state of your country, and great necessities. They informed us, that their general court was to convene the Wednesday following, at which time they would debate and consider of the matter. Myself being bound home, Captain Converse was ordered to wait upon them, and bring you their resolves. I then took notice of the council that they looked upon me with an ill aspect, not judging me worthy to receive thanks for the service I had done in your parts; nor as much as asked me whether I wanted money to bear my expenses, or a horse to carry me home. But I was forced, for want of money, being far from friends, to go to Roxbury on foot; but meeting there with a Rhodeisland gentleman, acquainted him of my wants; who tendered me ten pounds, whereby I was accommodated for my journey home. And being come home, I went to

---
* About 1716.

the minister of our town,* and gave him an account of the transactions of the great affairs I had been employed in, and the great favour God was pleased to show me, and my company, and the benefit I hoped would accrue to yourselves; and desired him to return publick thanks; but at the same interim of time a paper was presented unto him from a court of Plymouth, which was holden before I came home, to command a day of humiliation through the whole government, "because of the frown of God upon those forces sent under my command, and the ill success we had, for want of good conduct." All which was caused by those false reports which were posted home by those ill affected officers that were under my conduct; especially one, which yourselves very well know, who had the advantage of being at home a week before me, being sick of action, and wanting the advantage to be at the bank, which he was every day mindful of more than fighting the enemy in their own country.

"After I came home, being informed of a general court at Plymouth, and not forgetting my faithful promise to you, and the duty I lay under, I went thither. Where waiting upon them I gave them an account of my Eastward transactions, and made them sensible of the falseness of those reports that were posted to them by ill hands, and found some small favourable acceptance with them; so far that I was credited. I presented your thanks to them for their seasonably sending those forces to relieve you, of the expense and charge they had been at; which thanks they gratefully received; and said a few lines from yourselves would have been well accepted. I then gave them an account of your great necessities, by being imprisoned in your garrisons, and the great mischief that would attend the pub-

---

* Bristol. The Rev. Samuel Lee, I suspect, was then the minister, as he did not leave America until sometime the next year. See note 4, page xii.

lick concerns of this country by the loss of their Majesties' interest, and so much good estate of your's and your neighbours, as doubtless would be, on the deserting of your town. I then moved for a free contribution for your relief, which they with great forwardness promoted; and then ordered a day of thanksgiving through the government upon the twentysixth day of this instant. Upon which day a collection was ordered for your relief, and the places near adjacent, in every respective town in this government; and for the good management of it that it might be safely conveyed unto your hands, they appointed a man in each county for the receipt and conveyance thereof. The persons nominated and accepted thereof, are, for the county of Plymouth, Captain Nathaniel Thomas, of Marshfield; for the county of Barnstable, Captain Joseph Lathrop, of Barnstable; and for the county of Bristol, myself. Which when gathered, you will have a particular account from each person, with orders of advice how it may be disposed of for your best advantage, with a copy of the court's order.* The gentlemen [that] the effects are to be sent to, are yourselves that I now write to, viz., John Wheelwright, Esq., Captain John Littlefield, and Lieutenant Joseph Story. I deferred writing, expecting every day to hear from you concerning the Indians, coming to treat about their prisoners that we had taken. The discourse I made with them at Ameresscogen, I knew would have that effect as to bring them to a treaty, which I would have thought myself happy to have been improved in, knowing that it would have made much for your good. But no intelligence coming to me from any gentleman in your parts,

---

* The people of Connecticut were forward, also, in contributing to those distressed inhabitants. A contribution was ordered by the general court throughout the colony, and the clergy were directed to exhort the people to liberal contributions for these charitable purposes. Hist. Con. I, 387

and hearing nothing but by accident, and that in the latter end of the week by some of ours coming from Boston, informed me that the Indians had come into your town to seek for peace; and that there was to be a treaty speedily; but the time they knew not. I took my horse, and upon the Monday set out for Boston, expecting the treaty had been at your town, as rationally it should; but on Tuesday night coming to Boston, I there met with Captain Elisha Andros, who informed me that the place of treaty was Sacatyhock,* and that Captain Alden was gone from Boston four days before I came there, and had carried all the Indian prisoners with him; and that all the forces were drawn away out of your parts, except twelve men in your town, and twelve in Piscataqua, which news did so amuse me, to see, that wisdom was taken from the wise, and such imprudence in their actions as to be deluded by Indians. To have a treaty so far from any English town, and to draw off the forces upon what pretence soever, to me looks very ill. My fear is that they will deliver those we have taken, which, if kept, would have been greatly for your security, in keeping them in awe, and preventing them from doing any hostile action or mischief. I knowing that the English being abroad are very earnest to go home, and the Indians are very tedious in their discourses; and by that means will have an advantage to have their captives at very low rates, to your great damage.† Gentlemen, as to Rhodeisland,

---

* Sagadahock. On the south side of Kennebeck river, 20 miles southwest of Pemmaqued. Hubbard.

† The treaty here alluded to, was agreed upon by those sachems that came into "Wells garrison," mentioned on page 194, "with a flag of truce." Major Hutchinson and Capt. Townsend went from Boston to Wells, as commissioners, and after some time, a conference was agreed upon at Sagadahock, 23 November. They met according to appointment and a truce only, was obtained, and that till 1 May.

I have not concerned myself as to any relief for you, having nothing in writing to show to them; yet, upon discourse with some gentlemen there they have signified a great forwardness to promote such a thing. I lying under great reflections from some of yours in the eastward parts, that I was a very covetous person, and came there to enrich myself, and that I killed their cattle and barrelled them up, and sent them to Boston, and sold them for plunder, and made money to put into my own pocket; and the owners of them being poor people begged for the hides and tallow, with tears in their eyes; and that I was so cruel as to deny them! which makes me judge myself incapable to serve you in that matter; yet, I do assure you, that the people are very charitable at the island, and forward in such good actions; and therefore, I advise you to desire some good substantial person to take the management of it, and write to the government there, which I know will not be labour lost. As for what I am accused of, you all can witness to the contrary, and I should take it very kindly from you to do me that just right, as to vindicate my reputation; for the wise man says, "A good name is as precious ointment." When I hear of the effects of the treaty, and have an account of this contribution, I intend again to write to you, being very desirous, and should think myself very happy, to be favoured with a few lines from yourself, or any gentleman in the eastward parts. Thus leaving you to the protection and guidance of the great God of Heaven and earth, who is able to protect and supply you in your great difficulties, and to give you deliverance in his own due time. I remain, gentlemen, your most assured friend, to serve you to my utmost power.

BENJAMIN CHURCH."

However, 10 captives were redeemed, and at the end of the truce they were to bring the rest to Wells, and make a final peace. Magnalia, II, 529.

"Postscript. Esquire Wheelwright.* Sir, I entreat you, after your perusal of these lines, to communicate the same to Captain John Littlefield,† Lieutenant Joseph Story, and to any other gentlemen, as in your judgment you see fit; with the tender of my respects to you, &c., and to Major Vaughan, and his good lady and family. To Captain Fryer, and good Mrs. Fryer, with hearty thanks for their kindness whilst in those parts, and good entertainment from them. My kind respects to Major Frost, Captain Walton, Lieutenant Honeywel, and my very good friend little Lieutenant Plaisted; with due respects to all gentlemen, my friends in the eastward parts, as if particularly named. Farewell.

B. C."

"To Major Pike.

Honoured Sir,   Bristol, Nov. 27, 1690.

These come to wait upon you, to bring the tenders of my hearty service to yourself, and lady, with due acknowledgment of thankfulness for all the kindness, and favour I received from you in the eastward parts, when with you. Since I came from

---

* A son, it is presumed, of the Rev. John Wheelwright, of whom so much has been said and written concerning Antinomian principles and land titles. Being contented with the history of the father, I have not disturbed the ashes of the son. The venerable ancestor held a deed of certain lands in Exeter, N. H., from certain Indian Sagamores under date, 1629, the "authenticity" of which, has of late, been examined by two able criticks. The late Governour Plumer of N. H., first endeavoured to vindicate its genuineness, and James Savage of Boston, seems to have proved the contrary. The deed may be seen in I Belknap, App. No. I. Governour Plumer's argument in N. H. Hist. Soc. Col. 299. And that of Mr. Savage in his edition of Winthrop's Journal, I, 412.

† A Lieut. Littlefield is named by Penhallow, 71, as being slain in 1712, at Wells. It might be he.

those parts, I am informed by Captain Andros, that yourself and most all the forces, are drawn off from the eastward parts. I admire at it, considering that they had so low esteem of what was done, that they can apprehend the eastward parts so safe before the enemy were brought into better subjection. I was in hopes, when I came from thence, that those who were so desirous to have my room, would have been very brisk in my absence, to have got themselves some honour, which they very much gaped after, or else they would not have spread so many false reports to defame me; which had I known before I left the bank* I would have had satisfaction of them. Your honour was pleased to give me some small account, before I left the bank, of some things that were ill represented to you, concerning the eastward expedition, which being rolled home like a snowball through both colonies, was got to such a bigness, that it overshadowed one from the influence of all comfort, or good acceptance amongst my friends in my journey homeward. But through God's goodness [I] am come home, finding all well, and myself in good health; hoping, that those reports will do me the favour, to quit me from all other publick actions; that so I may the more peaceably, and quietly, wait upon God, and be a comfort to my own family, in this dark time of trouble; being as one hid, till his indignation is overpast. I shall take it as a great favour, to hear of your welfare. Subscribing myself as I am, sir,

   Your most assured friend and servant,
    BENJAMIN CHURCH."

Major Church did receive, after this, answers to his letters, but hath lost them, except it be a letter from several of the gentlemen in those parts, in June following, which is as followeth.

---

* Portsmouth. See page 196, note 2.

"*Portsmouth, June* 29, 1691.

Major Benj. Church,

Sir, your former readiness to expose yourself in the service of the country, against the common enemy, and particularly the late obligations, you have laid upon us, in these eastern parts, leave us under a deep and grateful sense of your favour therein. And forasmuch as you were pleased when last here, to signify your ready inclination to further service of this kind, if occasion should call for it. We therefore presume, confidently to promise ourselves compliance accordingly; and have sent this message on purpose to you, to let you know, that notwithstanding the late overture of peace, the enemy have approved themselves as perfidious as ever, and are almost daily killing and destroying upon all our frontiers. The Governour and council of the Massachusetts have been pleased to order the raising of one hundred and fifty men, to be forthwith despatched into those parts; and, as we understand, have written to your Governour and council of Plymouth for further assistance, which we pray you to promote, hoping if you can obtain about two hundred men, English and Indians, to visit them at some of their head quarters, up Kennebeck river, or elsewhere, which for want of necessaries was omitted last year; it may be of great advantage to us. We offer nothing of advice, as to what methods are most proper to be taken in this affair. Your acquaintance with our circumstances as well as the enemy's, will direct you therein. We leave the conduct thereof to your own discretion. But that the want of provision, &c., may be no *remora* to your motion, you may please to know Mr. Geafford, one of our principal inhabitants, now residing in Boston, hath promised to take care to supply to the value of *two or three hundred pounds*, if occasion require. We pray a few lines by the bearer, to give us a prospect of what we may expect for our further encouragement, and remain,

Sir, your obliged friends and servants,
WILLIAM VAUGHAN,
RICHARD MARTYN,
NATHANIEL FRYER,
WILLIAM FERNALD,
FRANCIS HOOKE,
CHARLES FROST,
JOHN WINCOL,
ROBERT ELLIOTT."

(*A true copy of the original letter; which letter was presented to me by Captain Hatch, who came express.*)

Major Church sent them his answer, the contents whereof was, that he had gone often enough for nothing, and especially to be ill treated with scandals and false reports, when last out, which he could not forget. And signified to them, that doubtless some amongst them, thought they could do without him, &c. And to make short of it, [they] did go out, and meeting with the enemy at Maquait, were most shamefully beaten, as I have been informed.*

---

* I will lay before the reader an account of the affair hinted at, as I find it in Mather, and will only observe, that, that author is enough inclined to favour the side of the English. "About the latter end of July [1691] we sent out a small army under the command of Capt. March, Capt. King, Capt. Sherburn, and Capt. Walten, who landing at Maquoit, marched up to Pechypscot, but not finding any signs of the enemy, marched down again. While the commanders were waiting ashore till the soldiers were got aboard, such great numbers of Indians poured in upon them, that though the commanders wanted not for courage or conduct, yet they found themselves obliged, with much ado, (and not without the death of worthy Capt. Sherburn) to retire into the vessels which then lay aground. Here they kept pelting at one another all night; but unto little other purpose than this, which was indeed remarkable, that the enemy was at this time going to

FRENCH AND INDIAN WARS. 207

THE THIRD EXPEDITION EAST.

THIS was in the year 1692. In the time of Sir William Phips'* government, Major Walley being at Boston, was requested by his excellency to treat with Major Church about going east with him. Major Walley coming home, did as desired; and to encourage the said Major Church, told him, that now

take the isle of Shoals, and no doubt had they gone they would have taken it, but having exhausted all their ammunition on this occasion, they desisted from what they designed." Magnalia, II, 530.

* Governour Phips "was a Newengland man," born at Pemmaquid, in 1650-1; being, as we are told, a younger son among twentysix children, of whom twentyone were sons. By profession he was a ship carpenter. That business he soon left; and being an industrious and persevering man, and applying himself to study, soon acquired an education competent for the discharge of common affairs, and then went to sea. On hearing of a Spanish ship's being wrecked near the Bahamas, proceeded to England, and gave so flattering an account of its value, and the practicability of obtaining it, that he was despatched in one of the King's ships in search of it; but returned without success. Yet he believed the treasure might be obtained; and soon after, the Duke of Albemarl sent him with two ships on the same business. After much excessive toil, and nearly on the point of abandoning the object, the treasure was discovered, and he succeeded in bringing from the wreck *three hundred thousand pounds*. But after deducting the Duke's share and the outfits, and his own great generosity to his men, he had left only *sixteen thousand*. He now had conferred on him the order of knighthood. In 1690 he commanded an expedition against Quebeck, but from unavoidable obstacles did not arrive until too late in the season, and was obliged to abandon the expedition. See note 1, on page 177, where some particulars are given. The King now for the first time complimented the Newengland agents with the nomination of their Governour, and they nominated Sir William Phips, and he arrived at Boston, 14 May, 1692, invested with the proper authority. In 1694, he was sent for to answer some complaints in England, but fell sick before he had his trial and died, 18 Feb. 1695. All represent him as a strictly honest man, and a real friend to his country. Mather, Holmes, Eliot, and Allen.

was the time to have recompense for his former great expenses; saying also, that the country could not give him less than *two or three hundred pounds.*

So upon his excellency's request, Major Church went down to Boston, and waited upon him, who said he was glad to see him, &c. After some discourse [he] told the said Church, that he was going east, himself, and that he should be his second, and in his absence, command all the forces. And being requested by his excellency to raise what volunteers he could of his old soldiers in the county of Bristol, both English and Indians, received his commission, which is as followeth.

" *Sir William Phips, Knight, Captain General and Governour in Chief, in and over his Majesty's province of the Massachusetts bay, in Newengland,*
To Benjamin Church, *Gent., Greeting.*

Reposing special trust and confidence in your loyalty, courage and good conduct; I do by these presents constitute and appoint you to be Major of the several companies of militia, detached for their Majesties' service against their French and Indian enemies. You are therefore authorized and required in their Majesties' names, to discharge the duty of a Major by leading, ordering and exercising the said several companies in arms, both inferiour officers and soldiers, keeping them in good order and discipline, commanding them to obey you as their Major. And diligently to intend the said service, for the prosecuting, pursuing, killing and destroying of the said common enemy. And yourself to observe and follow such orders and directions as you shall from time to time receive from myself, according to the rules and discipline of war, pursuant to the trust reposed in you for their Majesties' service.

Given under my hand and seal at Boston, the twentyfifth day of July, 1692. In the fourth year of the reign of our sovereign Lord and Lady, William and Mary, by the grace of God, King and Queen of England, Scotland, France and Ireland, defender of the faith, &c.

WILLIAM PHIPS.

By his Excellency's command.

Isaac Addington, *Secr.*"

Returning home to the county aforesaid, he soon raised a sufficient number of volunteers, both English and Indians, and officers suitable to command them, marched them down to Boston. But there was one thing I would just mention, which was, that Major Church, being short of money, was forced to borrow *six pounds* in money of Lieutenant Woodman, in Littlecompton, to distribute by a *shilling*, and a *bit** at a time, to the Indian soldiers, who, without such allurements, would not have marched to Boston. This money Major Church put into the hands of Mr. William Fobes, who was going out [as] their commissary in that service.

[He]¹ was ordered to keep a just account of what each Indian had, so that it might be deducted out of their wages at their return home. Coming to Boston, his excellency having got things in readiness, they embarked on board their transports, his excellency going in person with them; being bound to Pemaquid.† But in their way stopped at Casco, and buri-

¹ [who]

---

* Six pence.

† This word is better written Pemmaquid as it was formerly pronounced, and now generally. This place is celebrated as the birth place of Sir WILLIAM PHIPS. Several places are known by this name, but are all in the same vicinity, and on the east side of Kennebeck river, and about 20 miles from its mouth. Hubbard.

ed the bones* of the dead people there, and took off the great guns that were there, then went to Pemaquid.

Coming there his excellency asked Major Church to go ashore and give his judgment about erecting a fort† there? He answered, that his genius did not incline that way, he never had any value for them, being only nests for destructions. His excellency said, [that] he had a special order from their Majesties, King William and Queen Mary, to erect a fort there, &c. Then they went ashore and spent some time in the projection thereof. Then his excellency told Major Church that he might take all the forces with him, (except one company to stay with him and work about the fort.) The Major answered, that if his excellency pleased, he might keep two companies with him, and [that] he would go with the rest‡ to Penobscot, and places adjacent. Which his excellency did, and gave Major Church his orders, which are as followeth.

"*By his excellency*, Sir WILLIAM PHIPS, Knight, *Captain General and Governour in Chief, in and over their Majesties' province of the Massachusetts bay, in Newengland, &c.*

Instructions for Major Benjamin Church.

Whereas you are Major, and so chief officer of a body of men, detached out of the militia, appointed for an expedition against the French and Indian ene-

---

* See page 175, and note 3, where an account of the destruction of Casco is related.

† This fort was called the William Henry, and was the best then in these parts of America. It was built of stone of a quadrangular figure, and about 737 feet in compass, mounting 14 (if not 18) guns. Whereof 6 were 18 pounders. About 60 men were left to man the fort. Mather, Magnalia, II, 536, 537.

‡ Their whole force was 450 men. Ib.

my; you are duly to observe the following instructions.

Imprimis. You are to take care that the worship of God be duly and constantly maintained and kept up amongst you; and to suffer no swearing, cursing, or other profanation of the holy name of God; and, as much as in you lies, to deter and hinder all other vices amongst your soldiers.

Secondly. You are to proceed, with the soldiers under your command to Penobscot, and, with what privacy, and what undiscoverable methods you can, there to land your men, and take the best measures to surprise the enemy.

Thirdly. You are, by killing, destroying, and all other means possible, to endeavour the destruction of the enemy, in pursuance whereof, being satisfied of your courage and conduct, I leave the same to your discretion.

Fourthly. You are to endeavour the taking what captives you can, either men, women or children, and the same safely to keep and convey them unto me.

Fifthly. Since it is not possible to judge how affairs may be circumstanced with you there, I shall therefore not limit your return, but leave it to your prudence, only that you make no longer stay than you can improve for advantage against the enemy, or may reasonably hope for the same.

Sixthly. You are also to take care and be very industrious by all possible means to find out and destroy all the enemy's corn, and other provisions in all places where you can come at the same.

Seventhly. You are to return from Penobscot and those eastern parts, to make all despatch hence for Kennebeck river and the places adjacent, and there prosecute all advantages against the enemy as aforesaid.

Eighthly. If any soldier, officer, or other shall be disobedient to you as their commander in chief, or other their superiour officer, or make, or cause any mutiny, commit other offence or disorders, you shall call a council of war amongst your officers, and having tried him or them so offending, inflict such punishment as the merit of the offence requires, death only excepted, which if any shall deserve, you are to secure the person, and signify the crime unto me by the first opportunity.

Given under my hand this 11th day of August, 1692.

WILLIAM PHIPS."

Then the Major and his forces embarked and made the best of their way to Penobscot. And coming to an island in those parts in the evening, landed his forces at one end of the island. Then the Major took part of his forces and moved (toward day) to the other end of the said island, where they found two Frenchmen and their families, in their houses; and, that one or both of them had Indian women to their wives, and had children by them. The Major presently examining the Frenchmen, [demanded] where the Indians were? They told him, that there was a great company of them upon an island just by. And showing him the island, [he] presently discovered several of them.

Major Church and his forces still keeping undiscovered to them, asked the Frenchmen where their passing place was? Which they readily showed them. So presently they placed an ambuscade to take any that should come over. Then sent orders for all the rest of the forces to come; sending them an account of what he had seen and met withal; strictly charging them to keep themselves undiscovered by the enemy. The ambuscade did not lie long before an Indian man and woman came over in a canoe, to the place for landing, where the ambuscade was laid. [They][1] hauled up their canoe, and came right into the hands of our ambuscade, who so suddenly surpris-

[1] [who]

ed them that they could not give any notice to the others from whence they came. The Major ordering that none of his should offer, to meddle with the canoe, lest they should be discovered. Hoping to take the most of them, if his forces came as ordered, (he expecting them to come as directed.) But the first news [that] he had of them, was, that they were all coming, [and][1] not privately as ordered, but the vessels fair in sight of the enemy, which soon put them all to flight. And our forces not having boats suitable to pursue them, they got all away in their canoes, &c. [This][2] caused Major Church to say, [that] he would never go out again without [a] sufficient number of whale boats, [the][3] want of which was the ruin of that action.*

Then Major Church, according to his instructions, ranged all those parts, to find all their corn, and carried aboard their vessels what he thought convenient, and destroyed the rest. Also finding considerable quantities of plunder, viz., beaver, moose skins, &c.

Having done what service they could in those parts, he returned back to his excellency at Pemequid. Where being come, staid not long, (they being short of bread) his excellency intended [going] home for Boston for more provisions. [In the way][4] going with Major Church and his forces to Kennebeck river; and coming there gave him further orders, which are as followeth.

"*By his Excellency the Governour,*
To Major BENJAMIN CHURCH.

You having already received former instructions, are now further to proceed with the soldiers under

[1] [though]   [2] [which]   [3] [for]   [4] [but before]

---

* Mather, II, 537, says that five prisoners were taken at this time.

your command for Kennebeck river, and the places adjacent, and use your utmost endeavours to kill, destroy and take captive the French and Indian enemy wheresoever you shall find any of them; and at your return to Pemequid (which you are to do as soon as you can conveniently; after your best endeavour done against the enemy, and having destroyed their corn and other provisions) you are to stay with all your soldiers and officers, and set them to work on the fort, and make what despatch you can in that business, staying there until my further order.
                            WILLIAM PHIPS."

Then his excellency taking leave went for Boston, and soon after, Major Church and his forces had a smart fight with the enemy in Kennebeck river; pursued them so hard that they left their canoes, and ran up into the woods. [They] still pursued them up to their fort at Taconock,* which the enemy perceiving, set fire to their houses in the fort, and ran away by the light of them; and when Major Church came to the said fort, [he] found about half their houses standing, and the rest burnt; also found great quantities of corn, put up into Indian cribs, which he and his forces destroyed, as ordered.

Having done what service he could in those parts, returned to Pemequid. And coming there, employed his forces according to his instructions. Being out of bread [and] his excellency not coming, Major Church was obliged to borrow bread of the Captain of the man of war, that was then there, for all the forces under his command; his excellency not coming as expected. But at length his excellency came, and brought very little bread, more than

---

* This fort was about 64 miles from the sea. Taconock, or as Sullivan has it, Taconnet is a great fall of water in the Kennebeck. At this place, by order of Gov. Shirley, a fort was built on the east bank of the river (in 1754) and called fort Halifax. Minot's Hist. I, 186.

FRENCH AND INDIAN WARS. 215

would pay what was borrowed of the man of war; so that in a short time after Major Church, with his forces, returned home to Boston, and had their wages for their good service done.

Only one thing, by the way, I will just mention; that is, about the *six pounds* [which] Major Church borrowed as beforementioned, and put into the hands of Mr. Fobes, who distributed the said money, all but *thirty shillings*, to the Indian soldiers, as directed, which was deducted out of their wages, and the country had credit for the same. And the said Fobes kept the *thirty shillings* to himself, which was deducted out of his wages. Whereupon Major Walley and [the] said Fobes had some words. In short Major Church was obliged to expend about *six pounds* of his own money in marching down the forces both English and Indians, to Boston, having no drink allowed them upon the road, &c So, that instead of Major Church's having the allowances aforementioned by Major Walley, he was out of pocket about *twelve pounds* over and above what he had; all which had not been, had not his excellency been gone out of the country.

THE FOURTH EXPEDITION EAST.

In 1696, Major Church being at Boston, and belonging to the house of representatives, several gentlemen requesting him to go east again, and the general court having made acts of encouragement, &c. He told them, [that] if they would provide whale boats, and other necessaries convenient, he would. Being also requested by the said general court, he proceeded to raise volunteers; and made it his whole business, riding both east and west in our province and Connecticut, at great charge and expenses. And in about a month's time, raised a sufficient number out of those parts, and marched them down to Boston. Where he had the promise that every thing should be ready in three weeks, or a month's time; but was obliged to stay considerably longer. Being now at Boston, he received his commission and instructions, which are as followeth.

"WILLIAM STOUGHTON,* *Esquire, Lieutenant Governour, and Commander in Chief, in and over his Majesty's province of Massachusetts bay, in Newengland,*

To Major BENJAMIN CHURCH, Greeting.

Whereas there are several companies raised, consisting of Englishmen and Indians, for his Majesty's service, to go forth upon the encouragement given by the great and general court, or assembly of this his Majesty's province, convened at Boston, the 27th day of May, 1696, to prosecute the French and Indian enemy, &c. And you having offered yourself to take the command and conduct of the said several companies. By virtue, therefore, of the power and authority in and by his Majesty's royal commission to me granted, reposing special trust and confidence in your loyalty, prudence, courage

---

* Mr. Stoughton was the son of Israel Stoughton of Dorchester, at which place he was born in 1632. He graduated at Harvard college, 1650, and engaging in the study of divinity, is said to have made an excellent preacher, but was never settled. Is also said to have possessed good talents and great learning. It may be allowed that he had a *great* deal of some kind of learning, and yet, destitute of much solid understanding or science. This no one will doubt, when informed that he was one of the principal judges, who sat and condemned so many unfortunate persons for the imaginary crime of *witchcraft*, in the *witch age* of Salem; and to add to his misfortunes, Dr. Eliot says, that "he was more obstinate in his errour than others on the bench." When Phips left the government, he was the commander in chief. In 1700 he was again in the office. He died in 1702. At his expense was the college called Stoughton hall built N. E. Biog. 444, 5.

and good conduct. I do by these presents constitute and appoint you to be Major of the said several companies, both Englishmen and Indians, raised for his Majesty's service upon the encouragement aforesaid. You are therefore carefully and diligently to perform the duty of your place, by leading, ordering, and exercising the said several companies in arms, both inferiour officers and soldiers, keeping them in good order and discipline, commanding them to obey you as their Major. And yourself diligently to intend his Majesty's service for the prosecuting, pursuing, taking, killing or destroying the said enemy by sea or land; and to observe all such orders and instructions as you shall from time to time receive from myself, or commander in chief for the time being, according to the rules and discipline of war, pursuant to the trust reposed in you. Given under my hand and seal at arms, at Boston, the third day of August, 1696, in the eighth year of the reign of our sovereign Lord WILLIAM the III, by the grace of God, of England, Scotland, France, and Ireland, King, defender of the faith, &c.

    WILLIAM STOUGHTON
 By command of the Lieut. Governour, &c.
    Isaac Addington, *Secr.*"

"*Province of Massachusetts bay. By the Right Honourable the Lieutenant Governour and Commander in Chief.*

Instructions for Major BENJAMIN CHURCH, *Commander of the forces raised for his Majesty's service, against the French and Indian enemy and rebels.*

 Pursuant to the commission given you, you are to embark the forces now furnished and equipped for his Majesty's service on the present expedition to the eastern parts of this province, and with them, and such others as shall offer themselves to go forth on the said service, to sail unto Piscataqua, to join those lately despatched thither for the same expedition, to await your coming. And with all care and diligence to improve the vessels, boats and men under your command in search for, prosecution and pursuit of, the said enemy at such places where you may be informed of their abode or resort, or where you may probably expect to find, or meet with them, and take all advantages against them which providence shall favour you with.

You are not to list or accept any soldiers that are already in his Majesty's pay, and posted at any town or garrison within this province, without special order from myself.

You are to require and give strict orders that the duties of religion be attended on board the several vessels, and in the several companies under your command, by daily prayers unto God, and reading his holy word, and observance of the Lord's day to the utmost you can.

You are to see that your soldiers have their due allowance of provisions, and other necessaries, and that the sick or wounded be accommodated in the best manner your circumstances will admit. And that good order and command may be kept up and maintained in the several companies, and all disorders, drunkenness, profane cursing, swearing, disobedience of officers, mutinies, omissions or neglect of duty, be duly punished according to the laws martial. And you are to require the Captain or chief officer of each company, with the clerk of the same, to keep an exact journal of all their proceedings from time to time.

In case any of the Indian enemy and rebels offer to submit themselves, you are to receive them, only at discretion; but if you think fit to improve any of them, or any others which you may happen to take prisoners, you may encourage them to be faithful by the promise of their lives, which shall be granted upon approbation of their fidelity.

You are carefully to look after the Indians which you have out of the prison, so that they may not have opportunity to escape, but otherwise improve them to what advantage you can, and return them back again to this place.

You are to advise, as you can have occasion, with Captain John Gorham, who accompanies you in this expedition, and is to take your command in case of your death. A copy of these instructions you are to leave with him, and to give me an account from time to time of your proceedings.

WILLIAM STOUGHTON.

Boston, August 12*th,* 1696."

In the time [that] Major Church lay at Boston, the news came of Pemequid fort's being taken.* It came

---

* Thus the fort which had cost the country an immense sum of money, was entirely demolished. This was fort William Henry, built in the last expedition. Two men of war were sent from Boston, early this year, (1696) to cruise off the river St. Johns, for an expected French store ship; but unhappily, the French at Quebeck had despatched two men of war for the capture of the above said fort. These fell in with the two English vessels, and being more than a match for them, captured one, called the Newport, the other, taking advantage of a fog, got back to Boston. The French now proceeded to attack the fort, being strengthened by the addition of the Newport, and Baron Castine with 200 Indians. The French were commanded by one Iberville, " a brave and experienced officer," and the English fort by one Chubb, without bravery or experience. On the 14 July, Iberville arrived before the fort, and immediately sent in a summons for its surrender. Chubb returned a mere gasconade for an answer. Says he, " If the sea were covered with French vessels, and the land with Indians, yet I would not give up the fort." Some firing then commenced with the small arms, and thus closed the first day. The night following Iberville landed some cannon and mortars, and by the next day at 3 of the clock, had so raised his works as to throw 5 bombs into the fort, to the great terror of Chubb and his men. And to add to their terror, Castine found means to convey a letter into

by a shallop that brought some prisoners to Boston
who gave an account, also, that there was a French
ship at Mountdesart* that had taken a ship of ours.
So the discourse was, that they would send the man
of war,† with other forces to take the said French
ship, and retake ours. But in the mean time Major
Church and his forces being ready, embarked, and on
the fifteenth day of August, set sail for Piscataqua,
where more men were to join them. (But before
they left Boston, Major Church discoursed with the
Captain of the man of war, who promised him, [that]
if he went to Mountdesart, in pursuit of the French
ship, that he would call for him and his forces at Piscataqua, expecting that the French and Indians
might not be far from the said French ship, so that
he might have an opportunity to fight them while he
was engaged with the French ship.)

Soon after the forces arrived at Piscataqua, the
Major sent his Indian soldiers to Colonel Gidney,‡ at

---

the fort, importing, that "if they held out the Indians would
not be restrained, for he had seen such orders from the King
to Iberville." Upon this Chubb surrendered and the French
demolished the fort. Hutchinson, II, 88 to 90. Mather,
Magnalia, II, 549, says, that the fort contained "95 men
double armed which might have defended it against nine
times as many assailants." Chubb lived at Andover, where
in February following he was killed by a small party of
about 30 Indians, who fell upon the place. Ib. 554.

* Desert it should be. A very large island covering the
area of about 180 square miles, and nearly all the waters of
the bay of Fundy or Frenchman's bay. It was named Monts
Deserts by Champlain, in honour, perhaps, of De Monts
with whom he had formerly sailed. It was once called Mt.
Mansell by the English, which, Mr. Savage (in Winthrop,
I, 23) thinks was so called in honour of Sir Robert Mansell
named in the great Charter.

† There were two men of war *now* at Boston, which with
some other vessels were sent in pursuit of the enemy and
came in sight of them, but effected nothing. Hutchinson,
II, 91.

‡ Bartholomew Gidney, one of the judges of 1692, whose
name is sufficiently perpetuated in Calef's "More Wonders

York, to be assisting for the defence of those places,* who gave them a good commend for their ready and willing services done; in scouting and the like.

Lying at Piscataqua with the rest of our forces near a week, waiting for more forces who were to join them, to make up their complement.† In all which time heard never a word of the man of war. On the twentysecond of August, they all embarked [from]¹ Piscataqua. And when they came against York, the Major went ashore, sending Captain Gorham‡ with some forces in two brigantines and a sloop, to Winterharbour. Ordering him to send out scouts, to see if they could make any discovery of the enemy, and to wait there till he came to them.

Major Church coming to York, Colonel Gidney told him, [that] his opinion was, that the enemy was drawn off from those parts; for that the scouts could not discover any of them, nor their tracks. So having done his business there, went with what forces he had there, to Winterharbour, where he had the same account from Captain Gorham, [viz.,] that they had not discovered any of the enemy, nor any new tracks. So, concluding [that] they were gone from those parts towards Penobscot, the Major ordered all the vessels to come to sail, and make the best of their

¹ [for]

of the Invisible World." He was an associate with Hawthorn and Curwin, in executing the laws against witchcraft. Small time has been spent for more information of him, and as little has been found.

* The French were expected to make other attempts along the coast, which they threatened after their success at Pemmaquid.

† Their whole force, it appears from Hutchinson, II, 91, was 500 men.

‡ Captain John Gorham seems from this time through this and the other expeditions to have acted a conspicuous part. I have found no other accounts of him.

way to Monhegin,* which being not far from Penobscot, where the main body of our enemy's living was. Being in great hopes to come up with the army of French and Indians, before they had scattered and gone past Penobscot, or Mountdesart, which is the chief place of their departure from each other after such actions.

Having a fair wind, made the best of their way, and early next morning they got into Monhegin. And there lay all day fitting their boats, and other necessaries to embark in the night at Mussleneck† with their boats. Lying there all day to keep undiscovered from the enemy. At night the Major ordered the vessels all to come to sail, and carry the forces over the bay‡ near Penobscot. But having little wind, he ordered all the soldiers to embark on board the boats with eight days provision, and sent the vessels back to Monhegin, that they might not be discovered by the enemy; giving them orders, when and where they should come to him.

The forces being all ready in their boats, rowing very hard, got ashore at a point near Penobscot.§ just as the day broke. [They][1] hid their boats, and keeping a good look out by sea, and sent out scouts by land, but could not discover either canoes or Indians. What tracks and fire places they saw were judged to be seven or eight days before they came. As soon as night came, that they might go undiscovered, got into their boats, and, went by Mussleneck, and so amongst Penobscot islands, looking very sharp as they went, for fires on the shore, and for canoes but found neither.

[1] [and]

---

* An island on the east side of Kennebeck river, and about 10 miles from the main, celebrated as the place where Capt. John Smith landed in 1614; here he built some houses, the remains of which were to be seen when Judge Sullivan wrote his history. It is spelt Monheagan.

† A point in Monheagan island.

‡ The bay of Penobscot.　　§ Mouth of the river.

Getting up to Mathebestucks hills, [and] day coming on, landed and hid their boats; looking out for the enemy, as the day before, but to little purpose. Night coming on, to their oars again, working very hard; turned night into day, [which] made several of their new soldiers grumble. But telling them [that] they hoped to come up quickly with the enemy put new life into them. By daylight they got into the mouth of the river, where landing, found many rendezvous, and fireplaces, where the Indians had been; but at the same space of time as beforementioned. And no canoes passed up the river that day. Their pilot, Joseph York,* informed the Major, that fifty or sixty miles up that river, at the great falls, the enemy had a great rendezvous, and planted a great quantity of corn, when he was a prisoner with them, four years ago; and that he was very well acquainted there. This gave great encouragement to have had some considerable advantage of the enemy at that place.

So using their utmost endeavours to get up there undiscovered. And coming there found no enemy, nor corn planted; they having deserted the place. And ranging about the falls on both sides of the river, leaving men on the east side of the said river, and the boats just below the falls, with a good guard to secure them, and to take the enemy if they came down the river in their canoes. The west side being the place where the enemy lived and best to travel on, they resolved to range as privately as they could. A mile or two above the falls, [they] discovered a birch canoe coming down with two Indians in it. The Major sent word immediately back to those at the falls, to lie very close, and let them pass down the falls, and to take them alive, that he might have intelligence where the enemy were, (which would

---

* York probably belonged here, for it appears from Sullivan, 146, that persons of this name were among the early proprietors of the lands of Kennebeck.

have been a great advantage to them.) But a foolish soldier seeing them pass by him, shot at them, contrary to orders given, which prevented them [from] going into the ambuscade, that was laid for them. Whereupon several more of our men being near, shot at them. So that one of them could not stand when he got ashore, but crept away into the brush. The other stepped out of the canoe with his paddle in his hand, and ran about a rod and then threw down his paddle, and turned back and took up his gun, and so escaped. One of our Indians swam over the river, and fetched the canoe, wherein was a considerable quantity of blood on the seats that the Indians sat on, [and] the canoe had several holes shot in her. They stopped the holes, and then Captain Bracket* with an Indian soldier, went over the river, [and][1] tracked them by the blood about half a mile, [where they] found his gun, took it up and seeing the blood no further, concluded that he stopped [it,][2] and so got away.

In the mean time, another canoe with three men were coming down the river, [and being][3] fired at by some of our forces, ran ashore, and left two of their guns in the canoe, which were taken; and also a letter from a priest to Casteen, [giving][4] him an account of the French and Indians returning over the lake to Mountroyal,† and of their little service done upon the Maquas‡ Indians westward; only de-

[1] [who]   [2] [his blood]   [3] [were]   [4] [that gave]

---

* The same person mentioned at page 166.

† Montreal.

‡ This was the name given by the Dutch to the Fivenations of Indians. See N. Y. Hist. Soc. Col. II, 44. By the French they were called Iroquois, between whom their wars were almost perpetual. An account of what is hinted at in the text may be seen in Smith's Newyork, 147, 149, and N. Y. Hist. Soc. Col. II, 67, 68. The expedition was executed under count De Frontenac now (1696) Governour of Canada. He had assembled a great body of his friend Indians from different nations, which he joined with two battalions

FRENCH AND INDIAN WARS. 225

molishing one fort, and cutting down some corn, &c. He desiring to hear of the proceedings of Deborahuel, and the French man of war. And informed him that there were several canoes coming with workmen from Quebeck, to St. Johns.* Where since, we concluded, it was to build a fort at the river's mouth, when the great guns were taken, &c.

It being just night, the officers were called together to advise, and their pilot, York, informed them of a fort up that river, and that it was built on a little island in that river; and that there was no getting to it, but in canoes, or on the ice in the winter time. This with the certain knowledge that we were discovered by the enemy that escaped out of the upper canoe, concluded it not proper, at that time, to proceed any further up; and that there was no getting any further with our boats; and the enemy being alarmed, would certainly fly from them (and do as they did four years ago at their fort at Taconock. Having fought them in Kennebeck river, and pursued them about thirty miles to Taconock, they then set their fort on fire, and ran away by the light of it, ours not being able to come up with them at that place.)

---

of regulars. They left Montreal about the first of July, and with the greatest difficulty penetrated about 200 miles into the wilderness. Nothing was effected by this great army, but the burning of a few Indian huts, and torturing a few prisoners. One circumstance of the latter, as a striking example of magnanimity, on the one side, and more than savage barbarity on the other, shall be related. On the approach of the Count with his army to an Indian town, it was deserted by all its inhabitants, except an aged chief, of near 100 years. He was immediately put to torment. One stabbed him with a knife, at which he exclaimed, "You had better make me die by fire, that these French dogs may learn how to suffer like men," &c. He continued firm until he expired under the most excruciating torture that could be invented.

* At the mouth of the river St. Johns, in what is now N. Brunswick.

Major Church then encouraging his soldiers, told them, [that] he hoped they should meet with part of the enemy in Penobscot bay, or at Mountdesart, where the French ships were. So, notwithstanding they had been rowing several nights before, with much toil, besides were short of provisions, they cheerfully embarked on board their boats, and went down the river both with and against the tide. And next morning came to their vessels, where the Major had ordered them to meet him, who could give him no intelligence of any enemy. Where being come they refreshed themselves. Meeting then with another disappointment; for their pilot, York, not being acquainted any further, they began to lament the loss of one Robert Cawley, whom they chiefly depended on for all the service to be done now eastward. He having been taken away from them the night before they set sail from Boston (and was on board Mr. Thorp's sloop) and put on board the man of war unknown to Major Church, notwithstanding he had been at the trouble and charge of procuring him. Then the Major was obliged to one Bord,* procured by Mr. William Alden, who being acquainted in those parts, to leave his vessel, and go with him in the boats, which he readily complied with, and so went to Nasket† point, where being informed was a likely place to meet the enemy. Coming there, found several houses and small fields of corn, the fires having been out several days, and no new tracks. But upon Penobscot island they found several Indian houses, corn and turnips. Though the enemy still being all gone, as beforementioned.

Then they divided, and sent their boats some one way, and some another, thinking, that if any straggling Indians, or Casteen himself, should be there-

---

* The name of Bord or rather Boad as Sullivan has it, is found among the first inhabitants of Saco. Hist. Maine, 218.

† Or Nauseag, in the town of Woolwich on the east side of the Kennebeck.

about, they might find them, but it proved all in
vain. Himself and several boats went to Mountdesart, to see if the French ships were gone, and
whether any of the enemy might be there, but to no
purpose; the ships being gone and the enemy also.
They being now got several leagues to the westward
of their vessels, and seeing that the way was clear
for their vessels to pass; and all their extreme rowing, and travelling by land and water, night and day,
to be all in vain. (The enemy having left those
parts as they judged, about eight or ten days before.)
And then returning to their vessels, the commander
calling all his officers together, to consult and resolve what to do; concluding that the enemy, by
some means or other, had received some intelligence
of their being come out against them; and that they
were in no necessity to come down to the sea side
as yet, moose and beaver now being fat.

They then agreed to go so far east, and employ
themselves, that the enemy belonging to these parts,
might think [that] they were gone home. Having
some discourse about going over to St. Johns. But
the masters of the vessels said, [that] [they][1] had as
good carry them to old France, &c., which put off
that design. (They concluding that the French ships
were there.) Then the Major moved for going over
the bay towards Lahane,* and towards the gut of
Cancer,† where was another considerable fort of Indians, who often came to the assistance of our enemy, the barbarous Indians. Saying, that by the
time they should return again, the enemy belonging
to these parts would come down again, expecting
that we were gone home. But in short, could not
prevail with the masters of the open sloops to ven-

[1] [he]

---

* This name is spelt Layhone in a succeeding page.

† Properly, Canceau, and pronounced Canso. It is the
strait between Cape Breton island and Novascotia connect-
ing the Atlantic with the gulf of St. Lawrence.

ture across the bay.* [They]¹ said [that] it was very dangerous so late in the year, and as much as their lives were worth, &c.

Then they concluded and resolved to go to Senactaca,† wherein there was a ready compliance. (But the want of their pilot, Robert Cawley, was a great damage to them, who knew all those parts.) However, Mr. John Alden, master of the brigantine Endeavour, piloted them up the bay to Senactaca. And coming to *Grinstone*‡ point, being not far from Senactaca, then came to, with all the vessels, and early next morning came to sail, and about sunrise got into town. But it being so late before we landed, that the enemy, most of them, made their escape. And as it happened [we] landed where the French and Indians had some time before killed Lieutenant John Paine,§ and several of Captain Smithson's men, that were with said Paine. They seeing our forces coming, took the opportunity, fired several guns, and so ran all into the woods, [and] carried all or most part of their goods with them. One Jarman Bridgway‖ came running towards our forces, with a

¹ [who]

---

* Bay of Fundy.

† This, I presume, is what is called Signecto in Gov. Dudley's instructions to Col. Church for the fifth expedition. It is since written Chignecto, and is the northern arm of the bay between Novascotia and Newbrunswick. Here the tide rises and falls 60 feet.

‡ I suppose the reader would get over this word better, were it spelt *better*. But the alteration would be immaterial, as it is the name of a place.

§ The same, I presume, who, in 1676–7, assisted Major Waldron in settling a treaty with the eastern Indians. I learn no more of him than is found in Mr. Hubbard's Nar 349, &c. Of Smithson I learn nothing.

‖ Charlevoix, who was better acquainted with French names than our author, calls him *Bourgeois*. He was one of the principal inhabitants of the place. See Hist. Mas. II. 92, 93. Hutchinson, ib., says, that "Church calls him Bridgman." Perhaps he did in his despatches, but it is not so spelt in my copy.

gun in one hand, and his cartridge box in the other, [and] calling to our forces to stop, that he might speak with them. But Major Church thinking [that this]¹ was [done] that they might have some advantage, ordered them to run on. When the said Bridgway saw [that] they would not stop, turned and ran. But the Major called unto him, and bid him stop, or he should be shot down. Some of our forces being near to the said Bridgway, said, [that] it was the General that called to him. He hearing that, stopped and turned about, laying down his gun, stood, till the Major came up to him. His desire was, that the commander would make haste with him to his house, lest the savages* should kill his father and mother, who were upward of four score years of age, and could not go. The Major asked the said Bridgway whether there were any Indians amongst them, and where they lived? He shaked his head, and said, he durst not tell, for if he did, they would take an opportunity, and kill him and his. So all that could be got out of him was, that they were run into the woods with the rest.

Then orders were given to pursue the enemy, and to kill what Indians they could find, and take the French alive, and give them quarter if they asked it.

Our forces soon took three Frenchmen, who, upon examination, said, that the Indians were all run into the woods. The French firing several guns, and ours at them. But they being better acquainted with the woods than ours, got away. The Major took the abovesaid Jarman Bridgway for a pilot, and with some of his forces went over a river, to several of their houses, but the people were gone, and [had] carried their goods with them. In ranging the woods [they] found several Indian houses,

¹ [it]

---

* Church's savages.

their fires being just out, but no Indians. Spending that day in ranging to and fro, found considerable of their goods, and but few people. At night the Major wrote a letter, and sent out two French prisoners, wherein was signified, that if they would come in, they should have good quarters. The next day several came in, which did belong to that part of the town where our forces first landed, [and]¹ had encouragements given them by our commander, [viz.,] that if they would assist him in taking those Indians, which belonged to those parts, they should have their goods returned to them again, and their estates should not be demnified; [but]² they refused.* Then the Major and his forces pursued their design.†

¹ [who]   ² [which]

---

* What Hutchinson, II, 92, observes concerning this very severe requisition, is too just to be unnoticed. "This was a hard condition, and in effect, obliging them to quit their country; for otherwise, as soon as the English had left them without sufficient protection, the incensed Indians would have fell upon them without mercy."

† "Charlevoix says, (in Hist. Mas. II, 92, 93,) that Bourgeois produced a writing, by which Sir William Phips had given assurances of protection to the inhabitants of Chignecto, whilst they remained faithful subjects of King William; and that Church gave orders that nothing in their houses, &c., should be touched; but whilst he was entertained by Bourgeois, together with the principal officers, the rest of the army dispersed themselves among the other houses and behaved as if they had been in a conquered country." And, "that many of the inhabitants, not trusting to the promises of the General [Church] refused to come in, and that it was very well they did; for soon after he broke through all bounds, and left only the church and a few houses and barns standing; and having discovered, posted up in the church, an order of Frontenac, the Governour of Canada, for the regulation of trade, he threatened to treat them as rebels, set fire to the church, and the houses which he had spared and which were now all reduced to ashes; and having done this, he presented a writing which he told them was an acknowledgement of their having renewed their subjection to King William, and would be a security to them in case any English should again land among them." Before regarding this

And went further ranging their country, found several more houses, but the people [had] fled, and carried what they had away. But in a creek [they] found a prize bark, that was brought in there by a French privateer. In ranging the woods, took some prisoners, who upon examination gave our commander an account, that there were some Indians upon a neck of land, towards Menis.*

So a party of men was sent into those woods. In their ranging about the said neck, found some plunder, and a considerable quantity of whortleberries, both green and dry, which were gathered by the Indians. [They]¹ had like to have taken two Indians; [but]² by the help of a birch canoe [they] got over the river, and made their escape. Also they found two barrels of powder, and near half a bushel of bullets. The French denying [them]³ to be theirs, [and] said [that] they were the savages; but sure it might be a supply for our enemies. Also, they took from Jarman Bridgway several barrels of powder, with bullets, shot, spears and knives, and other supplies to relieve our enemies. He owned that he had been trading with those Indians along Cape Sable† shore, with Peter Assnow; and, that there he met with the French ships, and went along with them to St. Johns, and helped them to unload the said ships, and carried up the river provisions, ammunition and other goods to Vilboon's fort.‡

The Major having ranged all places that were thought proper, returned back to the place where

¹ [and]   ² [who]   ³ [it]

---

account as perfectly correct, it should be remembered that the Jesuit Charlevoix ever portrays the affairs of the French in amiable colours.

* On a basin of the east arm of the bay between Novascotia and Newbrunswick. Morse spells the word two ways viz., Mines and Minas.

† The southwest point of Novascotia.

‡ This fort was upon the river St. Johns.

they first landed. And finding several prisoners come in, who were troubled to see their cattle, sheep, hogs and dogs lying dead about their houses, chopped and hacked with hatchets, (which was done without order from the Major.) However, he told them, [that] it was nothing to what our poor English, in our frontier towns, were forced to look upon. For men, women and children were chopped and hacked so, and left half dead, with all their scalps taken off; and that they and their Indians served ours so; and our savages would be glad to serve them so too, if he would permit them, which caused them to be mighty submissive. And [they] begged the Major that he would not let the savages serve them so.

Our Indians being somewhat sensible of the discourse, desired to have some of them to roast, and so to make a dance. And dancing in a hideous manner, to terrify them, said, that they could eat any sort of flesh, and that some of theirs would make their hearts strong. [And] stepping up to some of the prisoners, said that they must have their scalps, which much terrified the poor prisoners, who begged for their lives. The Major told them [that] he did not design the savages should hurt them; but it was to let them see a little what the poor English felt, saying, [that] it was not their scalps [that] he wanted, but the savages; for he should get nothing by them; and told them, that their fathers, the friars and Governours encouraged their savages, and gave them money to scalp our English, notwithstanding they were with them, which several of our English, there present, did testify to their faces, that their fathers and mothers were served so in their sight.

But the Major bid them tell their fathers, (the friars and Governours,) that if they still persisted, and let their wretched savages kill and destroy the poor English at that rate, he would come with some hundreds of savages, and let them loose amongst them, who would kill, scalp, and carry away every French person in all those parts; for they were the root from whence all the branches came, that hurt us. For the Indians could not do us any harm, if they [the French] did not relieve and supply them. The French being sensible of the Major's kindness to them, kissed his hand, and were very thankful to him for his favour to them in saving their lives. [They] owned that their priests* were at the taking of Pemequid fort, and were now gone to Layhone, with some of the Indians, to meet the French ships, but for what, they would not tell.

The commander, with his forces, having done all they could in those parts, concluded to go to St. Johns river, to do further service for their King and country; [so] embarked all on board their transports.† And having a fair wind, soon got to Monogenest,‡ which lies a little distance from the mouth of St. Johns river.

Next morning early, the Major with his forces, landed to see what discovery they could make; [so they] travelled across the woods to the old fort or falls at the mouth of St. Johns river, keeping themselves undiscovered from the enemy. Finding that there were several men at work, and having informed themselves as much as they could, (the enemy being on the other side of the river, could not come at them) returned back. But night coming on, and dark wet weather, with bad travelling, were obliged to stop in the woods till towards next day morning, and then went on board.

Soon after the Major ordered all the vessels to come to sail, and go into the mouth of the river. [That] being done, it was not long before the Major and his forces landed on the east side of the river, the French firing briskly at them, but did them no

---

* Castine was mentioned as being there. See note, page 219.
† On the 20 September.
‡ On the north side of the river.

harm. And running fiercely upon the enemy, they soon fled into the woods. The Major ordered a brisk party to run across a neck to cut them off from their canoes, which the day before they had made a discovery of. So the commander, with the rest, ran directly towards the new fort [that] they were building, not knowing but [that] they had some ordnance mounted. The enemy running directly to their canoes, were met by our forces, who fired at them and killed one, and wounded Corporal Canton, who was taken. The rest threw down what they had, and ran into the woods. The said prisoner, Canton, being brought to the Major, told him, [that] if he would let his surgeon dress his wound and cure him, he would be serviceable to him as long as he lived. So being dressed, he was examined. [He][1] gave the Major an account of the twelve great guns which were hid in the beach, below high water mark. (The carriages, shot, and wheelbarrows, some flour and pork, all hid in the woods.)

The next morning the officers being all ordered to meet together, to consult about going to Vilboon's fort, and none amongst them being acquainted but the Aldens, who said, [that] the water in the river was very low, so that they could not get up to the fort; and the prisoner, Canton, told the Commander, that what the Aldens said was true. So not being willing to make a Canada expedition, concluded [that] it was not practicable to proceed.* Then ordered some of the forces to get the great guns on board the open sloops, and the rest to range the woods for the enemy, who took one prisoner and brought [him] in. [They][2] in their ranging, found there a shallop, hauled in a creek. And a day or two after there came in a young soldier to our forces,

[1] [Who]   [2] [who]

---

* The unsuccessful attempt on Quebeck by Sir William Phips, which was rendered abortive by the lateness of the season.

who upon examination, gave an account of two more which he left in the woods at some distance. So immediately the Major with some of his forces went in pursuit of them, taking the said prisoner with them, who conveyed them to the place where he left them, but they were gone. [They] then asked the prisoner, whether there were any Indians in those parts? [He] said No, [that] it was as hard for Vilboon, their Governour, to get an Indian down to the water side, as it was for him to carry one of those great guns on his back to his fort. For they having had intelligence by a prisoner out of Boston jail, that gave them an account of Major Church and his forces coming out against them.

Now, having with a great deal of pains and trouble, got all the guns, shot, and other stores aboard, intended [to proceed] on our design, which we came out first for. But the wind not serving, the commander sent out his scouts into the woods to seek for the enemy. And four of our Indians came upon three Frenchmen undiscovered, who concluded, that if the French should discover them, [they] would fire at them, and might kill one or more of them; which, to prevent, fired at the French, killed one, and took the other two prisoners. And it happened that he who was killed, was Shanelere, the chief man there, &c.

The same day they mended their whale boats, and the shallop which they took; fitting her to row with eight oars, that she might be helpful to their prosecuting their intended design against the enemy, in their returning homeward. Then the commander ordering all the officers to come together, informed them of his intentions; and ordered that no vessels should depart from the fleet, but to attend the motions of their Commodore, as formerly; except they were parted by storms, or thick fogs. And if so, it should happen that any did part, when they came to

Passamequady,* should stop there awhile; for there they intended to stop and do business, with the help of their boats against the enemy. And if they missed that, to stop at Machias,† which was the next place [that] he intended to stop at. Having an account by the prisoners taken that Mr. Lateril‡ was there, a trading with the Indians in the river. [And] encouraging them, said, [that] he did not doubt but to have a good booty there. And if they should pass those two places, be sure not to go past Naskege§ point; but to stop there till he came, and not to depart thence in a fortnight without his orders; having great service to do in and about Penobscot, &c.

Then Major Church discoursed with Captain Bracket, Captain Hunewell, and Captain Larking, (with their Lieutenants) commanders of the forces, belonging to the eastward parts, who were to discourse their soldiers about their proceedings, when they came to Penobscot. And the Major himself was to discourse his Indian soldiers, and their Captains, who with all the rest readily complied. The projection being such, that when they came to Penobscot, the commander designed to take what pro-

---

* Better written Passammaquaddy. Coasters call it Quoddy. It is a deep bay, which begins the separation of the British dominions from Maine.

† The bay of Machias is separated from Passammaquoddy by Pleasant point on the west. A river flows into this bay of the same name, on which is the town of Machias.

‡ Whoever this person might be, we hear no more of him, only that he was a Frenchman, and had a family at Mountdesert; that he was taken in the last expedition; and that his name was *old* Lateril or Lotriell according to the early writers who mention him, which of course, was all they knew about him.

§ What Sullivan calls Nauseag, I expect, almost up to the Kennebeck, but on the east side, and now within the town of Woolwich. See page 226, of this history, where it is spelt Nasket.

visions could be spared out of all the sloops, and put [it] on board the two brigantines, and to send all the sloops home with some of the officers and men that wanted to be at home. And then with those forces aforementioned, *to wit*, the eastward men, and all the Indians; and to take what provisions and ammunition was needful, and to march with himself up into the Penobscot country, in search of the enemy, and if posssible to take that fort in Penobscot river. Captain Bracket informing the Major, that when the water was low, they could wade over, which was at that time, the lowest that had been known in a long time.

And being there, to range through that country down to Pemequid, where he intended [that] the two brigantines should meet them; and from thence taking more provisions, viz., bread, salt, and ammunition suitable (to send those two vessels home also) to travel through the country to Nerigiwack,* and from thence to Amerascogen fort, and so down where the enemy used to plant. Not doubting but that in all this travel to meet with many of the enemy before they should get to Piscataqua. All which intentions were very acceptable to the forces that were to undertake it. [And][1] rejoicing, said, they had rather go home by land than by water, provided their commander went with them. [He,][2] to try their fidelity, said [that] he was grown ancient, and might fail them. [But] they all said they would not leave him, and when he could not travel any further, they would carry him.

Having done what service they could, at and about the mouth of St. Johns river, resolved on their

[1] [who]   [2] [who]

---

* Norridgewock. This name has been subject to almost as many methods of spelling, as its neighbour, Androscoggin. It was an ancient celebrated Indian town on the Kennebeck river, about 84 miles from its mouth by the course of the river Sullivan, 31, 32.

intended design. And the next morning, having but little wind, came all to sail. The wind coming against them they put into Mushquash cove. And the next day the wind being still against them, the Major with part of his forces landed, and employed themselves in ranging the country for the enemy, but to no purpose. [But][1] in the night the wind came pretty fair, and at twelve o'clock they came to sail. [They][2] had not been out long before they spied three sail of vessels; expecting them to be French, fitted to defend themselves. So coming near, hailed them, [and][3] found them to be a man of war, the province galley, and old Mr. Alden* in a sloop, with more forces, Colonel Hathorne† commander.

Major Church went aboard the Commodore, where Colonel Hathorne was, who gave him an account of his commission, and orders, and read them to him. Then his honour told Major Church, that there was a particular order on board Captain Southack for him, which is as followeth.

[*To Major Benjamin Church.*]
"*Boston, September 9th,* 1696.

Sir,

His Majesty's ship Orford, having lately surprised a French shallop, with twentythree of the soldiers

[1] [and]   [2] [and]   [3] [Who]

---

* The same often mentioned in the preceding pages. See note 3, on page 196. He was in 1692 imprisoned for witchcraft, and previously examined by Hawthorn, under whom he appears in this expedition. See Hutchinson, II, 50, and 94.

† Col. John Hathorne or Hawthorn. This gentleman, however unfit he might be to succeed Church, it is certain that he may now be better employed than when committing *witches* at Salem. I learn little of him, excepting what may be seen in Hutchinson, and Calef. Perhaps he was a son of William Hawthorn, the first speaker of the court of Massachusetts, upon record. Hist. Mas. I, 150. He was quite active in these wars, also in the former. Nothing very brilliant appears to have been performed under his command.

belonging to the fort upon Johns river, in Novascotia, together with Villeau, their Captain, providence seems to encourage the forming of an expedition to attack that fort, and to disrest and remove the enemy from that post, which is the chief source from whence the most of our disasters do issue, and also to favour with an opportunity for gaining out of their hands the ordnance, artillery, and other warlike stores, and provisions, lately supplied to them from France, for erecting a new fort near the river's mouth, whereby they will be greatly strengthened, and the reducing of them rendered more difficult. I have therefore ordered a detachment of two new companies, consisting of about an hundred men to join the forces now with you for that expedition, and have commissioned Lieutenant Colonel John Hathorne, one of the members of his Majesty's council, who is acquainted with that river, and in whose courage and conduct I repose special trust to take the chief command of the whole, during that service, being well assured that your good affections and zeal for his Majesty's service will induce your ready compliance and assistance therein, which, I hope, will take up no long time, and be of great benefit and advantage to these his Majesty's territories, if it please God to succeed the same. Besides, it is very probable to be the fairest opportunity, that can be offered unto yourself and men, of doing execution upon the Indian enemy and rebels, who may reasonably be expected to be drawn to the defence of that fort. I have also ordered his Majesty's ship Arundel, and the province Galley to attend this service.

Colonel Hathorne will communicate unto you the contents of his commission and instructions received from myself for this expedition, which I expect and order that yourself, officers and soldiers, now under you, yield obedience unto. He is to advise with yourself and others in all weighty attempts. Praying for a blessing from Heaven upon the said enterprise, and that all engaged in the same may be under the special protection of the Almighty. I am your loving friend,

WILLIAM STOUGHTON."

The Major having read his last orders, and considering his commission, found that he was obliged to attend all orders,* &c., was much concerned that he and his were prevented in their intended projection, if carried back to St. Johns. Then discoursing with Colonel Hathorne, gave him an account of what they had done at St. Johns, viz., that as to the demolishing the new fort, they had done it; and [had] got all their great guns and stores aboard their vessels. And, that if it had not been that the waters were so low, would have taken the fort up the river also, before he came away. Told him also, that one of the prisoners which he had taken at St. Johns, upon examination, concerning the Indians in those parts, told him, [that] it was as hard for Vilboon their Governour, to get one of their Indians down to the water side, as to carry one of those great guns upon his back. And that they had an account of him [Church,] and his forces' coming to those parts by a prisoner out of Boston jail. Also, told his honour, that if they went back it would wholly disappoint them of their doing any further service, which was [what]¹ they came for to Penobscot, and places adjacent. But all was to no purpose. His honour tell-

¹ [that]

---

* Church could not but be offended at such boyish conduct, which will more fully appear in the ensuing narration. Important service, perhaps, might have been done in the execution of the plan that Church and his forces were then about to enter upon. They would doubtless have relieved the eastern people from their garrisons in which they had most of the year been shut up. The savages had hovered around the settlements from Pascataqua to their extent eastward, and had between the 7 May, and 13 October, killed and taken about 34 of the inhabitants; 24 being of the former number. See Magnalia, II, 549, 50.

ing the Major that he must attend his orders then received.*

And to encourage the officers and soldiers, told them, [that] they should be wholly at the Major's ordering and command in the whole action. And to be short did go back, and the event may be seen in Colonel Hathorne's journal of the said action.†

Only I must observe one thing by the way, which was, that when they drew off to come down the river again, Colonel Hathorne came off and left the Major behind to see that all the forces were drawn off. And coming down the river, in or near the rear, in the night, heard a person halloo. Not knowing at

---

* The superceding of Church, says Hutchinson, II, 94, "was an impolitic measure, unless any misconduct in Church made it necessary that he should be superceded." But nothing of that kind is made appear, and can be accounted for, only, by supposing that Stoughton had not fully recovered from the debility he had received in the late *Witch Crusade.*

† The journal of Hathorne, referred to, is undoubtedly lost, which we have to regret. Perhaps Hutchinson had the use of it, as the account which he gives of the expedition is somewhat particular. He mentions, II, 94, 5, that Villebon had timely notice of their object, and the reinforcement; and accordingly had made the best arrangements he could to receive them. They effected a landing on the 7 October, not however without considerable opposition. The same day they raised a battery, and planted two fieldpieces upon it. With these and their small arms they commenced an attack upon the fort, which was answered. The following night being very cold, the English made fires to keep them from perishing. But this being a sure mark for the enemy's cannon, were obliged to put them out, and suffer the inclemency of the weather. Church's men suffering more extremely, being almost bare of clothing from their long service. Discouragement now seized them, and they drew off the next night. Mather makes no reflections on the planning and executing of this expedition. "The difficulty of the cold season so discouraged our men, that after the making of some few shot the enterprise found itself under too much *congelation* to proceed any further." So he says, Magnalia, II, 550. No account is given that any were killed.

L

first, but it might be a snare to draw them into; but upon consideration, sent to see who or what he was, and found him to be a Negro man belonging to Marblehead, that had been taken and kept a prisoner amongst them for some time. The Major asked him, whether he could give any account of the Indians in those parts? He said Yes, they were or had been all drawn off from the sea coast, up into the woods near an hundred miles. [They] having had an account by a prisoner out of Boston jail, that Major Church and his forces were coming out against them in four brigantines, and four sloops, with twentyfour *pettiaugers*, (meaning whale boats) which put them into [such] a fright, that notwithstanding they were so far up in the woods, were afraid to make fires by day, lest he and his forces should discover the smokes, and in the night lest they should see the light.

One thing more I would just give a hint of, that is, how the French in the eastward parts were much surprised at the motion of the whale boats. [They] said, [that] there was no abiding for them in that country. And I have been informed since, that soon after this expedition, they drew off from St. Johns fort and river.

But to return. Then going all down the river, embarked and went homeward. Only by the way, *candid reader*, I would let you know of two things that proved very prejudicial to Major Church and his forces. The first was, that the government should miss it so much as to send any prisoner away from Boston before the expedition was over. Secondly, that they should send Colonel Hathorne to take them from the service and business they went to do; who, by submission, doubtless thought [that] they did for the best though it proved to the contrary.

So [I] shall wind up with a just hint of what happened at their coming home to Boston. After all

FRENCH AND INDIAN WARS. 243

their hard service both night and day, the government took away all the great guns and warlike stores and gave them not a penny for them (except it was some powder, and *that* they gave what they pleased for.) And besides the assembly passed a vote that they should have but half pay. But his honour the Lieutenant Governour being much disturbed at their so doing, went into the town house, where the representatives were sitting, and told them, except they *did* reassume that vote, which was to cut Major Church and his forces off their half pay, they should sit there till the next spring. Whereupon it was reassumed. So that they had just their bare wages. But as yet, never had any allowance for the great guns and stores; neither has Major Church had any allowance for all his travel and great expenses in raising the said forces, volunteers.

THE FIFTH AND LAST EXPEDITION EAST.

In the year 1703-4, Major Church had an account of the miserable devastations made on Deerfield,* a town in the westward parts of this province,† and the horrible barbarities, and cruelties exercised on those poor innocent people by the French and Indians; especially of their cruelties towards that worthy gentlewoman Mrs. Williams, and several others, whom they marched in that extreme season; forcing them to carry great loads. And when any of them by their hard usage could not bear with it, [they] were knocked on the head, and so killed in cool blood. All which, with some other horrible instances done by those barbarous savages, which Major Church himself was an eye witness to in his former travel in the eastward parts, did much astonish him.

---

* A more particular account of the "Destruction of Deerfield" will be given in the IX Appendix to this history.
† On Connecticut river, about 90 miles from Boston.

To see a woman that those barbarous savages had taken and killed, exposed in a most brutish manner (as can be expressed) with a young child seized fast with strings to her breast. [The][1] infant had no apparent wound, which doubtless was left alive to suck its dead mother's breast, and so miserably to perish and die. Also to see other poor children hanging upon fences, dead, of either sex, in their own poor rags, not worth stripping them of, in scorn and derision.

Another instance was, of a straggling soldier, who was found at Casco, exposed in a shameful and barbarous manner. His body being staked up, his head cut off, and a hog's head set in the room; his body ripped up, and his heart and inwards taken out, and private members cut off, and hung with belts of their own, the inwards at one side of his body, and his privates at the other, in scorn and derision of the English soldiers, &c.

These and such like barbarities caused Major Church to express himself to this purpose. That if he were commander in chief of these provinces, he would soon put an end to those barbarities, done by the barbarous enemy, by making it his whole business to fight and destroy those savages as they did our poor neighbours, which doubtless might have been done if rightly managed, and that in a short time, &c. So that these with the late inhumanities done upon the inhabitants of Deerfield, made such an impression on his heart, as cannot well be expressed. So that his blood boiled within him, making such impulses on his mind, that he forgot all former treatments, which were enough to hinder any man, especially the said Major Church, from doing any further service.

Notwithstanding all which, having a mind to take some satisfaction on the enemy, his heart being full, took his horse and went from his own habitation,

[1] [which]

near seventy miles, to wait upon his excellency, and offered his service to the Queen,* his excellency and the country; which his excellency readily accepted of, and desired Major Church to draw a scheme for the ensuing action, or actions. So taking leave went home, and drew it, which is as followeth.

" Tiverton, February 5, 1703--4.
May it please your Excellency—

According to your request, when I was last with yourself, and in obedience thereunto, I present you with these following lines, that concern the preparation for next spring's expedition, to attack the enemy. According to my former direction; for it is good to have a full stroke at them first, before they have opportunity to run for it. For the first of our action will be our opportunity to destroy them, and to prevent their running away, in waylaying every passage, and make them know we are in good earnest. And so we being in a diligent use of means, we may hope for a blessing from the Almighty, and that he will be pleased to put a dread in their hearts, that they may fall before us and perish. For my advice is,

First. That ten or twelve hundred good able soldiers, well equipped, be in a readiness fit for action, by the first of April at farthest; for then will be the time to be upon action.

Secondly. That five and forty or fifty, good whaleboats be had ready, well fitted with five good oars and twelve or fifteen good paddles to every boat.

---

* Anne, who came to the throne of England in 1702. She reigned until her death in 1714, and then the line of Georges commenced. This war which began in 1703 is generally called Queen Anne's war. Dr. Douglass calls it " Dudley's Indian War." But this must be regarded as one of his loose denominations, for the war had already originated when Gov. Dudley entered upon his office.

And upon the wale of each boat, five pieces of strong leather be fastened on each side to slip five small ash bars through; that so, whenever they land, the men may step overboard, and slip in said bars across, and take up said boat that she may not be hurt against the rocks. And that two suitable brass kettles be provided to belong to each boat to dress the men's victuals in to make their lives comfortable.

Thirdly. That four or five hundred pairs of good Indian shoes be made ready, fit for the service for the English and Indians, that must improve the whale boats and birch canoes; for they will be very proper and safe for that service. And let there be a good store of cow hides well tanned, for a supply of such shoes, and hemp to make thread, and wax to mend and make more such shoes when wanted, and a good store of awls.

Fourthly. That there be an hundred large hatchets, or light axes, made pretty broad, and steeled with the best steel that can be got, and made by workmen, that [they] may cut very well, and hold, that the hemlock knots may not break or turn them, to widen the landing place up the falls. For it may happen that we may get up with some of our whaleboats to their falls or headquarters.

Fifthly. That there be a suitable quantity of small bags, or wallets provided, that every man that wants may have one to put up his bullets in, of such a size as will fit his gun, (and not be served as at Casco.*) That every man's bag be so marked that he may not change it. For if so, it will make a great confusion in action. That every man's store of ball be weighed to him, that so he may be accountable and may not squander it away and also his store of powder, that so he may try his powder and gun before action. And that every particular company may have a bar-

---

* There most of their shot was so large that it was useless, only as it was hammered, and was not discovered until an engagement took place with the enemy. See page 166.

rel of powder to themselves and so marked that it may by no means be changed. That men may know beforehand, and may not be cheated out of their lives, by having bad powder, or not knowing how to use it. And this will prove a great advantage to the action.

Sixthly. That Colonel John Gorham, if he may be prevailed with, may be concerned in the management of the whale boats, he having been formerly concerned in the eastern parts and experienced in that affair. And whalemen then will be very serviceable in this expedition, which having a promise made to them, that they shall be released in good season, to go home a whaling in the fall, your excellency will have men enough.

Seventhly. That there may be raised for this service three hundred Indians at least, and more if they may be had; for I know certainly, of my own knowledge that they exceed most of our English in hunting and skulking in the woods, being always used to it. And it must be practised if ever we intend to destroy those Indian enemies.

Eighthly. That the soldiers already out eastward in the service, men of known judgment, may take a survey of them and their arms, and see if their arms be good and they know how to use them in shooting right, at a mark, and that they be men of good reason and sense to know how to manage themselves in so difficult a piece of service as this Indian hunting is, for bad men are but a clog and hinderance to an army, being a trouble and vexation to good commanders, and so many mouths to devour the country's provision, and a hinderance to all good actions.

Ninthly. That special care be had in taking up the whaleboats that they be good, and fit for that service, so that the country be not cheated as formerly in having rotten boats and as much care that the owners may have good satisfaction for them.

Tenthly. That the tenders or transports, vessels

to be improved in this action, be good decked vessels, not too big because of going up several rivers having four or six small guns apiece for defence, and the fewer men will defend them, and there are enough such vessels to be had.

Eleventhly. To conclude all, if your excellency will be pleased to make yourself great and us a happy people, as to the destroying of our enemies and easing of our taxes, &c., be pleased to draw forth all those forces now in pay in all the eastward parts, both at Saco and Casco bay, for those two trading houses never did any good nor ever will, and are not worthy the name of Queen's forts; and the first building of them had no other effect but to lay us under tribute to that wretched pagan crew; and I hope will never be wanted for that they were first built; [—]¹ but sure it is, they are very serviceable to them; for they get many a good advantage of us to destroy our men and laugh at us for our folly, that we should be at so much cost and trouble to do a thing that does us so much harm, and no manner of good: but to the contrary when they see all our forces drawn forth, and in pursuit of them they will think that we begin to be roused up, and to be awake and will not be satisfied with what they have pleased to leave us, but are resolved to retake from them that they took formerly from us, and drive them out of their country also. The which being done, then to build a fort at a suitable time, and in a convenient place, and it will be very honourable to your excellency, and of great service to her Majesty, and to the enlargement of her Majesty's government (the place meant being at Portroyal.)

Twelfthly. That the objection made against drawing off the forces in the eastward parts will be no damage to the inhabitants, for former experience teacheth us that so soon as drawn into their country, they will presently forsake ours to take care of their own. And that there be no failure in making pre-

¹ [for]

paration of these things aforementioned; for many times the want of small things prevents the completing of great actions. And that every thing be in readiness before the forces be raised to prevent charges, and the enemy's having intelligence. And that the general court be moved to make suitable acts for the encouraging both English and Indians, that so men of business may freely offer estates and concerns to serve the publick.

Thus hoping what I have taken the pains to write in the sincerity of my heart, and good affection, will be well accepted, I make bold to subscribe as I am, your excellency's most devoted humble servant,
BENJAMIN CHURCH."

Then returning to his excellency, presented the said scheme, which his excellency approved of, and returned it again to Major Church, and desired him to see that every thing was provided; telling him he should have an order from the commissary General to proceed. Then returned home, and made it his whole business to provide oars and paddles, and a vessel to carry them round, and then returned again to his excellency, who gave him a commission which is as followeth.

" JOSEPH DUDLEY,* *Esq., Captain General and Governour in Chief, in and over her Majesty's pro-*

---

* A son of Thomas Dudley, who came to America in 1630, and who has been celebrated for his bitterness against toleration. Some poetry found in his pocket (says Morton, 151,) after his death, is so singular, and characteristick of the times, that I may be pardoned for so much digressing as to insert a clause of it.
  " Let men of God in courts and churches watch
  O'er such as do a toleration hatch;
  Lest that ill egg bring forth a cockatrice,
  To poison all with heresy and vice.
  If men be left, and otherwise combine,
  My epitaph's, *I dy'd no libertine.*"
The subject of this note was born in 1647, graduated at Harvard College, 1665, and is said to have been eminent for

vince *of the Massachusetts bay, in Newengland, in America, and Vice Admiral of the same,*

To BENJAMIN CHURCH, *Esq., Greeting.*

By virtue of the power and authority, in and by her Majesty's royal commission, to me granted, I do by these presents, reposing special trust and confidence in your loyalty, courage, and good conduct, constitute and appoint you to be Colonel of all the forces raised, and to be raised for her Majesty's service, against the French and Indian enemy and rebels, that shall be improved in the service to the eastward of Casco bay; and to be Captain of the first company of the said forces. You are therefore carefully and diligently to perform the duty of a Colonel and Captain, by leading, ordering and exercising the said regiment and company in arms, both inferiour officers and soldiers; and to keep them in good order and discipline. Hereby commanding them to obey you as their Colonel and Captain; and with them to do and execute all acts of hostility against the said enemy and rebels. And you are to observe and follow such orders and directions as you shall receive from myself, or other, your superiour officer, according to the rules and discipline of war, pursuant to the trust reposed in you. Given under my hand and

---

his learning. He was a commissioner in Philip's war, and his name may be seen among them at the head of the *long* treaty with the Narragansets, in July, 1675. When Andross was Governour, Mr. Dudley was president of the council, and was seized upon as belonging to his party, and imprisoned for some time, and treated with inhumanity. Being sent for by King William, he embarked in Feb., 1689. The next year he was sent over as chief justice of Newyork, but he was never satisfied any where but in the government of Massachusetts. He therefore exerted himself to injure Governour Phips, expecting to succeed him; but the people prevented him by procuring the appointment of the Earl of Bellomont, whose premature death gave him his beloved office, in which he continued from 1702 to 1716. Gov. Shute succeeded him, and he died in 1720, aged 73.

seal at arms, at Boston, the 18th day of March, in the third year of her Majesty's reign. Anno Dom. 1703-4.

J. DUDLEY.

By his Excellency's command.

ISAAC ADDINGTON, *Secr.*"

Colonel Church no sooner received his commission, but proceeded to the raising of men, volunteers, by going into every town within the three counties,* which were formerly Plymouth government; advising with the chief officer of each company, to call his company together, that so he might have the better opportunity to discourse and encourage them to serve their Queen and country. Treating them with drink convenient, told them, [that] he did not doubt but with God's blessing to bring them all home again. All which with many other arguments, animated their hearts to do service. So, that Colonel Church enlisted, out of some companies, near twenty men, and others fifteen.

He having raised a sufficient number of English soldiers, proceeded to the enlisting of Indians, in all those parts where they dwelt, which was a great fatigue and expense; being a people that need much treating, especially with drink, &c. Having enlisted the most of his soldiers in those parts, who daily lay upon him, [and] was not less than five pounds per day expenses, some days in victuals and drink; who doubtless thought, (especially the English) that the country would have reimbursed it again, otherwise they would hardly [have] accepted it of him.

Colonel Church's soldiers, both English and Indians, in those parts, being raised, marched them all

---

* Plymouth, Barnstable, and Bristol. This division was made in 1685, which before were all in one. Supplement to Morton, 207.

down to Nantasket,* according to his excellency's directions. Where being come, the following gentlemen were commissionated to be commanders of each particular company, viz., Lieutenant Colonel Gorham, Captains, John Brown, Constant Church, James Cole, John Dyer, John Cook, Caleb Williamson, and Edward Church, of the forces raised by Colonel Church; each company being filled up with English and Indians as they agreed among themselves, and by the Colonel's directions. Captain Lamb, and Captain Mirick's company, which were raised by his excellency's direction, were ordered to join those aforesaid, under the command of Colonel Church.

Matters being brought thus far on, Colonel Church waited upon his excellency at Boston to know his pleasure, what farther measures were to be taken; and did humbly move that they might have liberty in their instructions to make an attack upon Portroyal. Being very well satisfied in his opinion, that with the blessing of God, with what forces they had, or should have; and whaleboats so well fitted with oars and paddles, as they had with them, might be sufficient to have taken it. His excellency (looking upon Colonel Church) replied, [that] "he could not admit of that, by reason, [that] he had, by the advice of her Majesty's council, writ to her Majesty about the taking of Portroyal fort, and how it should be disposed of when taken," &c. However Colonel Church proceeded to get every thing ready for the forces down at Nantasket, which was the place of parade.

He happening one day to be at Captain Belch-

---

* The entrance into Boston harbour, south of the lighthouse. The winter of 1696 was so severe, that sleds and sleighs frequently passed from Boston to Nantasket upon the ice. The island of this name was the place of rendezvous and is nine miles from Boston. It contains the present town of Hull, and is connected to Hingham by a dam.

er's,* where his excellency happened to come. [He][1] was pleased to order Colonel Church to put on his sword, and walk with him up the common, which he readily complied with. Where being come, he saw two mortar pieces with shells, and an engineer trying with them, to throw a shell from them to any spot of ground where he said it should fall; which when Colonel Church had seen done, gave him great encouragement, and hopes [that] that would promote their going to Portroyal, which he had solicited for. And returning from thence, after they had seen them tried by the said engineer, and performing what was proposed, [and] coming near to Captain William Clark's house, over against the horse shoe, his excellency was invited by Captain Clark to walk over and take a glass of wine, which he was pleased to accept of, and took Colonel Church with him And in the time they were taking a glass of wine, Colonel Church once more presumed to say to his excellency; " Sir, I hope that now we shall go to Portroyal in order to take it; those mortars being very suitable for such an enterprise." His excellency was pleased to reply; " Colonel Church, you must say no more of that matter, for the letter I told you of, I writ by the advice of her Majesty's council, now lies at home on the board before the Lords commissioners of her Majesty's foreign plantations," &c.

After some days, every thing being ready to embark, Colonel Church received his instructions, which are as follows:

" *By his excellency* JOSEPH DUDLEY, *Esq., Captain General and Governour in Chief, in and over her Majesty's province of the Massachusetts bay, &c., in Newengland, and Vice Admiral of the same.*

[1] [who]

---

* Captain Andrew Belcher of Cambridge, and father of Governour Belcher, I suspect is meant. See page 62, note 3.

Instructions for COLONEL BENJAMIN CHURCH *in the present Expedition.*

In pursuance of the commission given you to take the chief command of the land and sea forces by me raised, equipped and sent forth on her Majesty's service, against her open declared enemies, the French and Indian rebels. You are to observe the following instructions.

First. You are to take care, that the duties of religion be attended on board the several vessels, and in the several companies under your command, by daily prayers unto God, and reading his holy word. And that the Lord's day be observed and duly sanctified to the utmost of your power, as far as the circumstances and necessity of the service can admit, that so you may have the presence of God with, and obtain his blessing on, your undertaking.

You are to take care, that your soldiers have their due allowance of provisions and other necessaries; that their arms be well fixed, and kept fit for service, and that they be furnished with a suitable quantity of powder and ball, and be always in readiness to pass upon duty.

That good order and discipline be maintained; and all disorders, drunkenness, profane swearing, cursing, omission or neglect of duty, disobedience to officers, mutiny, desertion, and sedition be duly punished, according to the rules and articles of war; the which you are once a month or oftener, to cause to be published, and made known to your officers and soldiers for their observance and direction in their duty. Let notorious and capital offenders be sent away to the next garrison, there to be imprisoned until they can be proceeded with.

Let the sick and wounded be carefully looked after, and accommodated after the best manner your circumstances will admit of, and be sent either to Casco fort, or to Mr. Peperel's at Kittery, which may be easiest, so soon as you can.

You are forthwith to send away the forces and stores by the transports, with the whaleboats to Piscataqua, on Kittery side there to attend your coming whither you are to follow them with all expedition.

You are to embark in the province galley, Captain Southack commander, and Lieutenant Colonel Gorham go on board Captain Gallop; who are both directed to attend your motion on the French side, after which they are to return. Let the commanders of all the store sloops and transports know that they sail, anchor and serve at your direction.

When you sail from Piscataqua, keep at such distance off the shore, that you be not discovered by the enemy to alarm them. Stop at Montinicus,* and there embark the forces in the whaleboats for the main, to range that part of the country, in search of the enemy, to Mountdesart, sending the vessels to meet you there; and after having refreshed and recruited your soldiers, proceed to Machias, and from thence to Passamequado; and having effected what spoils you possibly may, upon the enemy in those parts, embark on your vessels for Menis and Signecto, to Portroyal gut; and use all possible methods for the burning and destroying of the enemies houses, and breaking the dams of their corn grounds in the said several places, and make what other spoils you can upon them, and bring away the prisoners. In your return call at Penobscot and do what you can there, and so proceed westward.

This will probably employ you a month, or six weeks; when you will draw together again, and by the latter end of June, consider whether you can march to Norrigwack, or other parts of their planting, to destroy their corn and settlements and keep

---

* An island considerable distance from the coast of Maine, and the same, I suppose, called Martinicus or Mertinicus on the late maps. It is 15 or 20 miles from Vinalhaven island at the mouth of the Penobscot.

the expedition on foot until the middle of August next.

Notwithstanding the particularity of the aforegoing instruction, I lay you under no restraint, because I am well assured of your courage, care, caution and industry; but refer you to your own resolves, by the advice of your commission officers, not under the degree of Captains, and the sea commission Captains (whom you will, as often as you can, advise with) according to the intelligence you may receive, or as you may find needful upon the spot.

You are by every opportunity, and once a week certainly, by some means either by way of Casco, Piscataqua, or otherwise to acquaint me of your proceedings and all occurrences, and what may be further necessary for the service. And to observe such further and other instructions as you shall receive from myself.

As often as you may, advise with Captain Smith and Captain Rogers, commanders of her Majesty's ships.

Let your minister, commissary, and surgeons be treated with just respects. I pray to God to preserve, prosper and succeed you.

Given under my hand at Boston, the fourth day of May, 1704.

J. DUDLEY."

Pursuant to his instructions he sent away his transports and forces* to Piscataqua, but was obliged himself to wait upon his excellency by land to Piscataqua in order to raise more forces in the way thither; and did raise a company under the command of Captain Harridon.† Taking care to provide a

---

* This collected armament consisted of 550 soldiers, in 14 small transports, and was provided with 36 whale boats, and convoyed by three men of war; one of 48, one of 32, and one of 14 guns. Hutchinson, II, 132. Douglass, I, 557.

† This name is spelt Harreden in Penhallow's history; but his own signature to the resolve before Portroyal is Harradon. No other mention is made of him in the Indian wars that I have seen.

pilot for them in the bay of Fundy. (Colonel Church being directed to one Fellows whom he met with at Ipswich.) And going from thence to Piscataqua with his excellency, was there met by that worthy gentleman, Major Winthrop Hilton,* who was very helpful to him in the whole expedition, whose name and memory ought not to be forgot.

Being ready to embark from Piscataqua, Colonel Church requested the commanders of her Majesty's ships, Captain Smith,† and Captain Rogers‡ to tarry at Piscataqua a fortnight, that so they might not be discovered by the enemy before he had done some spoil upon them. Then moving§ in their transports, as directed, got safe into Montinicus,|| undiscovered by the enemy. Next morning early, fitted out two whaleboats with men, Captain John Cook in one, and Captain Constant Church in the other, and sent them to Green island¶ upon a discovery. And coming there, they parted, one went to one part, and the other to the other part, that so they might not miss

---

* Abundant materials are preserved for a biography of this gentleman. He was a direct descendant of one of the first settlers of Newhampshire in 1623. He was a successful officer, but like many others was doomed to fall by savage hands. In addition to what is found in this history, and Penhallow's Indian Wars, a memoir may be seen in I of Farmer and Moore's Col. 241, 251. He was engaged in the masting business in Exeter, where he lived, and having some fine trees fallen in the woods, went with 17 men to peel the bark off, to save them from the worms; but a party of Indians, on 23 June, 1710, fired upon them from an ambush, and killed the Colonel and two more. Colonel Daniel Plumer of Epping, informs me that the place where they were killed is in the present town of Epping, N. H. Perhaps not far from what is now called the *mast way*.

† Commander of the Jersey frigate.

‡ Commander of the frigate Gosport.

§ May 15. || See note on page 255.

¶ A small woody island about 5 miles south easterly from Montinicus.

of what could be discovered. [Here][1] they met with old Lafaure,* with his two sons, Thomas and Timothy, and a Canada Indian.

The enemy seeing that they were discovered, threw down their ducks and eggs, who had got a considerable quantity of each, and ran to their canoes, getting into them, stood directly for the main. [On] looking behind them perceived the whaleboats to gain so fast upon them, clapt side by side, and all four got into one canoe, which proved of little advantage to them. For the whaleboats gained so much upon them, and got so near, that Captain Cook, firing at the steersman, which was the Indian, and happened to graze his skull, and quite spoiled his paddling. Upon which old Lafaure, and sons, seeing their companion's condition, soon begged for quarter, and had it granted. The two Captains with their success presently returned to their commander taking care that their captives should not discourse together before they were examined. When brought to Colonel Church, he ordered them to be apart, and first proceeded to examine old Lafaure, whom he found to be very surly and cross; so that he could gain no intelligence by him.

Upon which the commander was resolved to put in practice what he had formerly done at Senecto.† Ordering the Indians to make two large heaps of dry wood, at some distance one from the other, and to set a large stake in the ground, close to each heap. Then [he] ordered the two sons Thomas and Timothy, to be brought, and to be bound to the stakes; also ordering his Indians to paint themselves with colours, which they had brought for that use. Then the Colonel proceeded to examine, first Timothy;

[1] [where]

---

* Penhallow, 33, in N. H. Hist. Col. I, calls him Monsieur Lafebure.

† The place, which on page 228, is spelt Senactaca. See note 2 of that page.

[he]¹ told him, [that] he had examined his father already, and that if he told him the truth he would save his life, and take him into his service; and that he should have good pay and live well. He answered, that he would tell him the truth. And [accordingly] gave him an account of every thing [that] he knew, which was all minuted down. He being asked whether his brother Thomas did not know more than he? His answer was, yes, for his brother Thomas had a commission sent him from the Governour* of Canada, to command a company of Indians, who were gathered together at a place where some French gentlemen, lately arrived from Canada, who were officers, to command the rest that were to go westward to fight the English;† and that there was sent to his father, and brother Tom, a considerable quantity of flour, fruit, ammunition and stores, for the supply of the said army. He being asked whether he could pilot our forces to them? said no; but his brother Tom could, for he had hid it, and that he was not then with him? The Colonel asked him what gentlemen those were that came from Canada? He

---

¹ [and]

* Vaudreuil.

† This is supposed by the historian of Newhampshire, to be the army of which Penhallow gives an account; who mutinied in their march "about the plunder that they had in view; forgetting the proverb about dividing the skin before the bear was killed." In consequence of their mutiny most of them returned; but a subdivision of them fell upon Lancaster and Groton, killed two or three persons, and got some plunder. But this army does not correspond with the statement given by Dr. Belknap. See page 161, note 2. After Mr. Penhallow has got quite through with the expedition of Church, and the affair under "Mr. Caleb Lyman" at the westward, he says, "The French in Canada were now forming another design on Northampton." Now it appears to me, that the Doctor is out in his conjecture, and that the army mentioned by Penhallow was not the one mentioned by our author. And had he looked into Dr. Douglass, Summary, I, 557, he would have found more particulars about it.

answered, "Monsieur Gourdan,* and Mr. Sharkee."
Being asked where they were? answered, "At Passamaquado, building a fort there." Being also asked
what number of Indians and French there were at
Penobscot? he answered, [that] there were several
families, but they lived scattering. Asked him farther, if he would pilot our forces thither? [He] answered [that] he would if the commander would not
let the savages roast him. Upon which the Colonel
ordered him to be loosed from the stake, and took
him by the hand, told him, he would be as kind to
him as his own father; at which he seemed to be
very thankful.

And then the Colonel proceeded to examine his
brother Tom. [He][1] told him that he had examined
his father and brother; and that his brother had told
him every tittle [that] he knew; and that he knew
more than his brother Timothy did; and that if
he would be ingenuous and confess all he knew, he
should fare as well as his brother. But if not, the
savages should roast him. Whereupon he solemnly
promised that he would, and that he would pilot him
to every thing he knew, to the value of a knife and
sheath (which without doubt he did.)

Then the Colonel immediately gave orders for the
whaleboats to be ready, and went directly over where
the said goods and stores were, and found them as
informed, took them on board the boats, and returned to their transports. And ordering provisions to
be put into every man's knapsack for six or eight days;
so in the dusk of the evening left their transports,
with orders how they should act, and went directly
for the main land of Penobscot, and mouth of that

[1] [and]

---

* Guorden appears to be the true orthography of this name.
He was afterward taken as will presently be seen. Sharkee
made a very narrow escape with his wife into the woods.
Penhallow, 17, says he was taken, but he must be mistaken.
This errour is not noted in the N. H. Hist. Soc. Col. See
page 24.

river, with their pilots, Tom and Timothy, who carried them directly to every place and habitation, both of French and Indians thereabouts, (with the assistance of one DeYoung* whom they carried out of Boston jail for the same purpose, [and he]¹ was serviceable to them.)

Being there we killed and took every one, both French and Indians; not knowing that any one did escape in all Penobscot. Among those that were taken was St. Casteen's daughter, who said that her husband was gone to France, to her father, Monsieur Casteen.† She having her children with her, the commander was very kind to her and them. All the prisoners that were then taken, held to one story in general, which they had from Lafaure's sons, [viz.,] that there were no more Indians thereabouts, but enough of them at Passamequado. Upon which they returned to their transports with their prisoners and plunder.

The commander giving order immediately for the soldiers in the whaleboats to have a recruit of provisions for a further pursuit of the enemy. Giving orders to the transports to stay a few days more there, and then go to Mountdesart, (and there to stay for her Majesty's ships, who were directed to come thither,) and there to wait his further order.

Then Colonel Church with his forces immediately embarked on board their whaleboats, and proceeded to scour the coast, and to try, if they could discover any of the enemy coming from Passamequado; making their stops in the day time at all the points and places where they were certain [that] the enemy would land, or come by with their canoes, and at night to their paddles. Then coming near where the

¹ [who]

---

* In Penhallow, 17, his name is written D'Young and not D. Young as *reprinted* in Col. N. H. Hist. Soc. I, 33.

† Baron De St. Castine. See note 1, on page 164.

vessels were ordered to come, having made no discovery of the enemy, went directly to Mountdesart, where the transports were just come. And taking some provisions for his soldiers, gave directions for the ships and transports in six days to come directly to Passamequado, where they should find him and his forces.

Then immediately moved away in the whaleboats, and made diligent search along shore, as formerly, inspecting all places where the enemy was likely to lurk: Particularly at Machias, but found neither fires nor tracks. Coming afterwards to the west harbour at Passamequado, where they entered upon action. An account whereof Colonel Church did communicate to his excellency, being as followeth.

"*May it please your Excellency,*

I received yours of this instant, October ninth, with the two inclosed informations, that concern my actions at Passamequado, which I will give a just and true account of, as near as possibly I can, viz On the seventh of June last, 1704, in the evening, we entered in at the westward harbour at said Passamequado. Coming up said harbour to an island, where landing, we came to a French house, and took a French woman and children. The woman upon her examination, said her husband was abroad a fishing. I asked her, whether there were any Indians thereabouts? she said 'Yes, there were a great many, and several on that island.' I asked her, whether she could pilot me to them? said 'No, they hid in the woods.' I asked her, when she saw them? answered, 'Just now, or a little while since.' I asked her whether she knew where they had laid the canoes? she answered 'No, they carried their canoes into the woods with them.' We then hastened away along shore, seizing what prisoners we could, taking old Lotriel and his family.

This intelligence caused me to leave Colonel Gorham, and a considerable part of my men, and boats with him at ·that island; partly to guard and secure those prisoners. Being sensible it would be a great trouble to have them to secure and guard at our next landing, where I did really expect, and hoped to have an opportunity, to fight our Indian enemies. For all our French prisoners that we had taken at Penobscot, and along shore, had informed us, that when we came to the place where these Canada gentlemen lived, we should certainly meet with the savages to fight us; those being the only men that set the Indians against us, or upon us, and were newly come from Canada, to manage the war against us. (Pleading in this account and information their own innocency.) And partly in hopes that he, the said Colonel Gorham, would have a good opportunity in the morning to destroy some of those our enemies, (we were informed [of,] by the said French women as above) with the use of his boats as I had given direction.

Ordering also Major Hilton to pass over to the next island, that lay east of us with a small party of men and boats, to surprise and destroy any of the enemy, that in their canoes might go here and there, from any place, to make their flight from us; and, as he had opportunity, to take any French prisoners.

We then immediately moved up the river, in the dark night, through great difficulty, by reason of the eddies and whirlpools, made with the fierceness of the current. And here it may be hinted, that we had information, that Lotriel had lost part of his family passing over to the next island, falling into one of those eddies were drowned, which the two pilots told to discourage me. But I said nothing of that nature shall do it. For I was resolved to venture up, and therefore, forthwith paddling our boats as privately as we could, and with as much expedition as we could make with our paddles and the help of a strong tide, we came up to Monsieur Gourdan's a little before day. Where taking notice of the shore, and finding it somewhat open and clear, I ordered Captain Mirick and Captain Cole, having English companies, to tarry with several of the boats to be ready, that if any of the enemy should come down out of the brush into the bay (it being very broad in that place) with their canoes, they might take and destroy them.

Ordering the remainder of the army, (being landed,) with myself and the other officers, to march up into the woods with a wide front, and to keep at a considerable distance; for that if they should run in heaps, the enemy would have the greater advantage. And further directing them, that if possible, they should destroy the enemy with their hatchets, and not fire a gun. This order I always gave at landing; telling them the inconveniency of firing, in that it might be, first, dangerous to themselves, they being many of them young soldiers. (As I had sometime observed, that one or two guns being fired many others would fire, at they knew not what, as happened presently after.) And it would alarm the enemy, and give them the opportunity to make their escape; and it might alarm the whole country, and also prevent all further action from taking effect.

Orders being thus passed, we moved directly towards the woods. Le Faver's* son directing us to a little hut or wigwam, which we immediately surrounded with a few men. The rest marching directly up into the woods, to see what wigwams or huts they could discover. Myself made a little stop, ordering the pilot to tell them in the hut, that they were surrounded with an army, and that if they would come forth and surrender themselves, they should have good quarter; but if not, they should be all knocked on the head and die.

One of them showed himself, [and] I asked who

---

* The same, who in the late preceding pages is called Lafaure. See note 1, on page 258.

he was? He said 'Gourdan;' and begged for quarter. I told him he should have good quarter; adding further, that if there were any more in the house, they should come out. Then came out two men. Gourdan said, they were his sons, and asked quarter for them, which was also granted. Then came out a woman, and a little boy. She fell upon her knees, begged quarter for herself and children, and that I would not suffer the Indians to kill them. I told them they should have good quarter, and not be hurt. After which I ordered a small guard over them, and so moved presently up with the rest of my company after them that were gone before. But looking on my right hand, over a little run, 1 saw something look black just by me; [I] stopped and heard a talking; [then] stepped over, and saw a little hut or wigwam, with a crowd of people round about it, which was contrary to my former directions. [I] asked them what they were doing? They replied, [that] there were some of the enemy in a house and would not come out. I asked what house they said, 'A bark house.' I hastily bid them pull it down, and *knock them on the head*, never asking whether they were French or Indians; they being all enemies alike to me.*

---

* The Colonel was much blamed for this hasty step; and Hutchinson says, II, 133, that he "excused himself but indifferently." Of which, however, the reader may judge as well as he. It does not appear from a long career of useful services, that Church was ever rash or cruel. From the extraordinary situation of his men, rendered doubly critical from the darkness of the night, and the almost certain intelligence, that a great army of the enemy were at hand, is thought to be sufficient excuse for the measure; the remark of Hutchinson to the contrary notwithstanding. The same author, II, 128, excuses the French and Indians for their cruelty in putting to death prisoners at the destruction of Deerfield; because it was necessary to their own preservation, and the English had done so too; and gives for example the action of Henry V, who, after the celebrated battle of Agincourt, put to death a multitude of his French priso-

And passing then to them, and seeing them in great disorder, so many of the army in a crowd together, acting so contrary to my command and direction, exposing themselves and the whole army to utter ruin, by their so disorderly crowding thick together. Had an enemy come upon them in that interim, and fired a volley amongst them, they could not have missed a shot. And wholly neglecting their duty in not attending my orders, in searching diligently for our lurking enemies in their wigwams, or by their fires, where I had great hopes, and real expectations to meet with them.

I most certainly know that I was in an exceeding great passion; but not with those poor miserable enemies; for I took no notice of a half a dozen of the enemy, when at the same time I expected to be engaged with some hundreds of them; of whom we had a continued account, who were expected from Portroyal side. In this heat of action, every word that I then spoke, I cannot give an account of; and I presume it is impossible.

I stopped but little here, but went directly up into the woods, hoping to be better employed with the rest of the army. I listened to hear, and looked earnestly to see what might be the next action. But meeting with many of the soldiers they told me [that] they had discovered nothing; we fetching a small compass round, came down again.

It being pretty dark, I took notice, [that] I saw two men lay dead, as I thought, at the end of the house where the door was; and immediately the

---

ners, that greatly exceeded the number of his own army. This was in a barbarous age; being 200 years before the settlement of Newengland. Hence it would have been much easier for him to excuse our hero than the enemy. For according to the usages of war, he would have been justified in putting to death prisoners at such a critical time. But these were enemies who would not submit; or what amounted to the same thing, they would not come out of their house when ordered by the forces.

guns went off, and they fired every man, as I thought, and most towards that place where I left the guard with Monsieur Gourdan. I had much ado to stop the firing, and told them, I thought they were mad; and [that] I believed they had not killed and wounded less than forty or fifty of our own men. And I asked them what they shot at? they answered, 'At a Frenchman that ran away.' But to admiration no man was killed but he, [the Frenchman] and one of our men wounded in the leg. And I turning about, a Frenchman spoke to me, and I gave him quarter.

Daylight coming on, and no discovery made of the enemy, I went to the place where I had left Monsieur Gourdan, to examine him and his sons, who agreed in their examinations; told me two of their men were abroad. It proved a damage. And further told me, that Monsieur Sharkee lived several leagues up, at the head of the river, at the falls, and all the Indians were fishing, and tending their corn there; and that Monsieur Sharkee had sent down to him, to come up to him, to advise about the Indian army* that was to go westward. But he had returned him answer, [that] his business was urgent, and he could not come up; and that Sharkee, and the Indians would certainly be down that day, or the next at the furthest, to come to conclude of that matter.

This was a short night's action, and all sensible men do well know, that actions done in the dark, (being in the night aforesaid) under so many difficulties, as we then laboured as before related, was a very hard task for one man, matters being circumstanced as in this action, which would not admit of calling a council; and at that time could not be confined thereunto. At which time I was transported above fear, or any sort of dread; yet, being sensible of the danger in my army's crowding so thick together, and of the great duty incumbent on me,

---

* See note 2, of page 259.

to preserve them from all danger [that] I possibly could, for further improvement in the destruction of our implacable enemies, am ready to conclude, that I was very quick and absolute in giving such commands and orders, as I then apprehended most proper and advantageous. And had it not been for the intelligence I had received from the French, we took at Penobscot, as before hinted; and the false report [that] the French women (first took) gave me, I had not been in such haste.

I question not, but those Frenchmen that were slain, had the same good quarter of other prisoners. But I ever looked on it, a good providence of Almighty God, that some few of our cruel and bloody enemies were made sensible of their bloody cruelties, perpetrated on my dear and loving friends and countrymen; and that the same measure (in part) meeted to them, as they had been guilty of, in a barbarous manner at Deerfield; and, I hope, justly. I hope God Almighty will accept hereof, although it may not be eligible to our French implacable enemies, and such others as are not our friends.

The foregoing journal, and this short annexment, I thought it my duty to exhibit, for the satisfaction of my friends and countrymen, whom I very faithfully and willingly served in the late expedition. And I hope will find acceptance with your excellency, the honourable council and Representatives now assembled, as being done from the zeal I had in the said service of her Majesty, and her good subjects here. I remain your most humble and obedient servant,
BENJAMIN CHURCH."

This night's service being over, immediately Colonel Church leaves a sufficient guard with Gourdan and the other prisoners, moved in some whaleboats with the rest; and as they were going, spied a small thing upon the water at a great distance, which proved to be a birch canoe with two Indians in her

FRENCH AND INDIAN WARS. 269

The Colonel presently ordered the lightest boat he had, to make the best of her way, and cut them off from the shore. But the Indians perceiving their design, ran their canoe ashore and fled. Colonel Church fearing [that] they would run directly to Sharkee, made all the expedition imaginable. But it being ebb, and the water low, was obliged to land, and make the best of their way through the woods, hoping to intercept the Indians, and get to Sharkee's house before them, which was two miles from where our forces landed.

The Colonel being ancient and unwieldy, desired Sergeant Edee to run with him. And coming to several trees fallen, which he could not creep under, or readily get over, would lay his breast against the tree, the said Edee turning him over, generally had *catluck*, falling on his feet, by which means [he] kept in the front. And coming near to Sharkee's house, discovered some French and Indians making a wear* in the river, and presently discovered the two Indians aforementioned, who called to them at work in the river, [and] told them, [that] "there was an army of English an Indians just by." [They][1] immediately left their work and ran, endeavouring to get to Sharkee's house. [He][2] hearing the noise, took his lady and child and ran into the woods. Our men running briskly, fired and killed one of the Indians, and took the rest prisoners.

Then going to Sharkee's house found a woman and child, to whom they gave good quarter. And finding that Madam Sharkee had left her silk clothes and fine linen behind her, our forces were desirous to have pursued and taken her. But Colonel Church forbade them; saying he would have her run and suffer, that she might be made sensible, what hardships our poor people had suffered by them, &c. [He] then pro-

---

[1] [who]   [2] [who]

* Or, wier, a rack to catch fish in.

ceeded to examine the prisoners newly taken, who gave him the same account [that] he had before, of the Indians being up at the falls, &c. It being just night, prevented our attacking them that night.

But next morning early, they moved up to the falls which was about a mile higher. But doubtless the enemy had some intelligence by the two aforesaid Indians, before our forces came, so that they all got on the other side of the river, and left some of their goods by the water side to decoy our men, that so they might fire upon them; which indeed they effected. But through the good providence of God, never a man of ours was killed, and but one slightly wounded. After a short dispute, Colonel Church ordered that every man might take what they pleased of the fish, which lay bundled up, and to burn the rest, which was a great quantity. The enemy seeing what our forces were about, and that their stock of fish was destroyed, and the season being over for getting any more, set up a hideous cry, and so ran all away into the woods. They being all on the other side of the river, ours could not follow them.

Having done, our forces marched down to their boats, at Sharkee's, and took their prisoners, beaver, and other plunder which they had got, and put it into their boats, and went down to Gourdan's house, where they had left Lieutenant Colonel Gorham, and Major Hilton, with part of the forces to guard the prisoners, (and kept a good look out for more of the enemy) who upon the Colonel's return, gave him an account that they had made no discovery of the enemy since he left them, &c.

Just then her Majesty's ships and transports arriving, the commanders of her Majesty's ships told Colonel Church, that they had orders to go directly for Portroyal gut, and wait the coming of some store ships,* which were expected at Portroyal from France.

---

* No ships arrived, or at least, we have no account of any. Holmes, II, 65, mentions, sub anno 1705, that a rich ship

And Colonel Church advising with them, proposed that it was very expedient and serviceable to the crown, that Captain Southack in the Province galley should accompany them, which they did readily acquiesce with him in.

Upon which, the Colonel immediately embarked his forces on board the transports, and himself on board Captain Jarvis, ordering the commissary of the stores, the minister, surgeons and pilots all to embark on board the same vessel with him. Ordering all the whaleboats to be put on board the transports, and then to come to sail. The ships standing away for Portroyal gut, and Colonel Church with the transports for Menis. In their way the Colonel inquired of their pilot, Fellows, what depth of water there was in the creek, near the town of Menis? he answered him, that there was water enough, near the town, to float that vessel, they were in, at low water.

So, when coming near, Colonel Church observed a woody island between them and the town, that they ran up on the back side of, (the said island) with all their transports, undiscovered to the enemy, and came to anchor. Then the Colonel and all his forces embarked in the whaleboats. It being late in the day, [they] moved directly for the town; and in the way asked for the pilot, who, he expected, was in one of the boats; but he had given him the slip, and tarried behind. The Colonel not knowing the difficulties that might attend their going up to the town, immediately sent Lieutenant Giles, who could speak French, with a flag of truce up to the town, (with a

---

named the Siene, was taken, the preceding autumn, by the English; and that she was bound to Quebeck, with a cargo amounting to nearly a million of livres. But this was in June, hence it does not agree with the supposition that said ship was taken by Church's convoy. He cites Charlevoix, and the Universal History. Dr. Douglass, I, 557, in this, as well as many other cases, comes happily to our relief. He informs us, that this ship "was taken by an English Virginia Fleet."

summons, which was written before they landed,) expecting their surrender; which is as followeth.

"*Aboard her Majesty's Ship Adventure, near the gut of Menis, June* 20, 1704.
An agreement made by the field officers commanding her Majesty's forces for the present expedition against the French enemies, and Indian rebels.

Agreed, that a declaration or summons be sent on shore at Menis and Portroyal, under a flag of truce.

Particularly, we do declare to you, the many cruelties and barbarities that you and the Indians have been guilty of towards us, in laying waste our country here in the east at Casco, and the places adjacent. Particularly, the horrid action at Deerfield, this last winter, in killing, massacreing, murdering and scalping, without giving any notice at all, or opportunity to ask quarter at your hands; and, after all, carrying the remainder into captivity in the height of winter, (of which they killed many in the journey) and exposed the rest to the hardships of cold and famine, worse than death itself. Which cruelties we are yet every day exposed unto and exercised with.

We do also declare, that we have already made some beginnings of killing and scalping some Canada men, (which we have not been wont to do or allow) and are now come with a great army of English and Indians, all volunteers, with resolutions to subdue you, and make you sensible of your cruelties to us, by treating you after the same manner.

At this time we expect our men of war and transport ships to be at Portroyal. (We having but lately parted with them.)

In the last place, we do declare to you, that inasmuch as some of you have shown kindness to our captives, and expressed a love to, and desire of being under the English government, we do therefore, notwithstanding all this, give you timely notice, and do demand a surrender immediately, by the laying down your arms, upon which, we promise very good quarter; if not, you must expect the utmost severity.

To the chief commander of the town of Menis, and the inhabitants thereof, and we expect your answer, positively, within an hour.

BENJAMIN CHURCH, *Col.*
JOHN GORHAM, *Lieut. Col.*
WINTHROP HILTON, *Maj.*"

Then moving to the creek, expecting to have had water enough for the boats, as the pilot had informed them, but found not water enough for a canoe. So [they] were obliged to land, intending to have been up at the town before the hour was out, that the summons expressed. For their return was, " that if our forces would not hurt their estates, then they would surrender, if otherwise intended, they should fight for them," &c.

But meeting with several creeks, near twenty or thirty feet deep, which were very muddy and dirty; so that the army could not get over them, [and] were obliged to return to their boats again, and wait till within night, before the tide served them to go up to the town. And then [they] intended to go up pretty near the town, and not to fall to, till morning; being in hopes that the banks of the creeks would shelter them from the enemy. But the tide's rising so high, exposed them all to the enemy; who had the trees and woods to befriend them; and so came down in the night, and fired smartly at our forces. But Colonel Church being in a pinnace, that had a small cannon placed in the head, ordered it to be charged several times with bullets, in small bags, and fired at the enemy; which made such a rattling amongst the trees, that [it] caused the enemy to draw off. And by the great providence of Almighty God, not one of our forces was hurt that night. But as I have been informed, [the enemy]¹ had one Indian killed, and some others wounded, which was some discouragement to [them.]²

Next morning, by break of day, Colonel Church ordered all his forces (and placed Major Hilton on the right wing) to run all up, driving the enemy before them; who leaving their town to our forces, but had carried away the best of their goods, which were soon found by our soldiers. The bulk of the enemy happening to lie against our right wing, caused the hottest dispute there. [They]³ lay behind logs and trees, till our forces, and Major Hilton, who led them, came [—]⁴ upon them, and forced them to run. And notwithstanding the sharp firing of the enemy at our forces, by the repeated providence of God, there was never a man of ours killed or wounded.

Our soldiers not having been long in town, before they found considerable quantities of strong drink, both brandy and claret; and being very greedy after it, especially the Indians, were very disorderly; firing at every pig, turkey, or fowl [that] they saw; of which [there] were very plenty in the town, which endangered our own men. Colonel Church perceiving the disorder, and firing of his own men, ran to put a stop to it, [and] had several shot come very near him. And finding what had occasioned this disorder, commanded his officers to knock out the heads of every cask of strong liquor they could find in the town, to prevent any further disturbance among his army; knowing, [that] it was impossible to have kept it from them, especially the Indians, if it were saved, &c.

Then some of the army who were desirous to pursue the enemy, having heard them driving away their cattle, requested the Colonel to let them go. [He]⁵ did, and gave them their orders. Captain Cooke, and Captain Church to lead the two wings

¹ [they] ² [the enemy] ³ [who] ⁴ [on] ⁵ [who]

and Lieutenant Barker,* who led the Colonel's company, in the centre. And the said Captain Cooke and Captain Church desired Lieutenant Barker not to move too fast; so that he might have the benefit of their assistance, if he had occasion. But the said Lieutenant not being so careful as he should have been, or at least was too eager, was shot down, and another man, which were all the men that were killed in the whole expedition.†

Towards night, Colonel Church ordered some of his forces to pull down some of the houses, and others to get logs and make a fortification for his whole army to lodge in, that night; that so they might be together. And just before night [he] ordered some of his men to go [and] see if there were any men in any of the houses in the town; [and] if [there were] not, to set them all on fire, which was done; and the whole town seemed to be on fire all at once, &c.

The next morning the Colonel gave orders to his men, to dig down the dams, and let the tide in, to destroy all their corn, and every thing that was good *according to his instructions;*‡ and to burn the fortification which they had built the day before; and when the tide served to put all the plunder which they had got into the boats. Then ordering his soldiers to march a good distance one from another, which caused the enemy to think that there were no less than a thousand men, as they said afterwards; and that the burning of the fortification, and doing as they did, caused the enemy to think that they were

---

* Charlevoix, in his account of the taking of Menis, says, that the Lieutenant General of the English forces, was killed, by which the Lieutenant of Church's company is meant.

† Penhallow in N. H. Hist. Col. I, 34, says "not above six died in the whole expedition."

‡ Thus do governments cause such horrid scenes. But is the crime lessened? They are considered right in the trade and custom of war. But is it so on that account?

gone clear off, and not to return again. But it proved to the contrary; for Colonel Church and his forces, only went aboard their transports, and there staid till the tide served. In the night [they]¹ embarked on board their whaleboats, landed some of their men, expecting they might meet with some of the enemy mending their dams; which they did. And with their boats went up another branch of the river to another town or village, [and] upon such a surprise, [that they] took as many prisoners as they could desire.

And it happened that Colonel Church was at the French Captain's house when two gentlemen came post from the Governour* of Portroyal to him, who was the chief commander at Menis, with an express to send away two companies of men to defend the King's fort there; and to give him an account, that there were three English men of war come into Portroyal gut, or harbour; and that the men sent for must be posted away with all speed. Colonel Church as was said before, being there, treated the two gentlemen very handsomely, and told them, [that] he would send them back again post to their master upon his business. And bid them give him his hearty thanks for sending him such good news, that part of his fleet was in so good a harbour. Then reading the summons to them that he had sent to Menis. Further added, that their master, the Governour of Portroyal, must immediately send away a post to the Governour of Canada, at Quebeck, to prevent his further sending any of his cruel and bloody French, and savages, as he had lately done upon Deerfield, where they had committed such horrible and bloody outrages upon those poor people, that never did

¹ [his]

---

* Monsieur De Subercase, this year came in to be governour of Acadie. Portroyal, I suspect, was his principal seat. The next year he drove the English from Newfoundland, and destroyed their settlements. Holmes II, 65.

them any harm, as is intolerable to think of; and that for the future, if any such hostilities were made upon our frontier towns, or any of them, he would come out with a thousand savages, and whaleboats convenient, and turn his back upon them, and let his savages scalp, and roast the French; or, at least, treat them as their savages had treated ours.

[He] also gave them an account of part of that action at Passamequado, and how that his soldiers had killed and scalped some Canada men there, and would be glad to serve them so too, if he would permit them, which terrified them very much,* &c. The two French gentlemen that came post, made solemn promises, that they would punctually do the Colonel's message to their Governour. So with the desire of the French people there, that the Governour might have this intelligence, Colonel Church dismissed them, and sent them away; telling the same story to several of the prisoners, and what they must expect, if some speedy course were not taken to prevent further outrages upon the English. The number of prisoners† then present, which were considerable, did unanimously entreat of Colonel Church, that he would take them under the protection of the crown of England; making great promises of their fidelity to the same; begging with great agony of spirit to save their lives, and to protect them from his savages, whom they extremely dreaded.

As to the matter of the savages, he told them, [that] it would be just retaliation for him to permit his savages to treat the French in the same manner, as the French with their savages treated our friends in our frontier towns. But as to his taking them under the protection of the crown of England, he ut-

---

* This, the commander of Portroyal, says Hutchinson, must know to be a gasconade.

† Penhallow says, that in this expedition one hundred prisoners were taken. So says Dr. Douglass, I, 307; probably on the same authority.

terly refused it; urging to them, their former perfidiousness. They also urging to him, that it would be impossible for any French to live any where in the bay of Fundy, if they were not taken under the English government. For with the benefit of the whale-boats, (as the English called them) they could take and destroy all their people in the town of Menis, in one night. But he replied to them, [that] it should never be. Alleging to them, that when they were so before, when Portroyal was taken last by the English,* that it proved of very ill consequence to the crown of England, and the subjects thereof in our frontiers. For that our English traders supplying them, enabled them (which opportunity they improved) to supply the Indians, our bloody enemies; and, therefore, he could make no other terms of peace with them, than, that if the French at Menis, Signecto, and Canada, would keep at home with their bloody savages, and not commit any hostilities upon any of our frontiers, we would return home and leave them. For that we lived at a great distance off, and had not come near them to hurt them now, had not the blood of our poor friends and brethren, in all the frontiers of our province cried for vengeance. Especially, that late unheard of barbarity committed

---

* It is situated on the west side of Novascotia, on a river of the same name, which flows into the bay of Fundy. Mention has been made of the expedition to Canada in 1690, under Sir William Phips; the reduction of Portroyal was executed under the same gentleman, in the same year, but previous. It was commanded by Gov. Menival, who built it about 1663. When Phips took it, it was both " ill fortified and ill provided." See note 1, on page 177. It was in no condition to stand a siege, and submitted without resistance. (Hutchinson, I, 352.) But it was, in 1705, retaken by the French. Again in 1710, a large armament under Col. Nicholson went against it, of which they made an easy conquest. There were but 260 men to defend it. The English had 5 frigates, 5 lower rates, and 24 transports. After it was taken the name was changed from Port Royal to Annapolis royal, which it yet retains.

upon the town of Deerfield; which wrought so generally on the hearts of our people, that our forces came out with that unanimity of spirit, both among the English and our savages, that we had not, nor needed a pressed man among them. The Colonel also telling them, that if ever hereafter any of our frontiers, east or west, were molested by them, as formerly, that he would, (if God spared his life) and they might depend upon it, return upon them with a thousand of his savages, (if he wanted them,) all volunteers, with our whaleboats, and pursue them to the last extremity.

The Colonel's warm discourse with them, wrought such a consternation in them, which they discovered by their panick fears and trembling, their hearts sensibly beating, and rising up, as it were, ready to choke them. [They] confessed, that they were all his prisoners, and begged of him, for JESUS' sake, to save their lives, and the lives of their poor families, with such melting terms, as wrought relentings in the Colonel's breast towards them. But however, he told them, that his intent was to carry as many prisoners home as he could; but that he had taken so many, they were more than he had occasion for, nor desired any more; and, therefore, he would leave them.

The Colonel resolving the next day to complete all his action at Menis, and so draw off. Accordingly, [he] sent his orders to Colonel Gorham and Major Hilton, with all the English companies, both officers and soldiers, except some few, which he thought he might have occasion for, to go with the Indians in the whaleboats, up the eastward river, where a third part of the inhabitants lived. That so he might prevent any reflection made on them, in leaving any part of the service undone. And therefore, in the evening, ordered all the whaleboats to be laid ready for the night's service. And, accordingly when the tide served, he went with his Indians up the river, where they did some spoil upon the enemy going up.

In the morning, several of their transports came to meet them, to their great rejoicing, whom they went on board [of] and soon came up with the whole fleet, with whom they joined, bending their course directly towards Portroyal, where they were ordered. Coming to Portroyal gut, where their ships were, and calling a council according to his instructions, drew up their result, which is as followeth.*

\ "*Present all the Field Officers and Captains of the land forces, aboard the province Galley, 4th July, 1704, in Portroyal harbour.*

We whose names are hereunto subscribed, having deliberately considered the cause in hand, whether it be proper to land all our forces, to offend and destroy as much as we can at Portroyal, all or any part of the inhabitants thereof, and their estates, we are of opinion, that it is not for our interest and honour, and the sountry's whom we serve, to land and expose ourselves; but quit it wholly, and go on about our other business, we have to do; for this reason, that we judge ourselves inferiour to the strength of the enemy; and, therefore, the danger and risk we run, is greater than the advantage we can, or are likely to obtain; seeing, the enemy hath such timely notice, and long opportunity to provide themselves against us; by our ships' lying here in the road about twelve days before we could join them from Menis, where we were during that time, and being so meanly provided with necessaries, convenient for such an undertaking with so small a number of men, not being four hundred, capable and fit for service to land; and, understanding, by all the intelligence we can

---

* That any steps should be taken, or even any thing said about reducing Portroyal, may seem strange, after they had been so peremptorily refused, by the Governour, as has been related in the preceding history. See page 253.

get, from both English, and French prisoners, that the fort is exceeding strong.

     JOHN GORHAM, *Lieut. Col.*
     WINTHROP HILTON, *Major,*
     JNO. BROWN,
     JAMES COLE,
     JOHN COOK,
     ISAAC MYRICK,
     JOHN HARRADON,
     CONSTANT CHURCH,
     JOHN DYER,
     JOSHUA LAMB,
     CALEB WILLIAMSON,
     EDWARD CHURCH."

"Having pursuant to my instructions, taken the advice of the gentlemen above subscribed, and considering the weight of their reasons, I do concu therewith.   BENJAMIN CHURCH."

"Whereas Colonel Church hath desired our opinions, as to the landing the forces at Portroyal, they being but four hundred effective men to land; and by all the information, both of French and English prisoners, the enemy having a greater number of men, and much better provided to receive, than they are to attack them, we do believe, it is for the service of the crown, and the preservation of her Majesty's subjects, to act as above mentioned.

     THOMAS SMITH,
     GEORGE ROGERS,
     CYPRIAN SOUTHACK"

After this they concluded what should be next done, which was, that the ships should stay some days longer at Portroyal gut, and then go over to Mountdesart harbour, and there stay till Colonel Church with his transports, came to them.

Being all ready, the Colonel with his transports and forces went up the bay to Signecto, where they needed not a pilot, being several of them well acquainted there. (And [they] had not met with so many difficulties at Menis, had it not been that their pilot deceived them, who knew nothing of the matter, [and] kept out of the way, and landed not with them, &c.) And coming to Signecto, the enemy were all in arms to receive them. Colonel Church landing his men, the commander of the enemy waving his sword over his head, bid a challenge to them. The Colonel ordering his two wings to march up apace, and come upon the backs of the enemy. Himself being in the centre, and the enemy knowing him, (having been there before) shot chiefly at him. But through God's goodness, received no harm; neither had he one man killed, nor but two slightly wounded; and then all ran into the woods, and left their town with nothing in it. Having had timely notice of our forces' [coming, they] had carried all away out of the reach of our army; for Colonel Church while there with part of his forces, ranged the woods, but to no purpose. Then returning to the town, did them what spoil he could, according to his instructions, and so drew off, and made the best of their way for Passamequado. And going in, in a great fog, one of their transports ran upon a rock, but was soon got off again.

Then Colonel Church with some of his forces embarked in their whaleboats, and went amongst the islands, with an intent to go to Sharkee's where they had destroyed the fish. But observing a springy place in a cove, went on shore to get some water to drink. It being a sandy beach, they espied tracks; the Colonel presently ordered his men to scatter and make search. [They] soon found De Boisses'* wife, who had formerly been Colonel Church's prisoner, and carried to Boston, but returned; who seemed very glad to see him. She had with her, two sons, that were near men grown The Colonel ordering them apart, examined the woman first, who gave him this account following. That she had lived there-

---

* Dubois. Pronounced Duboy.

FRENCH AND INDIAN WARS. 283

abouts ever since the fleet went by; and that she had never seen but two Indians since, who came in a canoe from Norrigwock;* [and that they]¹ asked her, 'what made her to be there alone?' she told them [that] she had not seen a Frenchman nor an Indian, except those two, since the English ships went by. Then the Indians told her, 'there was not one Indian left, except those two, who belonged to the gut of Canso, on this side of Canada. For those friars coming down with the Indians to Monsieur Gourdan's; and finding the Frenchmen slain, and their hair spoiled, being scalped, put them into a great consternation. And the friars told them it was impossible for them to live thereabouts; for the English with their whaleboats would serve them all so; upon which they all went to Norrigwock.' Also told her that 'when the English came along through Penobscot, they had swept it of the inhabitants, as if it had been swept with a broom; neither French nor Indians escaping them.' [And,] further told her, that when their fathers, the friars, and the Indians met together at Norrigwock, they called a council, and the friars told the Indians, that they must look out for some other country, for that it was impossible for them to live there.' Also told them [that] 'there was a river called Mossipee,† where they might live quietly, and no English come near them; it being as far beyond Canada as it was to it, &c., and if they would go and live there; they would live and die with them; but if not they would leave them, and never come near them again.' Whereupon they all agreed to go away, which they did; and left their rough household stuff, and corn behind them; and went all, except those two, for Canada. Also her sons giving the same intelligence, so we had no reason to think, but that it was true.

¹ [who]

* Norridgewock. See note 1, on page 287.
† The river Mississippi I suppose was meant.

Colonel Church having done what he could there, embarked on board the transports, and went to Mountdesart. [He] found no ships there, but a rundlet, rid off by a line in the harbour, which he ordered to be taken up. And opening of it, found a letter, which gave him an account that the ships were gone home for Boston.

Then he proceeded and went to Penobscot. Where being come, [they] made diligent search in those parts for the enemy; but could not find, or make any discovery of them; or that any had been there, since he left those parts; which caused him to believe what De Boisses' wife had told him was true.

I will, only by the way, just give a hint of what we heard since, of the effects of this expedition, and then proceed. First, that the English forces that went next to Norrigwock, found that the enemy was gone, and had left their rough household stuff, and corn behind them.*

Also, not long after this expedition, there were several gentlemen† sent down from Canada, to con-

---

* Reference is here made, it is thought, to the expedition under Col. Hilton, in the winter of 1705. He with 250 English, and 20 Indians (Dr. Douglass says he had but 220 men) repaired to Norridgewock on snow shoes, but found no enemies to contend with. They burned the deserted wigwams, and a chapel, and then returned. See Belknap, I, 268, and Penhallow, 28.

About the same time an express was ordered with snow shoes for the frontiers, but was intercepted by a scout from Montreal, who robbed him of 50 pounds in money; which, on being taken to Canada, the Governour converted it into a bowl, and called it the Newengland gift. Ib., or N. H. Hist. Soc. Col. I, 43.

† Hutchinson, II, 141, sub anno 1706, mentions that 4 or 5 persons were sent to Canada " for the exchange of prisoners, who brought back Mr. Williams, the minister, and many of the inhabitants of Deerfield, with other captives." He mentions no more than one's being sent from Canada, and that, after ours had been sent there. Hence it appears that he was not very well acquainted with the affair; for Penhallow's history was extant before he wrote, who gives the particulars about it, viz., that on " the 4 May 1705, Capt. Hill,

cert with our Governour about the settling of a cartel for the exchange of prisoners; and that the Governour* of Canada has never since sent down an army upon our frontiers, (that I know of) except sometimes a scout of Indians to take some prisoners, that he might be informed of our state, and what we were acting, &c. And always took care that the prisoners so taken, should be civilly treated, and safely returned, as I have been informed. [Also,] that some of the prisoners that were taken gave an account [to this effect;] so that we have great cause to believe, that the message [which] Colonel Church sent by the two French gentlemen from Menis, to the Governour of Portroyal, took effect, and was a means to bring peace in our borders, &c.

Then Colonel Church with his forces embarked on board the transports, and went to Casco bay, where they met with Captain Gallop, in a vessel from Boston, who had brought Colonel Church further orders; which were, to send some of his forces up to Norrigwock, in pursuit of the enemy. But he being sensible that the enemy were gone from thence, and that his soldiers were much worn out, and fatigued in the hard service they had already done, and wanted to get home, [he] called a council, and agreed, all to go home; which, accordingly they did.

To conclude this expedition, I will just give a hint of some treatment,† [which] Colonel Church had be-

---

who was formerly taken at Wells and carried to Canada, was from thence sent to concert the exchange of prisoners." He gave information that there were about 187 English prisoners with the French and Indians. "Upon the advice hereof," the persons mentioned by Hutchinson, were sent to Canada, and succeeded in rescuing about 60 captives. The French Governour was kept in suspense by the management of Governour Dudley. He wished for a neutrality, and during the time, the frontiers enjoyed peace and tranquillity. Hutchinson, ib.

* Vaudreuil.

† It appears that Church was censured wrongfully, and for some time, bore the faults, due only to others. For it

fore and after he came home. For all his great expenses, fatigues and hardships, in and about this expedition, viz., he received of his excellency *fifteen pounds*, as an earnest penny, towards raising volunteers. And after he came to receive his debenture for his Colonel's pay, there were *two shillings and four pence* due to him. And as for his Captain's pay* and man Jack; he has never received any thing as yet.

Also, after he came home, some ill minded persons did their endeavour to have taken away his life; for there were some of the French enemy killed,† [in] this expedition. But his excellency the Governour, the honourable council, and the house of representatives, saw cause to clear him, and gave him thanks for his good service done.‡

---

was generally thought by the people, that Col. Church went on this expedition, for the express purpose of reducing Portroyal, as it was, by the government, styled the "Portroyal expedition," or, as entered on the council books " an expedition to Portroyal," not knowing that he was strictly ordered to the contrary; therefore, we are not surprised that he should be blamed, until the truth should be known. The Governour was accused of preserving that place to benefit himself by an illegal trade with the inhabitants. However this may be, he excused himself by saying, that he had no orders from the Queen to go against it ; and that her Majesty was to send over in the spring, a force expressly for that purpose, as has been previously stated in this history.

* It will be recollected that he was commissioned Colonel and Captain at the same time, and in the same warrant.

† See page 265. Some of the enemy that would not surrender.

‡ Thus ends the military achievements of the justly celebrated BENJAMIN CHURCH. [The reader is requested to correct an errour in Dr Douglass' History, I, 557, 8, where he observes, that Col. Church made an expedition in 1707–8; it was Col. March.]

APPENDIX

I.—SOME ACCOUNT OF THE EARLY VOYAGES TO, AND SETTLEMENTS IN NORTH AMERICA, AND THE TREATMENT OF THE INDIANS BY THOSE VOYAGERS.

As early as 1508, the natives of North America began to be carried away by voyagers, sometimes by force, and sometimes by flattery. At this early period, one Aubert, a Frenchman, sailed up the river St. Lawrence, and on his return to France, conveyed off a number of the natives.* In 1585, a colony was sent out from England, under the direction of Sir Walter Ralegh, and was settled at Roanoke. This was the first English colony planted in America.† Through their misconduct to the natives, and to one another, they found themselves in a miserable condition before the end of a year. Sir Francis Drake returning that way from a cruise against the Spaniards, gave them a passage to England in his fleet. Just before the arrival of Drake, a chief, and many of his men were killed, and afterwards an Indian town was burned, by order of Sir Richard Grenville, who brought supplies to the colonists.

In 1602, Bartholomew Gosnold sailed from England, and was the first Englishman that came in a direct course to this part of America.‡ He fell in with the coast near Cape Cod, which he discovered. Being met near the shore, by the natives in their ca-

---
* American Annals, I, 37.   † Ib. I, 119.
‡ Belknap, Biog. I, 231.

noes, was kindly treated by them, and they helped him load his vessels.*

The next year, Martin Pring arrived on the coast, and collected a cargo of Sassafras.† The Indians appeared hostile to this company, and caused them to leave the coast, sooner than they would otherwise have done. But this was not without a cause. A canoe had been stolen from them, and they were sported with by the sailors, who, to get rid of them, when they had amused themselves sufficiently, would set their dogs to chase them away.

In 1605, Captain George Weymouth carried off five of the natives from the coast of Newengland, against their consent; one of whom was a chief.

In 1607, the first permanent colony of Virginia arrived in the Chesapeak, the twentysixth of April, and the thirteenth of May, they took a position for a town; which, soon after, in honour of King James, was named James Town. They were annoyed by the Indians at first, and one person was killed. A peace was concluded in June following, but it was of short duration. An attempt, also, to settle a colony on Kennebeck river was made this year, but was relinquished the next.‡

In 1614, Captain John Smith made a profitable voyage to Newengland, and made an accurate survey of its coast. The Newengland Indians, in this voyage, were justly incensed against the English, to a great degree. When Smith went for England, he left one Hunt to complete his cargo of fish. This perfidious man enticed twentyfour Indians on board his vessel, put them in confinement, and sold them at Malaga, to the Spaniards, for slaves. In the course of the year, another vessel came on the coast to trade with two of those taken off by Hunt, to assist in the

---

* Sassafras and furs were then the articles of exportation.

† See Belknap's life of Pring. Sassafras was collected about the islands. Pring found it on what is now Edgar town.

‡ See page 171 and note 5.

business. It was now designed to settle a trading house, but the Indians soon discouraged them in the attempt. One of the prisoners had died, and the other was not permitted to go on shore. But some approached the ship under pretence of trade, and he jumped overboard. His friends in the canoes discharged their arrows so thick at the same time, that in defiance of the English guns, they got him on board, and paddled off. A number of the English were badly wounded, and some of the Indians killed. The English were discouraged, and sailed for England.* Two other natives, carried away by Hunt, found means, in time, to get back to Newengland, and in some measure, allayed the vengeance of their countrymen; by assuring them that the English, in general, were highly displeased at the conduct of Captain Hunt.†

These, and many other insults on the Indians though small, in comparison with those suffered by their race in South America, were more than enough to cause them to entertain fearful apprehensions of every stranger.

Before 1619, perhaps it would have been altogether impracticable to have attempted a settlement in Newengland, without great risk. The natives, before which, were extremely numerous and warlike; but this year,‡ a mortal sickness prevailed among them, that almost entirely desolated the country; insomuch, that the living could not bury the dead. For when the Pilgrims arrived at Plymouth, the ground was strewed with human bones. The extent of this pestilence was from Penobscot to Narraganset.§

---

* American Annals, I, 184, 185.   † Hist. N. H. I, 10, 11.

‡ It is not certain that this plague happened in 1619, though from Johnson and others cited by Holmes, (I, 207, 208,) it appears probable. Morton, 25, says that it was two or three years before the settlement of Plymouth. Prince. Chron. 119, thinks this plague raged as early as 1616 or 17.

§ Prince, Chron. 138, and Belknap, Biog. I, 356.

II.—ORIGIN OF THE SETTLEMENT OF NEWENGLAND.

BIGOTRY and superstition began to lose some ground in England, as early as 1550. And the persecutions, and sufferings of the early martyrs of religious freedom, have been the subject of many massy volumes. In 1549, a liturgy had been prepared by the bishops, and a law passed both houses of Parliament, " that all divine offices should be performed according to it."* The clergy were ordered to conform to the liturgy, under pain of fines and imprisonment. And, as has always since been the case, among all sects, the new sect, then denominated *Puritans*, grew more numerous, in proportion, as the severity of persecution increased.

In 1607, a congregation fled from England into Holland, and in 1608, were joined by others, and a church was there established, according, as they believed, to the principles of the primitive church of Christ; having Mr. John Robinson for their pastor. Their removal from England into Holland, was attended with the greatest difficulties, and though overlooked by the chief historians, who have written upon their history, is certainly among the first articles that should be related. It formed a part of a Manuscript History, written by Mr. William Bradford, one of their number, which, though since lost†, was in possession of Governour Hutchinson, who copied this valuable part into his "summary of the affairs of the colony of New Plymouth,"‡ which is as follows.

"There was a large company of them proposed to get passage at Boston in Lincolnshire, and for that

---

* Holmes' Annals, I, 50.

† At least, it has not been seen since 1775, when the British *Vandals* under Gen. Gage, in a sacrilegious manner, disturbed the contents of the old south church, where it was deposited.

‡ In his Hist Mass. II, No. I Appendix

APPENDIX. 291

end had hired a ship wholly to themselves, and made agreement with the master to be ready at a certain day, and take them and their goods in at a convenient place, where accordingly they would all attend in readiness. So after long waiting and large expense, though he kept not day with them, yet he came at length and took them in, in the night. But when he had them and their goods aboard he betrayed them, having beforehand complotted with the searchers and other officers so to do, who took them and put them into open boats, and then rifled and ransacked them, searching them to their shirts for money, yea, even the women, further than became modesty, and then carried them back into the town, and made them a spectacle and wonder to the multitude, which came flocking on all sides to behold them. Being thus, first by the catch-poles, rifled and stript of their money, books, and much other goods, they were presented to the magistrates, and messengers sent to inform the lords of the council of them, and so they were committed to ward. Indeed the magistrates used them courteously, and showed them what favour they could, but could not deliver them till order came from the council table; but the issue was, that after a month's imprisonment, the greatest part were dismissed, and sent to the places from whence they came, but seven of the principal men were still kept in prison and bound over, to the assizes. The next spring after, there was another attempt made, by some of these and others, to get over at another place. And so it fell out, that they light of a Dutchman at Hull, having a ship of his own belonging to Zealand. They made agreement with him, and acquainted him with their condition, hoping to find more faithfulness in him, than in the former of their own nation. He bade them not fear, for he would do well enough. He was by apppointment to take them in, between Grindstone* and Hull, where was a large

---
* Grimsby says Belknap.

common, a good way distant from any town. Now against the prefixed time, the women and children, with the goods, were sent to the place in a small bark, which they had hired for that end, and the men were to meet them by land; but it so fell out, that they were there a day before the ship came, and the sea being rough and the women very sick, prevailed with the seamen to put into a creek hard by, where they lay on ground at low water. The next morning the ship came, but they were fast and could not stir till about noon. In the mean time, the ship master perceiving how the matter was, sent his boat to get the men aboard, whom he saw ready, walking about the shore, but after the first boat-full was got aboard, and she was ready to go for more, the master espied a great company both horse and foot, with bills and guns and other weapons, for the country was raised to take them. The Dutchman seeing that, swore his country oath, '*Sacramente*,' and having the wind fair, weighed anchor, hoisted sails, and away. After enduring a fearful storm at sea, for fourteen days or more, seven whereof they never saw sun, moon nor stars, and being driven near the coast of Norway, they arrived at their desired haven, where the people came flocking, admiring their deliverance, the storm having been so long and sore, in which much hurt had been done, as the master's friends related to him in their congratulations. The rest of the men that were in greatest danger, made a shift to escape away before the troop could surprise them, those only staying that best might be assisting unto the women. But pitiful it was to see the heavy case of these poor women in distress; what weeping and crying on every side, some for their husbands that were carried away in the ship, others not knowing what should become of them and their little ones, crying for fear and quaking with cold. Being apprehended, they were hurried from one place to another, till in the end they knew not what to do with them; for, to imprison so

APPENDIX. 293

many women with their innocent children for no other cause, many of them, but that they would go with their husbands, seemed to be unreasonable, and all would cry out of them; and to send them home again was as difficult, for they alleged, as the truth was, they had no homes to go to, for they had either sold or otherwise disposed of their houses and livings: To be short, after they had been thus turmoiled a good while, and conveyed from one constable to another, they were glad to be rid of them in the end upon any terms, though, in the mean time, they, poor souls, endured misery enough."

After remaining several years in Holland, they began to fear that their company would finally become lost, by their connexion with the Dutch; and that their efforts to establish the true religion, also lost. Some of their young men had already engaged in the military service of the Dutch, and marriages with their young women had taken place. These things caused much grief to the pious Forefathers; more especially, because the Dutch were dissolute in their morals.

Under these considerations, their thoughts were turned towards America; but, never so far north as Newengland. Sir Walter Ralegh was about this time,* projecting a settlement in Guiana, and this place was first taken under consideration. Here a perpetual spring was promised, and all the beauties of a tropical summer. But considering the diseases which were so fatal to Europeans, and their near vicinity to the Spaniards,† the majority were against a removal thither.

At length, they resolved to make their settlement in north Virginia,‡ and accordingly they sent agents

---

* 1617.

† The Spaniards had not actually taken possession of this country, but claimed it. Belknap, Biog. II, 167.

‡ North America was then known under the general names of north and south Virginia, divided by the parallel of 40 d.

to England, to obtain a grant from the Virginia company, and to know whether the King would grant them liberty of conscience, in that distant country. The Virginia company were willing to grant them such privileges as were in their power, but the bigotted James would agree no further, than " to connive at them, provided they should conduct peaceably."*

The agents returned the next year, 1618, to the great discouragement of the congregation. Resolved, however, to make another trial, agents were sent again the next year, and after long and tedious delays,† a grant was obtained, under the seal of the company, which, after all this great trouble and expense, was never used.‡

Notwithstanding, their removal was not given up, and they made ready for their voyage, with what expedition they could. It was agreed that a part should go before, to prepare the way; and, accordingly, two ships were got ready, one named the Speedwell, of sixty tons, the other the Mayflower, of one hundred and eight tons. They first went from Leyden to England, and on the fifth of August, 1620, they left Southampton for America;§ but, they were twice forced to return, by reason of the bad state of the lesser ship.

It was now agreed to dismiss the Speedwell, and they embarked on board the Mayflower, and, on the *sixth of September*, again sailed on their intended voyage.‖

N. Prince, 180. Its whole extent was from Florida to the bay of Fundy.

* Belknap, Biog. II, 170. American Annals, I, 198.

† Occasioned by dissensions among the Virginia company. One treasurer having resigned was displeased with his successor. See Bradford in Prince, 151, 153.

‡ Because it was taken out in the name of a gentleman, whom " providence" separated from them.

§ They intended to have settled somewhere near Hudson's river.

‖ The last port they left was Plymouth.

APPENDIX. 295

Such were the transactions, and such the difficulties, attending this persevering company of Pilgrims, (as they are truly called) in the great attempt, to settle a colony in America. As no particulars are preserved of their voyage, we may now leave them until they appear on the coast.*

III.—LANDING OF THE PILGRIMS AT PLYMOUTH.

AFTER some difficulties, in a voyage of two months and three days, they fell in with the land of Cape Cod, on the ninth of November. Finding themselves further north than they intended to settle, they stood to the southward; but soon finding themselves nearly encompassed with dangerous shoals, the Captain† took advantage of their fears, and bore up again for the cape; and, on the tenth of November, anchored in cape Cod harbour.‡

On observing their latitude, they found themselves out of the limits of the south Virginia company. Upon which it was hinted by some, that they should now be under no laws, and every servant would have as much authority as his master. But the wisdom that had conducted them hither, was sufficient to provide against this evil; therefore, an instrument was drawn and signed, by which they unanimously formed themselves into a body politic. This instrument was executed November the eleventh, and signed by fortyone persons; that being the number of men, qualified to act for themselves. Their whole number

---

* It is related that in a storm a beam of the ship was thrown out of its place, and that they began to despair, but some gentleman having a large iron screw, by means of which it was again forced into its place.

† Jones.

‡ The Captain of the ship was hired by the Dutch to land them thus far north, because they claimed the country at Hudson's river, and were unwilling that the English should get any footing there. See Morton, 13.

consisted of *One hundred and one.** John Carver was chosen Governour for one year.

---

* As it must be ever gratifying to posterity to know the first form of government ever drawn up in their country, and the names of those who first ventured upon the great undertaking, both are here presented to their view, as I find them in Mr. Prince's N. Eng. Chronology. In my first edition I copied from Morton, but on account of some errours in the names of the signers as given in his Newengland's Memorial I copy from Mr. Prince. However, it is possible that some small errours may exist, even in his list; for we know, that the chirography of 1620, was vastly different from that a hundred years after; insomuch, that what Mr. Morton read for an *r*, might have been taken afterward for a *t* by Mr. Prince, &c., as will appear by comparing those names, in which a difference is seen. Mr. Morton writes No. 25, John Craxton, No. 27, Joses Fletcher, No. 29, Digery Priest, No. 34, Richard Bitteridge, and No. 40, Edward Doten. He also has No. 32, Edmund Morgeson, but that I suppose to be a misprint. Both of those authors copied from Gov. Bradford's MS., as Hutchinson perhaps did, who differs from both. He writes Nos. 15 and 16, Tilley, No. 20, Ridgsdale, No. 25, Croxton, No. 37, Gardner. But the most unaccountable differences exist between authors who have copied from Mr. Prince's printed book. I need not name any one, in particular, as all that I have met with, differ in some respect, except the Editors of the N. H. Hist. Collections, who seem to have been particularly careful.

"In the name of God, Amen. We, whose names are under written the loyal subjects of our dread sovereign Lord King James, by the grace of God, of Great Britain, France and Ireland, King, defender of the faith, &c.

Having undertaken for the glory of God, and advancement of the christian faith, and honour of our King and country, a voyage to plant the first colony in the northern parts of Virginia, do by these presents, solemnly and mutually in the presence of God, and one of another, covenant and combine ourselves together, into a civil body politick, for our better ordering and preservation, and fartherance of the ends aforesaid; and by virtue hereof, to enact, constitute, and frame such just and equal laws, ordinances, acts, constitutions, and offices, from time to time, as shall be thought most meet and convenient for the general good of the colony. Unto which we promise all due submission and obedience. In witness whereof we have hereunder subscribed our names at cape Cod, the 11th of November, in the year of the reign of our sovereign Lord, King James, of England, France and Ire-

APPENDIX. 297

The day answering to the *Eleventh of December*, is celebrated as the day of the landing of the Pilgrims;* but on that day, a place was discovered, and fixed upon for their settlement. Parties before had landed and made some discoveries.

The same day that the memorable instrument was signed, a party left the ship, and landed to explore the country, and get wood, but returned without making any particular discovery. But a few days after, (November fifteenth) sixteen men, under Captain Myles Standish, were permitted to go in search

land, the XVIII, and of Scotland the LIV. Anno Domini, 1620."

No.		No.	
1 Mr. John Carver,*		8	23 Francis Eaton,*	3
2 William Bradford,*	2	24 James Chilton,*§	3
3 Mr. Edward Winslow,*	5	25 John Crackston,§	2
4 Mr. Wm. Brewster,*	6	26 John Billington,*	4
5 Mr. Isaac Allerton,*	6	27 Moses Fletcher,§	1
6 Capt. Miles Standish,*	2	28 John Goodman,§	1
7 John Alden,	1	29 Degory Priest,§	1
8 Mr. Samuel Fuller,†	2	30 Thomas Williams,§	1
9 Mr. Christopher Martin*§	4	31 Gilbert Winslow,	1
10 Mr. Wm. Mullins,*§	5	32 Edmund Margeson,§	1
11 Mr. Wm. White,*§	5	33 Peter Brown,	1
12 Mr. Richard Warren,†	1	34 Richard Britterige,§	1
13 John Howland, (*in Carver's family.*)		35 George Soule, (*of Mr. Winslow's family.*)	
14 Mr. Stephen Hopkins,*	8	36 Richard Clark,§	1
15 Edward Tilly,*§	4	37 Richard Gardiner,	1
16 John Tilly,*§	3	38 John Allerton,§	1
17 Francis Cook,†	2	39 Thomas English,§	1
18 Thomas Rogers,§	2	40 Edward Dorey, ⎫	
19 Thomas Tinker,*§	3	41 Edward Leister, ⎭	
20 John Ridgdale,*§	2	(*both of Mr. Hopkins family.*)	
21 Edward Fuller,*§	3		
22 John Turner,§	3		101

The above names having this mark * at the end brought their wives with them. Those with this † did not. Those with this § died before the end of March. The figures at the end of the names denote the number in each family.

* To reduce old style to new, eleven days are added; therefore, the 22 December is celebrated as the landing of the Forefathers.

of a convenient place for settlement. They saw five Indians whom they followed all day, but could not overtake them. The next day they discovered several Indian graves; one of which they opened, and found some rude implements of war; a mortar, and an earthen pot; all which they took care to replace; being unwilling to disturb the sepulchres of the dead. They found under a small mound of earth, a cellar curiously lined with bark, in which was stored a quantity of Indian corn.* Of this they took as much as they could carry, and returned to the ship.

Soon after, twentyfour others made the like excursion, and obtained a considerable quantity of corn, which, with that obtained before, was about ten bushels.† Some beans were also found.‡ This discovery gave them great encouragement, and perhaps prevented their further removal; it also saved them from famine.

After considerable discussion, concerning a place for settlement, in which some were for going to Agawam,§ and some not so far, it was concluded to send out a shallop, to make further discovery in the bay. Accordingly, Governour Carver, with eighteen or twenty men, set out on the sixth of December, to explore the deep bay of Cape Cod. The weather was very cold, and the spray of the sea lighting on them, they were soon covered with ice, as it were, like coats of mail. At night having got to the bottom of the bay, they discovered ten or twelve Indians, about a league off, cutting up a grampus; who, on

---

"*Of divers colours which seemed to them a very goodly sight, having seen none before." Morton, 18.

† Holmes' Annals, I, 201.

‡ This was not hardly right, perhaps, but Morton, N. E. Memorial, 19, says, that in "About six months after they gave them full satisfaction to their content."

§ Ipswich is supposed to have been meant, as it was known by that name in a former voyage.

APPENDIX. 299

discovering the English, ran away with what of the fish they had cut off. With some difficulty from shoals, they landed, and erected a hut, and passed the first night. In the morning they divided their company, some went by land, and others in the vessel, to make further discovery of the bay, to which they gave the name of Grampus, because that fish was found there. They met again at night, and some lodged on board the shallop, and the rest as before.*

The next morning, December the eighth, as they were about to embark, they were furiously beset by Indians. Some of the company having carried their guns down to the boat, the others discharged upon them, as fast as they could; but the Indians shouted, and rushed on, until those had regained their arms, and then they were put to flight. One, however, more courageous than the rest, took a position behind a tree, and withstood several volleys of shot, discharging arrows himself at the same time. At length a shot glancing upon the side of the tree, hurled the bark so about his head that he thought it time to escape. Eighteen arrows were picked up by the English, after the battle, which they sent to their friends in England, as curiosities. Some were headed with brass, and others with horn and bone. The place where this happened, was on this account, called the *First Encounter*.†

The company, after leaving this place, narrowly escaped being cast away; but they got safe on an uninhabited island,‡ where they passed the night.

---

* Morton and Belknap.

† Morton, 22. It was before called Namskeket. Ib. 21. Dr. Belknap, Biog. II, 202, says, "A creek which now bears the name of *Skakit*, lies between Eastham and Harwich; distant about 3 or 4 miles westward from *Nauset*; the seat of a tribe of Indians, who (as they afterwards learned) made this attack."

‡ This they called "Clark's Island, because Mr. Clark, the master's mate, first stepped ashore thereon." Morton, 24.

The next day, December the ninth, they dried their clothes, and repaired their vessel, which had lost her mast, and met with other damage. The next day they rested, it being Sunday. The day following, they found a place, which they judged fit for settlement; and, after going on shore,*´ and discovering good water, and where there had been cornfields, returned to the ship. This was on the *Eleventh of December*, 1620, and is the day celebrated as the Forefathers' Day.

On the fifteenth, the ship came into the new harbour. The two following days, the people went on shore, but returned at night to the ship.

On the twentythird, timber was begun to be prepared for building a common store house.† The next day, the cry of Indians was heard, but none appeared. On the twentyfifth, the first house was begun. A fort was built on the hill, soon after, (where the burying ground now is) which commanded the town and harbour; and, they were diligently employed, until a town was laid out; to which they gave the name Plymouth, on account of the kind treatment they received from the people of Plymouth in

---

* A large rock near the water, said to be the place where they first stepped ashore, is shown with a degree of veneration by the inhabitants of Plymouth. It is a granite of a redish cast, and has long since been nearly levelled with the surface of the ground. A large fragment has been placed near the head of the main street, where it is made a rendezvous for boys in pleasant evenings. This, as well as the part from which it was taken, suffers occasionally under the force of a dull axe, to add to the entertainment of the story of the traveller.

† Their provisions and goods were held in common by the company, at first, but it was soon found by the wise leaders, that this method was not practicable, and it was soon dropped. Perhaps the chief mover of this wise measure was Gov. Bradford, as it was adopted in his administration. See Belknap, Biog. II, 232, 3.

England, and that being the place in their native country from which they last sailed.*

In January, 1621, their store house took fire, and was nearly consumed. Most of the people now were sick, and Governour Carver and Mr. Bradford were confined in the store house, when it took fire. In March, an Indian came boldly into the town, and saluted them with these words, "Welcome Englishmen! Welcome Englishmen!" This was uttered in broken English, but was clearly understood. His name was Samoset, and he came from the eastward, where he had been acquainted with some fishermen, and had learned some of their language. They treated him with kindness, and he informed them, that the great Sachem, Massassoit,† was coming to visit them; and, told them of one Squanto, that was well acquainted with the English language. He left them, and soon after returned, in company with Massassoit, and Squanto.‡ This Indian continued with the English as long as he lived, and was of infinite service to them. He showed them how to cultivate corn, and other American productions.

About this time, (beginning of April) Governour Carver died. Soon after, Mr. William Bradford was chosen. The mortality that began soon after their arrival, had before the end of March, carried off fortyfour of their number.

Such was the beginning of NEWENGLAND, which is now, alone, a formidable nation. At the death of the first Governour, it contained *Fiftyseven* Europe-

---

* It is remarkable that Captain Smith had called this place Plymouth in his map of Newengland. Dr. Belknap says, that it was partly on this account that it was now so called.

† For the particulars of Massassoit's visit to the Pilgrims. see page 133, and note 1.

‡ He was one of those carried off by Hunt, (see page 288) and got from Malaga to England; and was entertained by a gentleman in London, who employed him to Newfoundland, and other parts. He was at last brought into these parts by Mr. Thomas Dermer. Morton, 27, 28.

an inhabitants, and at the end of two hundred years, it contained upwards of one million six hundred thousand.

As it was my design, only to accompany the Pilgrims until they were seated in the wilderness, I shall now dismiss the engaging subject, with a short reflection.

Perhaps the annals of the world do not furnish a parallel to the first peopling of Newengland; as it respects purity of intention, judgment and fortitude in its execution, and in sustaining for a series of years, a government, that secured the happiness of all. An object of admiration, justly increasing on every succeeding generation, in proportion to the remoteness of time. Founded on the genuineness of those authorities, who, without the least shade of fable, have transmitted to us their true history: rendered peculiarly interesting, from its minuteness of detail, even beyond what could have been expected. Insomuch, that no one can read, without the deepest interest in their situations; and seeming, as it were, to live over those days with them, and to gain a perfect acquaintance with a Carver, a Bradford, a Winslow, and, indeed, the whole train of worthies.

IV.—HISTORY OF THE PEQUOT WAR.

While the number of English inhabitants was small, their troubles with the Indians were easily settled. But as is natural to mankind, as they increased in numbers and wealth, they were too proud to court the favour of the natives. And notwithstanding, great tribute is due to the memory of our venerable forefathers, for their almost unexampled resolution, perseverance, and above all, fortitude and wisdom, yet they were men, and accountable only as men.

"There was a nation of Indians in the southern parts of Newengland, called Pequods seated on a fair navigable river,* twelve miles to the eastward of the mouth of the great and famous river of Connecticut; who (as was commonly reported about the time when Newengland was first planted by the English) being a more fierce, cruel, and warlike people than the rest of the Indians, came down out of the more inland parts of the continent, and by force, seized upon one of the goodliest places, near the sea, and became a terror to all their neighbours, on whom they had exercised several acts of inhuman cruelty; insomuch, that being flushed with victories over their fellow Indians, they began to thirst after the blood of foreigners, English and Dutch,† that accidentally came amongst them, in a way of trade or upon other accounts.

"In the year 1634, they treacherously and cruelly murdered Captain Stone‡ and Captain Norton,§ who came occasionally with a bark into the river to trade with them. Not long after within the compass of the next year,|| they in like treacherous manner, slew one Mr. Oldham,¶ (formerly belonging to New Plymouth, but at that time an inhabitant of Massachusetts) at Block island,** a place not far from the mouth of their harbour, as he was fairly trading with them."††

---

* Mystic river.

† Some of the Dutch that belonged to Manhattans, now Newyork, had a trading house on Connecticut river, and in some difficulties with the Indians some were killed.

‡ Captain Stone was from St. Christophers, and came to trade in Connecticut river at the Dutch house. Hist. Con. I, 70.

§ Norton was of Massachusetts and killed the same time. Ib. || It was in 1636.

¶ Some difficulty was occasioned with Mr. Oldham, on account of religious matters, and he was banished out of Massachusetts, but was afterward permitted to return. For a valuable memoir of him, see Mr. Savage's edition of Winthrop's Hist. I, 80.

** About 20 miles S. S. W. of Newport, R. I.

†† Hubbard's Narrative.

How much cause the Indians had for these outrages we cannot tell; they say, that captain Stone surprised some of their men, and forced them to pilot him up the river, and that on his coming ashore, with two others, was killed while asleep. The English account is as follows. Having entered the river, Stone hired some Indians to pilot two of his men up the river, who at night went on shore to sleep, and were murdered by their pilots. About a dozen of those Indians, who had been trading with Captain Stone, went on board his vessel, and murdered him, as he lay asleep in his cabin, and threw a covering over him. The men were murdered as they appeared, one after another, except captain Norton, who defended himself in the cook's room, until some powder that he had in an open vessel for the quick loading of his gun, took fire, and so burned him that he could resist no longer.

Mr. John Oldham was murdered at Block island by some of them, or at least the murderers were sheltered by them. One Gallop, in his passage from Connecticut, discovered Mr. Oldham's vessel, and on coming near, found the deck to be covered with Indians. Gallop now suspected that they had killed Mr. Oldham. He hailed them, and they gave no answer, but made off as fast as they could; he made for them, and was soon up with them; fired among them, and drove all from the deck. His crew being small, would not venture to board, and so stood off and took the force of the wind, and ran down upon them, and nearly overset their vessel. Six of them were so frightened, that they leaped overboard and were drowned. He again stood off, and so lashed his anchor, that when he came down upon them again, it bored through the bows of the Indians' vessel, and four or five more jumped overboard and were lost. The vessels now stuck fast together, and they fought side by side, until they drove all below again; and then Gallop boarded them, and as they ventured up, were taken and bound. He not having places convenient to keep them all, threw one into the sea. They found the body of Mr. Oldham, covered over with a sail, with his head cleft to the brains. In this action, Gallop had with him but one man, and two boys. On board of Mr. Oldham's vessel were fourteen Indians; two or three of whom got in a hole below, and could not be drove from it. Captain Gallop then fastened the vessel to his, in order to take her in, but in a gale she was broken off and lost.

The same year, 1636, the government of Massachusetts sent Captain Endicott with ninety men to avenge these murders, in case the murderers were not delivered up, and restitution made for the losses sustained. The Narragansets, who had some hand in the murder, now submitted to the terms offered by the English. Captain Endicott proceeded to Block island, having with him Captain John Underhill, and Captain Nathaniel Turner. At their arrival they were met by about forty Indians, who all fled into thickets, where they could not be found. They burned sixty wigwams, and destroyed about two hundred acres of corn, and all their canoes, then sailed for the Pequot country. On their arrival in Pequot harbour,* several hundreds collected on the shore, but on learning the business of the English, fled into the woods. The men were landed on both sides of the river, and the Indians fired some arrows at them from behind the rocks and bushes. One or two of the enemy were killed, but no object was effected, and the troops returned to Boston.

Captain Underhill and twenty men were to proceed from thence to Saybrook fort, and strengthen it. But being wind bound, they went on shore to take some Indian corn, and were surprised by a large

---

* At the mouth of Pequot river, now called the river Thames.

body of the enemy, who fought them most of the afternoon. They, however, put the Indians to flight, and embarked on board their vessel. One man only was wounded, but they concluded that a number of the enemy were killed.

As nothing now was expected but war, the English took measures to secure the friendship of the Narragansets, which they effected. They had much to fear, in case they should join with the Pequots, being very numerous, their warriors being estimated at five thousand.

Endicott's ill success rather emboldened them than otherwise, and in the next April, 1637, six men were killed near Weathersfield, and several women were captivated. In all thirty had been killed since the first disturbances took place.

Vigorous measures were now resolved upon by the people of Connecticut, who raised ninety men; and shortly after, the other colonies united in the common cause.* The Connecticut troops, under Captain John Mason, on the tenth of May, accompanied by about seventy Mohegan Indians, under Uncas their Sachem, embarked down the river for Saybrook fort; where, after making proper arrangements, they

---

* The Massachusetts forces were on their march to join those of Connecticut, "when they were retarded by the most singular cause that ever influenced the operations of a military force. When they were mustered previous to their departure, it was found that some of the officers, as well as the private soldiers, were still under a covenant of works; and that the blessing of God could not be implored or expected to crown the arms of such unhallowed men with success. The alarm was general and many arrangements necessary in order to cast out the unclean, and to render this little band* sufficiently pure to fight the battles of a people who entertained high ideas of their own sanctity." Robertson's Hist. America, II, Book X. Thus while the Boston men were at war with the spirits of darkness, as they imagined, the Connecticut men under Mason were left alone to fight the more dangerous Pequots, as will presently be seen.

*Consisting of 200.

marched to Narraganset bay. Here they engaged a large body of the Narragansets, as auxiliaries, and then proceeded to Nihantic,* where they arrived, May twentyfourth.

The next morning they were joined by another body of the Narragansets, which made their Indian force amount to near five hundred men. After marching twelve miles, to Pawcatuck river, Captain Mason halted to refresh his men. The weather was extremely hot, and the men suffered very much. His Narraganset men now learning that they were going to attack the Pequot's chief fort, were greatly amazed, and the most of them returned home. One Wequash, a deserter from the Pequots, now piloted the army to a fort at Mystic. At night they encamped by two large rocks,† and two hours before day, made ready to attack the fort. They yet had two miles to march, which took them until near the dawn of day. The fort was on the top of a hill, and no time must be lost in making the attack. Their friend Indians now chiefly deserted them, and they divided themselves into two divisions, for the benefit of attacking them in two particular points. The party under Mason pressed on to the east side, while that under Captain Underhill gained the west. As Mason approached the palisades, a dog gave the alarm, and an Indian cried out " *Owanux!* *Owanux!*" that is, " Englishmen! Englishmen!" Being now discovered, they instantly discharged through the palisades, and then rushed into the fort sword in hand. Here the battle was severe, and for some time doubtful. As the moment grew more critical, Mason thought of the last expedient, and cried out, " We must burn them! We must burn them!" and taking a brand of fire, communicated it to the mats, with which the wigwams were covered, they were all in a blaze in a

---

* In Lyme.

†"Between two large rocks in Groton, since called Porter's rocks." Trumbull, I, 83.

moment. The English then formed a circle about the fort, and all that ventured out to escape the flames, were immediately shot down. Dreadful now was the work of death. Some perishing in the flames, others climbing over the palisades, were no sooner up than shot down. Uncas, in the mean time, had come up and formed a circle in the rear, and in a little more than an hour, the work was complete. Six or seven hundred Indians were slain, and but two of the English, and sixteen wounded.

The army now began the retreat, and a body of the enemy were soon seen in pursuit; but a few shot kept them at a distance. This body of the enemy had not been in the battle, and on arriving at the fort, and beholding the dismal spectacle, beat the ground with rage, and tore their hair in despair.

The English arrived at their homes in about three weeks from the time they set out, and the people were greatly rejoiced at their success.

Sassacus, the chief of the Pequots, and most of his people, now fled and left their country. But after some time, it was discovered, that a great body of them were in a swamp to the westward. Troops, therefore, were sent from Massachusetts, who joined others from Connecticut, and they immediately marched under the command of the valiant Mason, in pursuit of them. On the thirteenth of July they arrived at the fatal swamp. Some of the English rushed in, but were badly wounded, and rescued with difficulty. At length they surrounded the swamp, and the fight continued through the most of the night. By the help of a thick fog, many of the warriours escaped. About twenty were killed, and one hundred and eighty captivated, who were divided among the Narragansets and Mohegans. Sassacus, with a few of his chief men, fled to the Mohawks, who, at the request of the Narragansets, cut off his

APPENDIX.

head; and thus terminated the Pequot war.* Nothing of great moment occurred until the time of Philip.

V.—REMAINS OF PHILIP'S WAR.

It is intended here, to narrate the most important circumstances in the progress of that war at the eastward, in Maine and Newhampshire.

It was generally thought, that Philip had excited all of the Indians throughout Newengland, to rise with him in the war. While this has been doubted by some, others think it probable, that his endeavours were used even among the distant tribes of Virginia.† However this might have been, it is certain, that within twenty days from the time the war began in Swanzey, it began to blaze at the distance of two hundred miles, even at the northeasterly extremity of Newengland. But the war at the eastward is said to have grown out of the foolish conduct of some of the inhabitants. An insult was offered to the wife of Squando, a chief Sachem on the river Saco. Some irregular sailors, having heard that young Indians could swim naturally, like those of the brute creation, met the wife of Squando with an infant child in a canoe, and to ascertain the fact, overset it. The child sunk to the bottom, but the mother diving down, immediately brought it up without apparent injury. However, it fell out, that the child died shortly after, and its death was imputed to the treatment it had received from the sailors. This so enraged the chief, that he only waited a fit time to commence hostilities. Other causes of the war were not wanting all along the eastern frontier. A letter was received at

---

* It was the reflection upon the fate of this once famous nation, that gave rise to those beautiful and sympathetick lines in Dwight's Greenfield hill, Part the fourth, which see in note 3 to page 146 of Philip's war.

† See Hubbard, Nar. 262.

Kennebeck, from York, the eleventh July, 1675, giving account of the war at the westward, and that means were using to disarm the natives along the shore. Had the Indians entertained no ideas of war before, they certainly would be justified in making war upon any that were about to deprive them of the means of self defence. How much have the Spartans, under Leonidas been celebrated for their answer to Xerxes, when he endeavoured to persuade them to give up their arms. But the English were not so generous as the Persian monarch, for he promised the Spartans a far better country than theirs, if they would comply. To which they replied, that no country was worth having unless won by valour; and, as to their arms, they should want them in any country. Perhaps the despised Indians deserve as much honour, in some instances, as the defenders of Thermopylæ.

In an attempt to force the Indians to deliver up their arms at Kennebeck, one belonging to the English came near being killed. This caused considerable tumult, but at length was settled, by promises and hostages on the part of the Indians. But through the supineness of their keepers, the hostages found means to escape; and, meeting with some of their fellows, proceeded to Pejepscot, where they plundered the house of one Purchase, an early planter, and known as a trader among them. The men were not at home, but no incivility was offered to the women. This was in September, 1675.

About twentyfive of the English marched out to take revenge for what had been done. They went up Casco bay, and landed near the mouth of the Androscoggin, where they had farms. On coming near the houses, "they heard a knocking," and presently saw some Indians; who it appears, were doing no harm; but without waiting to know, the English rushed on them, and some were killed. The Indians rallied, and wounded many of them before they could

APPENDIX. 311

gain their vesesls. Some it appears, even in those days, stood a little for the rights of the natives, and ventured to question the virtue of this action. "But," says Mr. Hubbard, "if this happened after the murder of old Mr. Wakely and family, the English can be blamed for nothing but their negligence."* But whether it was or not, does not appear.† The destruction of this family was horrid. Six persons, namely, the old gentleman, his son, and daughter in law, who was far advanced in pregnancy, and three grandchildren were killed, and mangled in a shocking manner. Some of them, when found the next day, were partly consumed in the flames of their dwelling, to which the Indians set fire when they drew off.

At Saco they met with a severe repulse, in an endeavour to take Major Phillips' garrison.‡ Captain Benython had got information by a friendly Indian, that something was intended against the place, so he retired into the garrison with Phillips. His house had not been deserted above an hour, when he saw it in flames. The savages soon crossed the river, and were seen skulking by the fences to get a shot at some about the garrison. Major Phillips went into a chamber to look out for the enemy, and was wounded. The Indians thought they had killed him, and openly began the attack; but their Captain being immediately shot down, they drew a little further off. They now employed a stratagem to fire the garrison. They took the large wheels, (used for lumbering, at a mill near by, which they burned) and erected a battery upon the axletree, then they ran it back by taking hold of the tongue or spear, very near the garrison; when one wheel stuck in the mud, and the

---

* Narrative, 269.
† Sullivan, Hist. Maine, 199, says it was in July, 1675, and that the name of the family was Wakefield.
‡ On Saturday, 18 September.

other rolling on, gave their helm an oblique direction, and they were all exposed to the fire of the English, They being in readiness, fired from every part of the fortification at once, killing and wounding about thirty. The rest gladly gave up the siege and fled. They next killed seven persons at Blue point, (Scarborough,) and burned twenty houses.* About the same time, five persons were killed by the same Indians, while going up Saco river. In the same month, they burned two houses at Oyster river, belonging to two families by the name of Chesly, killed two men passing in the river, and carried two captive. One Robinson and son were shot in the way between Exeter and Hampton, about this time. Within a few days, also, the house of one Tozer, at Newichwannock, was assaulted, wherein were fifteen women and children, all of whom except two, were saved by the intrepidity of a girl of eighteen. She first seeing the Indians, shut the door and stood against it, till the others escaped to the next house, which was better secured. The Indians chopped the door to pieces, then entering, knocked her down, and leaving her for dead, went in pursuit of the others; of whom, two children, who could not get over the fence, fell into their hands. The valiant heroine recovered of her wounds. The two next days, they showed themselves on both sides of the river, burned two houses and three barns, containing a great quantity of grain. And, at Oyster river, they burned five houses, and killed two men. The people were now determined to retaliate. About twenty young men, chiefly of Dover, obtained leave of Major Waldron, then commander of the militia, to hunt the enemy. Having divided themselves into small parties, one of these came upon five Indians in the woods, near a deserted house. Two of them were preparing a fire to roast corn, while the other three were gathering it. They were at a loss at first

---

* Sullivan, 215.

how to make their onset, as the Indians were the most numerous. But at length, concluded to creep up and knock the two on the head at the fire, without noise to alarm the others. The first part of their plan exactly succeeded, the two Indians being laid dead with the buts of their guns; but the others heard the blows and fled.

People in general, now retired to garrison houses, and the country was filled with consternation. October the seventh, Thursday, a man was shot off his horse, as he was riding between two garrisons at Newichwannock. Not far from the same place two others were shot dead the same day. About the same time, an old gentleman, by the name of Beard, was killed, and his head cut off and set upon a pole. This was at Oyster river. On Saturday, the sixteenth, about a hundred Indians appeared at Newichwannock, (Berwick now) a short distance from the upper garrison, where they killed one Tozer, and captured his son. The guns alarmed Lieutenant Plaisted at the next garrison, who, with seven men, went out on a discovery, but fell into an ambush; two or three were killed, and the others escaped to the garrison, where they were closely besieged. In this perilous situation, Lieutenant Plaisted wrote a letter to Major Waldron for help, but he was not able to afford any. The next day Plaisted ventured out with twenty men to bury the dead, but was again ambushed, and his men deserted him. He disdaining to fly, was killed upon the spot, with his eldest son, and one more. His other son died of his wounds. It appears that the Indians now drew off, for Captain Frost went up from Sturgeon creek, the next day, and buried the dead. The enemy next appeared at Sturgeon creek, about the latter end of the month, and attacked Captain Frost's house, which was preserved only by a stratagem. Frost had only three boys with him, but by giving orders in an imperious tone, for some to march here, and others to fire there, that the Indians thought he had a great many men, so went off and left him. The next day they appeared against Portsmouth, on the Kittery side, where they killed one man and burned his house. Some shot from a cannon being thrown among them from a battery on Portsmouth side, they thought best to disappear. A party of English pursued them, and recovered most of their plunder, but killed none. Soon after a house and two or three barns were burned at Quocheco, and three or four persons killed about Exeter and Lampreyeel river.

At Casco bay, Lieutenant Ingersol's son, with another man, were killed, while out hunting. Many houses were also burned. At Black point, Lieutenant Augur with his brother were killed. Captain Wincol of Newichwannock, marched this way for the relief of his friends, with about fourteen men. He soon had a skirmish with the enemy, and lost two or three of his men. Soon after, as they were marching along on the sea side, they were beset by a great body of Indians; but, chancing to get behind some timber, from whence they dealt with them with such effect, that they soon took to the woods, and the English escaped in a canoe. But nine men from Saco, having heard the firing, came out to assist their fellows, and fell into an ambush, and were all killed. Two persons were killed at Wells in the beginning of winter. At the same place, one Cross and one Isaac Cousins were also killed about a week after.

Depredations were suspended on account of the severity of winter. But before the suspension, upwards of fifty people had been killed and taken. In the mean time, a peace was concluded through the mediation of Major Waldron, which, says Mr. Hubbard, "might have remained firm enough to this day, had there not been too just an occasion given for the breaking of the same, by the wicked practice of some lewd persons which opened the door, and made way for the bringing in all those sad calamities and mischiefs, that have since fallen upon those parts of the country."

But this may be considered as the end of Philip's war in the east, although from other causes a war continued till 1678.

Many of Philip's Indians mixed with those at the eastward after the fall of that chief, in hopes of escaping detection. For they had seen even those who delivered themselves up, executed, therefore, they were apprised of their fate. Some that had killed Thomas Kimbal of Bradford, and carried off his family, soon after restored them with the hopes of pardon, but it being doubted whether this was a sufficient atonement for the whole, they (three of them) were thrown into Dover jail. The prisoners considering this only as a prelude to their future punishment, broke jail, and fled to join the Kennebeck and Androscoggin Indians. Through their influence another quarrel was begun.

The next remarkable occurrence was the capture of the four hundred Indians at Quocheco.* For other particulars the reader is referred to Mather's Magnalia, and Belknap's Newhampshire.

VI.—THE BOLD EXPLOIT OF HANNAH DUSTAN.

THIS took place in the latter part of *Castine's War*, or as others term it " *King William's War ;*" but as it is evident that Castine was the chief mover of it, it may very properly be called *Castine's War*.

On the fifth of March, 1698, the Indians made a descent on Haverhill in Massachusetts, in which they took and killed thirtynine persons, and burned about a half a dozen houses. In the onset, the house of a Mr. Dustan was fallen upon, and his wife, who had lain in but a week before, and her nurse, Mary Neff, were taken. Mr. Dustan was absent when the In-

---

* An account of the affair is given with the history of Major Waldron in the third note to page 161.

dians first appeared about the town, and on hearing the alarm, ran to the assistance of his family. Meeting seven of his children near his house, ordered them to run, and make their escape to some garrison in the town, while he entered the house with intent to help his wife escape. She left her bed at the warning, but the near approach of the Indians, would admit only of a flying retreat; this Mr. Dustan saw was impossible, from the weak state of his wife. A moment of horrour and despair brooded over him; in which he had to choose whether he would stay and suffer with her, or make his escape. He resolved on the latter, knowing that he could be no assistance to her, amidst an army of savages; and, that he might be to his children, in facilitating their escape. The Indians were now upon them, but he having a horse, fled before them, and overtook his children, about forty rods from the house; some one of which, he intended to have taken on the horse with him, and so escape. But now he was at a loss, for which one to take, he knew not; therefore, he resolved to face about, and defend them to the last. Some of the enemy drew near and fired upon them, and Mr. Dustan being armed, also fired upon the Indians, at which they gave over the pursuit, and returned to share the spoils of the house. Mr. Dustan and his seven children (from two to seventeen years of age) got safe to a garrison, one or two miles off, where we must leave him to bewail the many supposed deaths of his wife and infant child.

The Indians, being about twenty in number, in the mean time, seized the nurse, who was making her escape with the young child, and taking Mrs. Dustan, with what plunder could be found from the house, set it on fire, and took up their march for Canada. The infant was immediately taken from the nurse, and a monster taking it by the feet, dashed out its brains against a tree. Their whole number of captives was now about twelve, which gradually diminished on the march. Some, growing weary and faint, were killed, scalped, and otherwise mangled, and left in the wilderness. Notwithstanding the weakness of Mrs. Dustan, she travelled twelve miles the first day, and thus bore up under a journey of near one hundred and fifty miles, in a few days. On their march the Indians divided, according to their usual custom, and each family shifted for itself with their share of prisoners, for the convenience of hunting. Mrs. Dustan, her nurse and an English youth, taken from Worcester eighteen months before, fell to the lot of an Indian family, consisting of twelve persons; two stout men, three women, and seven children. The captives were informed, that when they arrived at a certain Indian town, they were to run the gauntlet, through a great number of Indians. But on the thirtieth of April, having arrived at the mouth of Contoocook river, they encamped upon a small island, and pitched their tents. As all lay asleep but Mrs. Dustan, she conceived the bold design of putting the Indians to death, and escaping. Accordingly, she silently engaged Miss Neff, and the English youth, to act a part in the dreadful tragedy; infusing her heroism into them, each took a tomahawk, and with such deadly effect were the blows dealt, that all were slain save two; one a woman, who fled desperately wounded, the other a boy, whom they intended to have kept. They then took off their ten scalps, and returned home in safety. The government voted them fifty pounds reward, and Colonel Nicholson, the Governour of Maryland, made them a valuable present. The island on which this memorable affair happened, justly bears the name of Dustan's island.*

---

* For the principal facts in this narrative I am indebted to the Magnalia.

VII.—-SCHENECTADA DESTROYED.

"In the dead of winter, three expeditions were planned, and parties of French and Indians despatched from Canada, on different routes, to the frontiers of the English colonies. One of these parties, on February the eighth, 1690, fell on Schenectada,* a village on the Mohawk river. Such was the fatal security of the people, that they had not so much as shut their gates. The enemy made the attack in the dead time of the night, when the inhabitants were in a profound sleep. Care was taken by a division of the enemy into small parties, to attack every house at the same instant. Before the people were risen from their beds, the enemy were in possession of their dwellings, and commenced the most inhuman barbarities. In an instant the whole village was wrapped in a general flame. Women were ripped up, and their infants dashed against the posts of their doors, or cast into the flames. Sixty persons perished in the massacre, and about thirty were captivated. The rest fled naked in a terrible storm and deep snow. In the flight, twentyfive of these unhappy fugitives lost their limbs, through the severity of the season.

The enemy consisted of about two hundred French, and a number of Caghnuaga† Indians, under the command of D'Aillebout, De Mantel, and Le Moyne. Their first design was against Albany, but having been two and twenty days on their march, they were reduced to such straits, that they had thoughts of surrendering themselves prisoners of war. The In-

---

* About 14 miles above Albany, on the west side of the Mohawk. The country around is a sandy barren, on which account it was called Schenectada.

† This Caghnuaga is in Canada. There is another on the Mohawk river, 6 miles below Johnston, but the inhabitants here spell it Caughnewaga.

dians, therefore, advised them to Schenectada : and it seems that the accounts, which their scouts gave them of its fatal security, was the only circumstance which determined them to make an attempt, even upon this. The enemy pillaged the town, and went off with the plunder, and about forty of the best horses. The rest, with all the cattle they could find, were left slaughtered in the streets. The success of the enemy seems to have been principally owing to the dispute between Leisler* and the people of Albany, in consequence of which this post was neglected.

The Mohawks joining a party of young men from Albany, pursued the enemy, and falling on their rear, killed and captivated nearly thirty."†

VIII.—SCHUYLER'S EXPEDITION, AND OTHER EVENTS.

THE success of the French and Indians against the frontier settlements of Newengland, had been great, and the inactivity of the people to repel them, had justly been an object of blame with the Sixnations; for their country must at all times afford a pass to them. Steps, therefore, must now be taken to retain the confidence of those people.

Major Peter Schuyler, the Washington of his day, lived at Albany, where with incredible industry and perseverance, he made himself acquainted with all the plans and undertakings of the Sixnations, and as studiously maintained a friendship with them, which extended to all Americans. They had received repeated injuries from the French for a long time, and something was now necessary to prove to them, that the English were not afraid to meet them on their own ground. Accordingly, in 1691, Major Schuyler, " with about three hundred men, nearly half Mo-

* Afterwards executed for assuming the government of Newyork. See Smith's Hist. N. Y. 121 to 129.
† Trumbull's Hist. U. S. I, 215 to 217.

hawks and Schakook* Indians, passed Lake Champlain, and made a bold attack on the French settlements north of the lake. Meanwhile, De Callieres, the Governour of Montreal, spared no pains to give him a proper reception. He crossed the river with twelve hundred men, and encamped at La Praire. Schuyler attacked and put to flight his out posts and Indians, pursued them to the fort, and on that commenced a brisk attack. He had a sharp and brave action with the French regulars, and afterward forcing his way through a body of the enemy, who intercepted him, on his return, made good his retreat. In these several conflicts, the Major slew of the enemy, thirteen officers, and in the whole three hundred men; a greater number than he carried with him into the field."†

Before this, in 1688, twelve hundred warriors of the Sixnations, made a descent on the island of Montreal, slew a thousand of the inhabitants, and carried off twentysix prisoners, whom they burnt alive. About three months after, they attacked the island again, and went off with nearly the same success. "These expeditions had the most dismal consequences on the affairs of the French in Canada." They had a garrison at lake Ontario, which they now abandoned, and fled in canoes down the Cadarackui in the night; and, in descending the falls, a great number of men were lost. The warriors then took possession of the garrison, and twentyseven barrels of powder fell into their hands. Nothing but the ignorance of the Sixnations, in the European art of war, saved Canada from total ruin; and, what will ever be lamented, the colonies, through the caprice of their European lords, were unable to lend them any assistance. With a little help from the English, a period would have been put to the torrents of blood that

---

* Trumbull, I, 221, but at 301, he spells it as seen in Philip's war, page 68 except that he used but one *t*

† Ibid. 221–225.

APPENDIX. 321

flowed until, the conquest by the immortal Wolf and Amherst, in 1760.

IX.—DESTRUCTION OF DEERFIELD.

In 1703, the plan was laid to cut off the frontier inhabitants of Newengland, from one extremity to the other, but it was not fully executed. Though the eastern settlements from Casco to Wells were destroyed, and one hundred and thirty people killed and taken, the western frontiers remained unmolested, and were lulled into a fatal security. From the Indians that traded at Albany, Colonel Schuyler received intelligence of a design in Canada to fall upon Deerfield, of which the inhabitants were informed in May. "The design not being carried into execution in the course of the summer, the intelligence was not enough regarded. But the next winter, 1704, M. Vaudrieul, [Vaudreuil] Governour of Canada, resumed the project with much attention."

The history of this affair from the accomplished historian of Vermont, Dr. Samuel Williams, is perhaps more particularly interesting, as he is an immediate descendant of a principal sufferer, the Rev. John Williams, I give it in his own words.

"Deerfield, at that time, was the most northerly settlement on Connecticut river, a few families at Northfield excepted. Against this place, M. Vaudrieul sent out a party of about three hundred French and Indians. They were put under the command of Hertel de Rouville, assisted by four of his brothers; all of which had been trained up to the business by their father, who had been a famous partizan in their former wars. The route they took, was by the way of Lake Champlain, till they came to the French river, now called Onion river. Advancing up that stream, they passed over to Connecticut river, and travelled on the ice till they came near to Deerfield. Mr. Williams, their minister, had been much apprehensive of danger, and attempted to make the same impression on the minds of his people, but not with sufficient success; but upon his application, the government of the province had sent a guard of twenty soldiers for their assistance. The fortifications were some slight works thrown round two or three garrison houses, but were nearly covered in some places with drifts of snow. To this place, Rouville with his party, approached on February the twentyninth. Hovering round the place, he sent out his spies for intelligence. The watch kept the streets of the town till about two hours before day, and then, unfortunately, all of them went to sleep. Perceiving all to be quiet, the enemy embraced the opportunity and rushed on to the attack. The snow was so high, that they had no difficulty in jumping over the walls of the fortification; and immediately separated into small parties, to appear before every house at the same time. The place was completely surprised, and the enemy were entering the houses at the moment the inhabitants had the first suspicion of their approach. The whole village was carried in a few hours, and with very little resistance; one of the garrison houses only, being able to hold out against the enemy.

Having carried the place, slain fortyseven of the inhabitants, captured the rest, and plundered the village, the enemy set it on fire; and an hour after sun rise on the same day, retreated in great haste. A small party of the English pursued them, and a skirmish ensued the same day, in which a few were lost on both sides. The enemy, however, completely succeeded in their enterprize, and returned to Canada on the same route, carrying with them one hundred and twelve of the inhabitants of Deerfield, as prisoners of war. They were twentyfive days on their march from Deerfield to Chambly; and like their masters, the savages, depended on hunting for their support. On their arrival in Canada, they found much hu-

APPENDIX

manity and kindness from the French, and from M. Vaudrieul their Governour; but complained much of the intolerance, bigotry, and duplicity of the priests."*

Among the captives was the minister of the town, Rev. John Williams. As the Indians entered his room, he took down his pistol, and presented it to the breast of the foremost, but it missed fire. They then laid hold on him, and bound him naked as he was, and thus kept him for the space of an hour. In the mean time two of the children were carried out and killed; also a negro woman. His wife, who was hardly recovered from childbed, was with the rest marched for Canada. The second day, in wading a river, Mrs. Williams fainted and fell, but with assistance was kept along a little farther; when at the foot of a hill she began to falter, her savage master, with one blow of his tomahawk, put an end to her miseries.

The distance they had to march was at least three hundred miles. At different times the most of the prisoners were redeemed and returned home. Mr. Williams and fiftyseven others arrived at Boston from Quebeck, in 1706. One of his daughters, Eunice, married an Indian, and became a convert to the Roman Catholick religion, which she never would consent to forsake. She frequently visited her friends in Newengland; "but she uniformly persisted in wearing her blanket and counting her beads."†

Mr. Williams, after his return, was invited to preach near Boston; but refused every offer, and returned again to Deerfield and collected his scattered flock, with whom he continued until 1728; "dying in peace, beloved by his people, and lamented by his country." He published a history of his captivity, which, when Dr. Williams, his grand son, wrote his

---

* Williams' Hist. Vermont, I, 304–307.
† Holmes' American Annals, II, 63.

history of Vermont, had passed through seven editions.*

X.—RAVAGES OF THE EASTERN INDIANS.

In 1707, the frontiers suffered extremely. Oyster river, Exeter, Kingstown, and Dover in Newhampshire; Berwick, York, Wells, Winterharbour, Casco, and even Marlborough in Massachusetts, were considerably damaged. In 1710, Col. Walton with one hundred and seventy men made an expedition to Norridgewock, in the beginning of winter. The chief of that place was taken and killed,† and many more. The next year is rendered memorable by the great expedition against Canada; memorable only for its bad success, and the monstrous debt it brought upon the Colonies. In 1713, a peace was concluded with France, in consequence of which the eastern Indians desired peace with the colonies, which was accordingly brought about.‡ It was however of short duration. In August 1717, it was renewed at Arrowsike,§ but was broken within two years after,

---

* Hist. Vermont.

† His name was Arruhawikwabemt, "an active bold fellow, and one of an undaunted spirit; for, when he was asked several questions, he made no reply; and when they threatened him with death, he laughed at it with contempt." Penhallow, 70.

‡ The delegates met at Portsmouth, N. H., 11 July, and a treaty was signed the 13. The articles are preserved entire in Penhallow's History, 82–85.

§ Penhallow, page 90, relates a story concerning the abundance of Ducks at this place, which, though we do not doubt it, is certainly equally astonishing to many *fish stories*. About three days after the renewal of the treaty, "a number of Indians went a duck hunting, which was a season of the year that the old ones generally shed their feathers in, and the young ones are not so well flushed as to be able to fly; they drove them like a flock of sheep before them into the creeks, where without either powder or shot, they killed at one time, four thousand and six hundred." The English bought for a penny a dozen.

and various hostilities committed. The government, in 1721, ordered a party of men to Norridgewock, their chief town, but on their approach, the Indians all fled into the woods. One Sebastian Ralle, or Rolle dwelt there, as a missionary among them, and was supposed to have stirred up the Indians to hostilities, as Castine formerly had. Nothing was effected by the expedition, except the bringing away of some of Ralle's papers, by which it was discovered, that he was instigator in the war. This was thought by the Indians to be such an insult on the divine agency, that they now made war their business. In June, 1722, a large body struck a deadly blow on Merrymeeting bay, a village on an arm of the Winnipissaukee,* where they took nine families.† Shortly after, at Passammaquaddy, they took a vessel with passengers, and burned Brunswick.

War was now declared on the part of the English, and in February, Col. Westbrook with one hundred and thirty men, ranged the coast with small vessels as far as Mountdesert. "On his return he sailed up the Penobscot, and about thirtytwo miles above the anchoring place, for the transports, discovered the Indian Castle. It was seventy feet long and fifty broad. Within were twentythree well finished wigwams. Without was a handsome church, sixty feet long and thirty broad. There was also a commodious house for their priest. But these were all destroyed, and nothing more was accomplished by the expedition, than the barbarous business of burning this Indian village.

---

* There are many ways used in writing this word, Douglass, on the same page has it two ways; and few early authors write it alike, but all, or nearly all, seem to aim at the sound which I have endeavoured to give it. And, as the inhabitants, who dwell around this lake, pronounce it so, I see no reason why we should not write it so; especially, as it was the most early way, and, no doubt, so called by the natives themselves

† Most of these were afterward set at liberty. Penhallow, 91.

Afterwards Captain Moulton went up with a party of men to Norridgewock, but the village was deserted. He was a brave and prudent man, and, probably, imagining that moderation and humanity might excite the Indians to a more favourable conduct towards the English, he left their houses and Church standing."

In April, 1723, eight persons were killed or taken at Scarborough and Falmouth. "Among the dead was a Sergeant Chubb, whom the Indians imagining to be Captain Harman, against whom they had conceived the utmost malignity, fifteen aiming at him at the same instant, lodged eleven bullets in his body.

Besides other mischiefs, the enemy, the summer following, surprised Casco, with other harbours in its vicinity, and captured sixteen or seventeen sail of fishing vessels. The vessels belonged to Massachusetts; but Governour Philips of Novascotia, happening to be at Casco, ordered two sloops to be immediately manned and dispatched in pursuit of the enemy. The sloops were commanded by John Eliot of Boston, and John Robinson of cape Anne. As Eliot was ranging the coast he discovered seven vessels in Winepang harbour. He concealed his men, except four or five, and made directly for the harbour. Coming nearly up to one of the vessels, on board of which was about sixty Indians, in high expectation of another prize, they hoisted their pendants and cried out 'Strike English dogs and come aboard for you are all prisoners.' Eliot answered that he would make all the haste he could. As he made no attempts to escape, the enemy soon suspected mischief, cut their cable and attempted to gain the shore; but immediately boarding them he prevented their escape. For about half an hour they made brave resistance, but Eliot's hand grenadoes made such a havock among them, that at length, those who had not been killed, took to the water where they were a fair mark for the English musketeers. Five only reached the shore. Eliot received three bad wounds, had one man killed and several wounded. He recovered seven vessels, several hundred quintals of fish, and fifteen captives. Many of the captives had been sent away, and nine had been murdered in cold blood. Robinson retook two vessels and killed several of the enemy.

The loss of such a number of men determined the enemy to seek revenge on the poor fishermen. Twenty of these yet remained in their hands, at the harbour of Malagash, [where the remainder of the vessels lay which they had taken from the English, and were inaccessible to Captain Eliot.] These were all destined to be sacrificed to the manes of the slaughtered Indians. At the very time, that the powawing and other ceremonies, attending such horrible purposes, were just commencing, Captain Blin, who sometime before had been a prisoner among them, arrived off the harbour; and made the signal, or sent in a token, which it had been agreed between them, should be the sign of protection. Three Indians came aboard, and an agreement was made for the ransom both of the ships and captives. These were delivered and the ransom paid. Captain Blin in his way to Boston, captivated a number of them, near cape Sable; and Captain Southack a number more, which they brought on with them to Boston."

In September they made a descent on the island of Arrowsike, where they burned the houses, killed the cattle, and then retired to their head quarters at Norridgewock. There was a garrison on the island of about forty men, but their number was so small compared with that of the enemy, that no sally was made.

The beginning of the next year, 1724, was altogether unfavourable to the English. People were killed at Cape Porpoise, Black Point, and Berwick; also at Lamprey, and Oyster rivers, and Kingston, in Newhampshire.

"Captain Josiah Winslow, who had been stationed at the fort on St. George's river, with part of his company, had been surprised and cut off. He went out from the fort with two whaleboats, fourteen white men, and three Indians. It seems the enemy watched their motions, and on their return, suddenly surrounded them, with thirty canoes, whose compliment was not less than a hundred Indians. The English attempted to land, but were intercepted, and nothing remained but to sell their lives as dearly as possible. They made a brave defence, but every Englishman was killed. The three Indians escaped to report their hapless fall. Flushed with these successes, the enemy attempted still greater feats on the water. They took two shallops at the isles of shoals. They then made seizures of other vessels in different harbours. Among others they took a large schooner carrying two swivel guns. This they manned and cruised along the coast. It was imagined that a small force would be able to conquer these raw sailors. A shallop of sixteen, and a schooner of twenty men, under Captains Jackson and Lakeman, were armed and sent in pursuit of the enemy. They soon came up with them, but raw as they were, they obliged the English vessels to sheer off, and leave them to pursue their own course, who took eleven vessels and fortyfive men. Twentytwo they killed, and the others they carried into captivity."

While these affairs were passing at sea, the inland country suffered also. "Mischief was done at Groton, Rutland, Northampton, and Dover. In all these places more or less were killed, some wounded, and others carried into captivity."

The scene is now to change. The English are resolved to visit the Indians at their head quarters, at Norridgewock. Accordingly, Captains Moulton, Harman, and Bourne, with two hundred and eighty men, arrived at Taconnock, up the Kennebeck river, the twentieth of August. Here they left their boats

APPENDIX. 329

and forty men to guard them, and proceeded the next day for Norridgewock. "In the evening they discovered two women, the wife and daughter of Bomazeen, the famous warriour and chieftain of Norridgewock. They fired upon them and killed his daughter, and then captivated his wife. By her they obtained a good account of the state of the village. On the twentythird they came near it, and as they imagined that part of the Indians would be in their corn fields, at some distance, it was thought expedient to make a division of the army." Captain Harman marched with eighty men into the fields — "Moulton with the remainder marched directly for the village. About three o'clock it opened suddenly upon them. The Indians were all in their wigwams entirely secure. Moulton marched his men in the profoundest silence, and ordered that not one of them should fire at random, through the wigwams, nor till they should receive the enemy's fire; as he expected they would come out in a panic and overshoot them. At length an Indian stepping out, discovered the English close upon them. He instantly gave the war hoop, and sixty warriours rushed out to meet them. The Indians fired hastily without injuring a man. The English returned the fire with great effect, and the Indians instantly fled to the river. Some jumped into their canoes, others into the river, which the tallest of them were able to ford. Moulton closely pursuing them, drove them from their canoes, and killed them in the river, so that it was judged, that not more than fifty of the whole village reached the opposite shore. Some of these were shot before they reached the woods.

The English then returning to the village, found father Ralle, the jesuit, firing from one of the wigwams on a small number of men who had not been in the pursuit of the enemy. One of these he wounded; in consequence of which, one Lieutenant Jaques burst the door and shot him through the head. Captain Moulton had given orders not to kill him. Jaques excused himself, affirming that Ralla was loading his piece, and refused to give or take quarter. With the English there were three Mohawks. Mogg,* a famous Indian warriour firing from a wigwam killed one of them. His brother in a rage flew to the wigwam, burst the door, and instantly killed Mogg. The English followed in a rage and killed his squaw and two helpless children." After the action Harman arrived and they all lodged in the village. "In the morning they found twentysix dead bodies, besides that of the jesuit. Among the dead were Bomazeen. Mogg, Wissememet, and Bomazeen's son in law, all famous warriours."†

The inhumanity of the English to the women and children cannot be excused. It greatly eclipses the lustre of the victory.‡

The Norridgewocks were now broken down, and they never made any figure afterwards.§

XI.—LOVEWELL'S FIGHT.

PERHAPS the celebrated story of "LOVEWELL'S FIGHT," cannot be given, to interest the present age, better than in the language of the old song, composed just after it happened. It is a simple and true narrative of the affair.

1 Of worthy Captain Lovewell,‖ I purpose now to sing,
  How valiantly he served his country and his King;

---

* In Philip's War there was a chief by this name. Mr. Hubbard called him " Mug the rogue."

† " The number in all that were killed [of the enemy] was supposed to be eighty." Penhallow, 108.

‡ " It may," says Penhallow, ib. " be as noble an exploit, (all things considered) as ever happend in the time of King Philip."

§ The above article is taken from Dr. Trumbull's Hist. U. S. Chap. IX.

‖ Captain John Lovewell lived in Dunstable, Newham-

APPENDIX. 331

He and his valiant soldiers, did range the woods full wide,
And hardships they endured to quell the Indians' pride.

2 'Twas nigh unto Pigwacket,* on the eighth day of May,†
They spied a rebel Indian soon after break of day;
He on a bank was walking, upon a neck of land,
Which leads into a pond‡ as we're made to understand.

3 Our men resolv'd to have him and travell'd two miles round,
Until they met the Indian, who boldly stood his ground;
Then spake up Captain Lovewell, "Take you good heed,"
says he,
" This rogue is to decoy us, I very plainly see.§

4 " The Indians lie in ambush, in some place nigh at hand,
" In order to surround us upon this neck of land;
" Therefore we'll march in order, and each man leave his
pack,‖
" That we may briskly fight them when they make their
attack."

5 They came unto this Indian, who did them thus defy,
As soon as they came nigh him, two guns he did let fly,¶

---

shire, then Massachusetts. " He was a son of Zacheus Lovewell, an Ensign in the army of Oliver Cromwell, who came to this country and settled at Dunstable, where he died at the age of one hundred and twenty years, the oldest white man who ever died in the state of Newhampshire." Farmer and Moore's Col. III, 64.

* Situated on the upper part of the river Saco, then 50 miles from any white settlement. Ib. I, 27. It is in the present town of Fryeburg, Maine.

† They set out from Dunstable about the 16 April, 1725. Symmes' narrative, in Farmer and Moore's Col. I, 27.

‡ Called Saco pond. Some call this Lovewell's pond, but Lovewell's pond is in Wakefield, where he some time before, captured a company of Indians, who were on their way to attack some of the frontier towns.

§ This Indian was out a hunting, and probably had no knowledge of the English, having two ducks in his hand, and his guns loaded with beaver shot. Symmes and Belknap.

‖ The Indians finding their packs, learned their number, and placed themselves to surround them, when they returned.

¶ It appears from Mr. Symmes, that the English saw the Indian coming, and secreted themselves, firing at him first.

Which wounded Captain Lovewell, and likewise one man
  more,* [gore.†
But when this rogue was running, they laid him in his

6 Then having scalp'd the Indian, they went back to the spot,
Where they had laid their packs down, but there they
  found them not,
For the Indians having spy'd them, when they them down
  did lay,
Did seize them for their plunder, and carry them away.

7 These rebels lay in ambush, this very place hard by,
So that an English soldier did one of them espy,
And cried out "Here's an Indian," with that they started
  out,
As fiercely as old lions, and hideously did shout.

8 With that our valiant English, all gave a loud huzza,
To shew the rebel Indians they fear'd them not a straw:
So now the fight began, and as fiercely as could be,
The Indians ran up to them, but soon were forc'd to flee.‡

9 Then spake up Captain Lovewell, when first the fight began,
"Fight on my valiant heroes! you see they fall like rain."
For as we are inform'd, the Indians were so thick,
A man could scarcely fire a gun and not some of them hit.

10 Then did the rebels try their best our soldiers to surround,
But they could not accomplish it, because there was a pond,
To which our men retreated and covered all the rear,§
The rogues were forc'd to flee them, altho' they skulk'd
  for fear.

He then, having two guns, discharged both, and wounded
the Captain mortally.
  * Samuel Whiting.
  † Ensign Wyman shot him, and Mr. Frye, the chaplain,
and another, scalped him. Symmes.
  ‡ Both parties advanced with their guns presented, and
when they came within "a few yards," they fired on both
sides. "The Indians fell in considerable numbers, but the
English, most, if not all of them, escaped the first shot." Ib.
Then advancing within twice the length of their guns, slew
nine. Penhallow.
  § Twelve were killed and wounded before they retreated
to the pond. There was a small bank, which served them

APPENDIX.

11 Two logs there were behind them, that close together lay,
   Without being discovered, they could not get away ;
   Therefore our valiant English, they travell'd in a row,
   And at a handsome distance as they were wont to go.

12 'Twas 10 o'clock in the morning, when first the fight begun,
   And fiercely did continue until the setting sun ,
   Excepting that the Indians, some hours before 'twas night,
   Drew off into the bushes and ceased awhile to fight.*

13 But soon again returned, in fierce and furious mood,
   Shouting as in the morning, but yet not half so loud ;
   For as we are informed, so thick and fast they fell,
   Scarce twenty of their number, at night did get home well.†

14 And that our valiant English, till midnight there did stay,
   To see whether the rebels would have another fray ;
   But they no more returning, they made off towards their
      home,   [come.‡
   And brought away their wounded as far as they could

15 Of all our valiant English, there were but thirtyfour,
   And of the rebel Indians, there were about four score.
   And sixteen of our English did safely home return,
   The rest were killed and wounded, for which we all must
      mourn.§

---

as a breastwork, and, perhaps, saved them from an immediate defeat. This is the more probable, as but few were killed afterward. Ib.

* They probably drew off to take care of the wounded. Symmes nor Penhallow makes no mention that they returned again to the fight, after they drew off.

† Forty were said to be killed upon the spot, and eighteen more died of their wounds. Penhallow.

‡ Solomon Keyes, after receiving three wounds, crawled along the shore of the pond, where he chanced to find an old canoe, into which he rolled himself, and the wind wafted him on several miles toward the fort, which he reached in safety. He felt his end approaching, when he was in the boat, into which he had crawled, only to die in peace, and to escape the scalping knife, but wonderfully revived. Symmes.

§ Eight were left in the woods, whose wounds were so bad that they could not travel, of whom two only returned. One ran away in the beginning of the fight.

16 Our worthy Captain Lovewell among them there did die
    They killed Lt. Robins,* and wounded good young Frye,
    Who was our English chaplain; he many Indians slew,
    And some of them he scalp'd when bullets round him flew

17 Young Fullam‡ too I'll mention, because he fought so well,
    Endeavouring to save a man, a sacrifice he fell;
    But yet our valiant Englishmen in fight were ne'er dis-
        may'd, [made,
    But still they kept their motion, and Wyman's§ Captain

18 Who shot the old chief Paugus,‖ which did the foe defeat,
    Then set his men in order, and brought off the retreat;
    And braving many dangers and hardships in the way,
    They safe arriv'd at Dunstable, the thirteenth day of
        May.¶

In the beginning of the war, one hundred pounds were offered by the government for every Indian scalp. Captain Lovewell and his company in about

---

* He belonged to Chelmesford. Being mortally wounded, desired to have two guns charged, and left with him, which they did. He said, " As the Indians will come in the morning to scalp me, I will kill one more of them if I can." Ib.

† He fell about the middle of the afternoon. He was the only son of Capt. James Frye of Andover, graduated at Harvard college in 1723, and was chaplain of the company. Ib.

‡ Only son of Major Fullam of Weston, was sergeant of the company, and fell in the beginning of the fight. Ib.

§ Ensign Seth Wyman of Woburn. He was presented with a silver hilted sword for his good conduct, and commissioned Captain. He died soon after.

‖ Many of Lovewell's men knew Paugus personally. A huge bear's skin formed a part of his dress. From Mr. Symmes' account, it appears that John Chamberlain killed him. They had spoken together some time in the fight, and afterward both happened to go to the pond to wash out their guns, which were rendered useless by so frequent firing. Here the challange was given by Paugus, " It is you or I." As soon as the guns were prepared they fired, and Paugus fell.

¶ Wyman and three others did not arrive until the 15th, but the main body, consisting of twelve, arrived the 13th.

three months made twelve hundred pounds. This stimulated them to attack the village of Pigwocket, where, if successful, they considered their fortunes sure. It was a heavy loss to the country, but this nearly finished the war. The Indians formed no considerable body in these parts afterward. A long and happy peace followed.

The above song is taken from the valuable Historical Collections of Farmer and Moore.

I cannot refuse the beautiful lines of Mr. Thomas C. Upham, "a N. Hampshire poet," a place in this work. They were occasioned by a visit to the place of Lovewell's Fight.*

Ah! where are the soldiers that fought here of yore?
The sod is upon them, they'll struggle no more.
The hatchet is fallen, the red man is low;
But near him reposes the arm of his foe.

The bugle is silent, the warhoop is dead;
There's a murmur of waters and woods in their stead
And the raven and owl chant a symphony drear,
From the dark waving pines o'er the combatant's bier.

The light of the sun has just sunk in the wave,
And a long time ago sat the sun of the brave.
The waters complain, as they roll o'er the stones,
And the rank grass encircles a few scatter'd bones.

The names of the fallen the traveller leaves
Cut out with his knife in the bark of the trees,
But little avail his affectionate arts,
For the names of the fallen are graved in our hearts.

The voice of the hunter is loud on the breeze,
There's a dashing of waters, a rustling of trees;
But the jangling of armour hath all pass'd away,
No gushing of lifeblood is here seen to day.

The eye that was sparkling, no longer is bright,
The arm of the mighty, death conquered its might,

---

* Taken from Farmer and Moore's Col. I, 35.

The bosoms that once for their country beat high,
To those bosoms the sods of the valley are nigh.

Sleep, soldiers of merit, sleep, gallants of yore,
The hatchet is fallen, the struggle is o'er.
While the fir tree is green and the wind rolls a wave,
The tear drop shall brighten the turf of the brave.

XII.—ANECDOTES, NARRATIVES, &C., OF THE INDIANS.

1. Among the first settlers of Brunswick, Maine, was Daniel Malcolm, a man of undaunted courage, and an inveterate enemy of the Indians, who gave him the name of Sungurnumby, that is, a very strong man. Early in the spring, he ventured alone into the forest for the purpose of splitting rails from the spruce, not apprehensive of Indians so early in the season. While engaged in his work, and having opened a log with small wedges about half its length he was surprised by Indians, who crept up and secured his musket, standing by his side. "Sungurnumby," said the chief, "now me got you; long me want you; you long speak Indian, long time worry him; me have got you now; look up stream to Canada."—"Well," said Malcolm, with true *sang froid*, "you have me; but just help me open this log before I go." They all (five in number) agreed. Malcolm prepared a large wooden wedge, carefully drove it, took out his small wedges, and told the Indians to put in their fingers to the partially clefted wood, and help pull it open. They did; he then suddenly struck out his blunt wedge, and the elastick wood instantly closed fast on their fingers, and he secured them.*

2. *Origin of the name of a bridge in Salisbury N. H., known by the name of "*Indian Bridge.*"*—In the fall of the year 1753, two Indians, named Sa-

---

* Farmer and Moore, III, 103.

batis and Plausawa, came into Canterbury with furs.
They here met two men from Newbury, whom they
knew, but were not pleased at seeing them, and began to make off. Sabatis seemed disposed to do
mischief, but was prevented by Plausawa. The two
Englishmen offered to buy their furs. They refused,
and said they would not sell furs to the English, but
would go to Canada; but afterward they offered to
trade for rum. They had rum, but would not sell
it to them, thinking that they were ill disposed. As
they were about to leave the Indians, one of them,
Plausawa, appeared friendly, and advised them to
avoid meeting with Indians. When they had gone
a little distance from the Indians, Sabatis called
them, and said, " No more you English come here;
me heart bad; me kill you." One of the English
replied, " No kill—-English and Indians now all
brothers." As they left the Indians, they met one
Peter Bowen going toward them. They told him of
the temper the Indians had showed, and tried to dis-
suade him. He replied, that he was not afraid of
them; that be was acquainted with Indians and knew
how to deal with them. The Indians had got into
their canoe, and were going up the river, when Bow-
en called to them, and invited them to go to his
house, and stay all night; and that he would give
them some rum. They went with him to his house,
which was in Contoocook. The night was spent in
a drunken frolick, in which Bowen did not fail to
act his part; being much accustomed to their modes
of life. In the midst of the frolick, Bowen took the
caution to unload their guns. The next morning he
took his horse to convey their packs to their boats.
As they were going, Sabatis proposed to Bowen to
run with his horse. A race being agreed upon and
performed, in which Sabatis beat Bowen on horseback, at which he was much pleased, and laughed
heartily. After proceeding along a little further,

P

Sabatis said to him, "Bowen walk woods," meaning that Bowen was his prisoner. Bowen said, "No walk woods, all one brothers." Another race soon followed, in which Sabatis fell in the rear, and Bowen hearing a gun snap, looked round and saw a flash from Sabatis' gun, which was pointed at him. He turned back and laid him dead with a blow of his tomahawk. Plausawa was further behind, and as Bowen came toward him, he leveled his gun and it snapped also; he then fell on his knees and begged for his life, but Bowen knew he should be in danger so long as the friend of Sabatis lived, so he despatched him in like manner. He then hid the bodies under a bridge, which were found the next spring and buried. From this affair is the name of Indian Bridge derived.*

3. *Origin of the peopling of Nantucket by the Indians.* It is told that in a remote period of antiquity, an eagle made a descent on some part of the coast of what is now Newengland, and carried off a young Indian in his talons. The weeping parents made bitter lamentations, and with eager eyes saw their child borne out of sight, over the trackless deep. They resolved to follow in the same direction. Accordingly they set out in their canoes, and after a perilous passage descried the island. They landed and after much search found the bones of the child.

4. *An anecdote of the colony of Sagadehock.*
"The Norridgewock Indians have this tradition; that this company engaged a number of Indians, who had come to trade with them, to draw a cannon, by a long rope; that the moment they were ranged in a strait line, the white people discharged the piece, which killed and wounded a number. Their story is, that the indignation of the natives for this barba-

---
* Ibid. III, 27.

APPENDIX. 339

rous treachery, compelled the company to embark to save their own lives."*

5. "*A letter from* KING PHILIP *to Governour Prince, copied from the original, which belongs to Mr. White, of Plymouth. The words are spelt as in the original letter.*"

KING PHILIP desire to let you understand that he could not come to the court, for Tom, his interpreter has a pain in his back, that he could not travil so far, and Philip sister is very sick.

Philip would intreat that favor, of you, and aney of the majestrates, if aney English or Engians speak about aney land, he preay you to give them no answer at all. This last sumer he made that promis with you, that he would not sell no land in 7 years time, for that he would have no English trouble him before that time, he has not forgot that you promis him.

He will come a sune as posible he can to speak with you, and so I rest, your verey loveing friend, Philip, dwelling at mount hope nek
    To the much honered
        Governer, Mr. Thomas Prince,
            dwelling at Plymouth.†

6. *Singularity of the Indian language.* Thus the word Nummatchekodtantamooonganunnonash signifies no more in English, than *our lusts;* and Noowomantammooonkanunonnash no more than *our loves.* A yet longer word (if so such an assemblage of letters may be called) Kummogkodonattoottummooetiteaongannunnonash is to express only *our question.*‡

7. *A proof of King Philip's humanity.* The ancester of Col. B. Cole, of Warren, Rhodeisland, came to this country and settled at Tuisset.§ He in time

---

* Morse and Parish's Hist. N. Eng. 17.

† Mass. Hist. Soc. Col. II, 40. The Editor writes at the bottom of the letter, " There is no date to the letter, it was probably written about 1660 or 1670."

‡ See Magnalia, I, 507.

§ A neck of land on the east side of Keekamuit river.

became acqainted with Philip, and always lived in habits of friendship with him. In June 1675, Philip informed him that his young men were very eager to go to war against the English; but when he could no longer restrain them he would let him know. Accordingly on an evening previous to the fatal 24, canoes arrived from Mounthope with advise from Philip, that Mr. Cole and family must go over to R. I., as his people would begin the war. They embarked, and the next morning their dwellings were burned. Col. B. Cole, is of the fourth generation.*

8. *An Indian Snare.* To take large animals they sometimes built two extensive fences, perhaps a mile apart at one extremity, and at the other nearly meeting, forming an angle, generally, something less than a right one. At this point or opening they contrived to bend down a tree of sufficient strength to suspend the largest animals. " An English mare having once strayed away, was caught, and like Mahomet's fabled coffin, raised between the heavens and earth, in one of these snares. The Indians arriving, and seeing her struggling on the tree, ran immediately, and informed the English that their *squaw horse* was hanging on a tree."†

9. *Anecdote of Massassoit.* "Mr. Winslow,‡ coming in his bark from Connecticut to Narraganset,— and he left her there,—and intending to return by land, he went to Osamekin the sagamore, [Massassoit] his old ally, who offered to conduct him home to Plimouth. But, before they took their journey, Osamekin sent one of his men to Plimouth to tell them that Mr. Winslow was dead; and directed him to show how and where he was killed. Whereupon there was much fear and sorrow at Plimouth. The next day, when Osamekin brought him home, they

---

* Oral account of Col. Cole.
† Morse and Parish's N. Eng. 222.
‡ Mr. Edward Winslow.

APPENDIX. 341

asked him why he sent such word, &c. He answered, that it was their manner to do so, that they might be more welcome when they came home."* This was in 1634.

10. *Singular descriptions.* Dr. Mather says there fell into his hands the manuscript of a jesuit, employed by the French to instruct the Iroquois Indians in religion; in which was " one chapter about *Heaven,* and another about *Hell,* wherein are such *thick skulled* passages as these." " ' *Q. How is the soyl made in Heaven?* A. 'Tis a very *fair soyl,* they want neither for *meats* nor clothes : 'tis but *wishing* and we have them. *Q. Are they employed in Heaven?* A. No; they do nothing; the fields yield corn, beans, pumpkins, and the like without any tillage." After a few others that amount to no more or less, it proceeds thus in the examination of Hell. " ' *Q. What sort of soyl is that of hell?* A. A very wretched *soyl;* 'tis a *fiery pit,* in the centre of the earth. *Q. Have they any light in hell?* A. No. 'Tis always dark; there is always *smoke* there; their eyes are always in pain with it; they can see nothing but the devils. *Q. What shaped things are the devils?* A. Very ill shaped things; they go about with *vizards* on, and they terrify men. *Q. What do they eat in hell?* A. They are always hungry, but the damned feed on hot ashes and serpents there. *Q. What water have they to drink?* A. Horid water, nothing but *melted lead. Q. Don't they die in hell?* A. No: yet they eat one another, every day; but anon, God restores and renews the man that was eaten, as a cropt plant in a little time repullulates.' "
" It seems they have not thought this divinity too *gross* for the barbarians. But I shall make no reflections on it."†

---

* Winthrop's Hist N. Eng. I, 138, 139.
† See Magnalia, I, 521, 522.

XIII.—MASSACRE OF THE CONESTOGOE INDIANS IN PENNSYLVANIA.

An almost uninterrupted friendship seems to have existed between the Indians and the inhabitants of Pennsylvania, until the year 1754. At this period the French had stirred up the Indians in the back country, and an Indian war commenced.

About ten years after that, when "many," says Mr. Proud, " who had been continually flocking into the province, in later years, having from their inexperience and ignorance, too despicable an opinion of that people, and treating them accordingly, were by this conduct foolishly enraged against the whole species indiscriminately; insomuch, that in the latter part of the year 1763, calling to their aid the madness of the wildest enthusiasm, with which, under pretence of religion, certain most furious zealots among the preachers of a numerous sect, in the province, could inspire their hearers, to cover their barbarity, a number of, not improperly named, *armed demi-savages*, inhabitants of Lancaster county, principally from the townships of Paxtang and Donnegal, and their neighbourhood, committed the most horrible *massacre*, that ever was heard of in this, or perhaps, any other province, with inpunity! and under the notion of extirpating the heathen from the earth, as Joshua did of old, that these saints might possess the land alone," &c. Thus begins the narrative.

" 'These Indians were the remains of a tribe of the Six Nations, settled at Conestogoe, and thence called Conestogoe Indians. On the first arrival of the English in Pennsylvania, messengers from this tribe came to welcome them, with presents of venison, corn and skins; and the whole tribe entered into a treaty of friendship with the first Proprietary, William Penn; *which was to last as long as the sun should shine, or the waters run in the rivers*

This treaty has been since frequently renewed, and the *chain brightened*, as they express it, from time to time. It has never been violated on their part, or ours, till now. As their lands, by degrees, were mostly purchased, and the settlement of the white people began to surround them, the Proprietor assigned them lands on the manor of Conestogoe, which they might not part with; there they have lived many years, in friendship with their white neighbours, who loved them for their peaceable, inoffensive behaviour.

It has always been observed, that Indians, settled in the neighbourhood of white people, do not increase, but diminish continually. This tribe accordingly went on diminishing, till there remained in their town, on the manor, but twenty persons, namely, seven men, five women, and eight children, boys and girls.

Of these, Shehaes was a very old man, having assisted at the second treaty, held with them by Mr. Penn, in 1701; and ever since continued a faithful friend to the English; he is said to have been an exceeding good man, considering his education, being naturally of a most kind, benevolent temper.

This little society continued the custom they had begun, when more numerous, of addressing every new Governour, and every descendant of the first Proprietary, welcoming him to the province, assuring him of their fidelity, and praying a continuance of that favour and protection, which they had hitherto experienced. They had accordingly sent up an address of this kind to our present Governour (John Penn, Esquire) on his arrival; but the same was scarce delivered when the unfortunate catastrophe happened which we are about to relate.

On Wednesday, the 14th of December, 1763, fiftyseven men from some of our frontier townships, who had projected the destruction of this little commonwealth came all well mounted, and armed with firelocks, hangers and hatchets, having travelled through the country in the night to Conestogoe manor. There they surrounded the small village of Indian huts, and just at break of day, broke in upon them all at once. Only three men, two women, and a young boy were found at home; the rest being out among the neighbouring white people; some to sell their baskets, brooms and bowls, they manufactured, and others, on other occasions. These poor defenceless creatures were immediately fired upon, stabbed and hatcheted to death! The good Shehaes, among the rest, cut to pieces in his bed! All of them were *scalped*, and otherwise horribly mangled. Then their huts were set on fire, and most of them burned down.

The Magistrates of Lancaster sent out to collect the remaining Indians, brought them into the town, for their better security against any further attempt; and, it is said, condoled with them on the misfortune, that had happened, took them by the hand, and *promised them protection.*

They were put into the workhouse, a strong building, as the place of greatest safety.

These cruel men again assembled themselves; and hearing that the remaining fourteen Indians were in the workhouse at Lancaster, they suddenly appeared before that town, on the twentyseventh of December. Fifty of them armed as before; dismounting, went directly to the workhouse, and by violence broke open the door, and entered with the utmost fury in their countenances. When the poor wretches saw they had *no protection* nigh, nor could possibly escape, and being without the least weapon of defence, they divided their little families, the children clinging to their parents; they fell on their faces, protested their innocence, declared their love to the English, and that, in their whole lives, they had never done them injury; and in this posture, they all received the hatchet! **Men, women** and children, were every one inhumanly murdered in cold blood!

The barbarous men, who committed the attrocious fact, in defiance of government, of all laws, human and divine, and, to the eternal disgrace of their country and colour, then mounted their horses, huzzaed in triumph, as if they had gained a victory, and rode off unmolested!

The bodies of the murdered were then brought out, and exposed in the street, till a hole could be made in the earth, to receive and cover them. But the wickedness cannot be covered, and the guilt will lie on the whole land, till justice is done on the *murderers*. *The blood of the innocent will cry to heaven for vengeance.*

Notwithstanding the proclamations and endeavours of the Governour on the occasion, the murderers having given out such threatenings against those that disapproved their proceedings, that the whole country seems to be in terror, and no one durst speak what he knows; even the letters from thence are unsigned, in which any dislike is expressed of the rioters.'"

Mr. Proud* adds to the above narrative, that, "So far had the infection spread, which caused this action, and so much had fear seized the minds of the people, or perhaps both, that neither the printer nor the writer of this publication, though supposed to be as nearly connected as Franklin and Hall were at that time, and men of the first character in their way, did not insert either their names, or places of abode, in it! It was printed while the insurgents were preparing to advance towards Philadelphia; or on their way thither; it appeared to have some effect, in pre-

---

* See his Hist. Pennsylvania, I, 326 to 328. [I would remind the reader, that no comparison should have been made, in note 2, to page 147, between the treatment of the Indians in Newengland, and Pennsylvania; for Mr. Makin wrote before any material difficulties had occurred in that province.]

P

venting the threatened consequences, by exciting an exertion of endeavours, in the citizens, for that purpose; and being a relation of real facts, though writ in a hurry, it was never answered or contradicted."

XV.—TROUBLES WITH THE INDIANS IN THE LATE WAR WITH ENGLAND.

Before the declaration of war took place between America and Great Britain, the Indians along the frontiers, very much alarmed the inhabitants by their hostile appearance.

The famous Indian warriour, Tecumseh, had been known for his enmity to civilization, and utter aversion to the white people, from the time of Harmer's defeat; and, like the celebrated Philip, had extended his endeavours, far and wide, among the various tribes of his countrymen, to unite them in making war on the Americans. His eloquence was irresistable, and his success was great. It is sufficient to observe, that the English had early engaged him in their cause. Much was also imposed on the credulity of those people by a brother of Tecumseh, who professed the spirit of prophecy, and the art of conjuration; in the exercise of which, much was effected. He was known by the name of "The Prophet."

In 1811, Governour Harrison of Indiana, met a large number of chiefs at Vincennes, to confer about the state of affairs. Tecumseh appeared there, to remonstrate against the sale of certain lands, made by the Kickapoos and others. In a speech of great eloquence, he urged the wrongs of his countrymen, by the encroachments of the whites, of which he gave a faithful history. In the Governour's answer, he advanced something which Tecumseh thought, or perhaps knew to be wrong. At which he raised his tomahawk, and twenty or thirty others followed his example. But Harrison had taken the precaution to have a sufficient force at hand, which prevented any acts of violence. This broke up the conference, and war was soon expected to follow.

APPENDIX. 347

Battle of Tippecanoe. Toward the latter end of the year 1811, the appearance of the Indians was so alarming, that Gov. Harrison, with an army of about 2000 men, marched into the Indian country. On arriving within a mile of the Prophet's town, they were met by a number of chiefs, who sued for peace, and begged for their lives. Harrison demanded the plunder taken from the Americans. It being near night, 6 November, they requested the army to encamp, and in the morning, they would accede to his proposals. The intrigue was mistrusted, and the Governour drew up his army in order of battle, and encamped for the night. About four o'clock their camp was attacked with great impetuosity, and the battle was for some time doubtful and bloody. But at length, the Indians were overpowered, and the victory was complete. About 300 of their warriours strewed the ground of battle. The behaviour of the Americans, many of whom had never seen an engagement before, cannot be too much applauded. When the battle began, each took his post without noise, and with calmness. Their loss in valuable officers was severe : They were these ; killed, Col. Abraham Owens, the Governour's aid ; Col. Joseph H. Davies, a very eminent lawyer ; Col. White, Capt. Warrick, Capt. Spencer, Lieut. McMahon, Lieut. Berry, and Capt. Bean.

An Expedition against the Western Indians.—For the purpose of driving the hostile Indians out of the limits of the U. States, an expedition was on foot early in October, consisting of 4000 men under Gen. Hopkins. After relieving fort Harrison, above mentioned, he crossed the Wabash and encamped but few miles distant. Here discontents were discovered among the soldiers, which very soon broke out into open disobedience of orders. This great army was composed of raw militia, of which little could be expected ; and, but for the assistance afforded fort Harrison, the expedition would have been rendered entirely abortive. A certain Major rode up to the General, and with great authority of expression, commanded him to return. Seeing the state of his men, the General told them, that if 500 would accompany him, he would proceed in quest of the enemy; but not a man would turn out. He then requested them to let him have the direction for a single day; to which they assented. He then put himself at their head, and ordered them to march; but they filed off in a contrary direction, and marched off to fort Harrison; and the General followed in the rear. At their encampment in a great prairie beyond the Wabash, the grass was discovered to be on fire, and driven by a fierce wind directly toward their camp. This was an Indian trap. But the Americans set fire to the grass about them, and were thereby delivered from a formidable onset by the flames. The same officer, afterward performed a successful expedition against the Indians.

Affair of the river Raisin. Out of sympathy for the inhabitants of Frenchtown, who were threatened with an Indian massacre, an imprudent step was taken by the Americans. Gen. Winchester had taken post at the rapids, when he received a pressing request from those inhabitants, for his protection. Accordingly, he despatched Col. Lewis with 300 men for their relief. On his arrival, he found the Indians already in possession of the place, but he attacked them in their works, and drove them from the place, and encamped on the same ground. Two days after, 20 December, Gen. Winchester arrived with the main army. Their force now consisted of 750 men. These operations went on without the knowledge of Gen. Harrison, the commander in chief, whose knowledge of the situation of the country, convinced him of their extreme danger. Frenchtown is situated only 20 miles from Malden, a strong British post, of a superiour force to the Americans,

APPENDIX. 349

and the intervening waters were covered with solid ice. It was also 70 miles from any American place, from whence they could expect supplies. Their situation did not escape the notice of the British. Col. Proctor, with 600 English and above 1000 Indians under the two Indian chiefs, Splitlog and Roundhead, appeared before their camp at day break, on the 22 January, 1813, and immediately began the attack. The Americans' works not being large enough to contain their small force, 150 were posted without. The numbers of the enemy enabled him to dispose of his force, as to cut off all means of retreat. The attack was first made on those without the fort, who were soon forced to give way. They fled across the river, and were pursued by the enemy, and cut to pieces. One hundred men, in two companies, left the works, and went over to their assistance, and shared the same horrid fate. General Winchester and Col. Lewis, in some manœuvre, were taken prisoners. The little army now in possession of the pickets, maintained the unequal fight until 11 of the clock, when Gen. Winchester capitulated for them. It was particularly stipulated that the wounded should be protected from the savages. The army still consisted of upwards of 500 men, and not until a flag had passed three times would they consent to surrender. But knowing their situation to be desperate, they consented under assurance from the British officer, that their lives and properties should be protected. We shall now see, with what faith the semi barbarian, Proctor, acted. No sooner had this brave band submitted, than they saw what was to follow. The tomahawk and scalping knife were indiscriminately employed among the dead and wounded; officer's side arms were wrested from them, and many stript and robbed. About 60 wounded Americans strewed the battle ground, who, by the kindness of the inhabitants were removed into houses. But horrid to tell, the next day a body of those savages were permitted to return, and after scalping and murdering to their content, set fire to the town, and all were buried beneath the conflagration, except a few that could travel, who were marched into the wilderness.

Defence of fort Meigs. General Harrison had established his head quarters at Franklintown, previous to the battle of the river Raisin, for the greater facility of transmitting orders, &c., to the different posts. After that affair took place, he concentrated his forces, consisting of 1200 men, at the Rapids, and there threw up a fort, which, in honour of the Governour of Ohio, was called fort Meigs. The enemy made their appearance about the 28 April, and soon after, began to construct batteries on the opposite side of the river. But in this business they proceeded slowly, from the annoyance of fort Meigs, and were obliged to perform their labours in the night. They at length succeeded in erecting two batteries of heavy cannon, and a mortar. These began furiously to play upon the American works, but were several times silenced. Proctor sent an insolent summons to Harrison, to surrender; he returned an answer according as it merited. The siege was continued, and the Indians from the tops of the trees fired into the fort and killed several men. General Harrison now received information, that two regiments from Ohio, which were expected, were near at hand. He despatched orders to their General for a party to attack the enemy's works at one point, while a party from the fort, should act simultaneously on another part. Eight hundred men under Col. Dudley of the Ohio men, and another body under Col. Miller, were immediately in motion. Col. Dudley led his men up in the face of the enemy's cannon, and every battery was carried, almost in an instant, and the British and Indians fled with great precipitation. These fugitives were met by a large body of Indians under Gen. Tecumseh. This famous warriour, expecting the Americans to pursue, formed an ambush, and waited their approach. Col. Dudley's men were so elated at their success, that they could not be restrained from pursuing the fugitives, although their Colonel used his utmost endeavours. They accordingly pressed on, and immediately found themselves surrounded by the savages. Here another horrid slaughter followed; but, different from that at Raisin, for Tecumseh interposed for the lives of those that surrendered, and not like Proctor, did he turn his back on those barbarities. He even laid a chief dead at his feet, for persisting in the massacre. About 650 men were killed and missing in this affair. The lamented Dudley was among the former. The party under Col. Miller, performed their part admirably, and after spiking the cannon, returned to camp with upwards of 40 prisoners. These operations made the enemy relinquish his design, and he immediately drew off. The distinguished names of Croghan, Todd, Johnson, Sedgwick, Ritzen, Stoddard, and Butler will live in the annals of their country. The last mentioned was a son of Gen. Butler, who fell in St. Clair's defeat.

Battle of the Moravian towns, and death of Tecumseh. After the great naval victory on the lake, achieved by the American fleet, under the gallant Perry, Proctor abandoned Malden, and took a position on the river Thames. His precipitate movements were displeasing to Tecumseh, who thought the situation of his brethren entirely disregarded, by their being left open to the Americans. In a speech to Proctor, he reprobates his conduct in very pointed terms. He says, "The war before this, [meaning the revolution] our British father gave the hatchet to his red children, when our old chiefs were alive. They are now dead. In that war our father [the king] was thrown on his back by the Americans, and he afterward took them by the hand without our knowledge, and we are afraid he will do so again at this time. Listen, you told us to bring our families to this place, and we did so. You promised to take care of them, and that they should want for nothing. Our ships have gone one way, and we are very much astonished to see our father [Proctor] tying up every thing, and preparing to run away the other. You always told us you never could draw your foot off British ground; but now, father, we see you are drawing back without seeing the enemy. We must compare our father's conduct to a fat animal, that carries his tail on his back, but when affrighted, drops it between its legs and runs off." This though a few detached paragraphs, will serve to give some acquaintance with the great chief. Proctor, after considerable manœuvring, was unable to escape with all his baggage, being hard pressed by Harrison in every move up the Thames. At length the two armies met in the vicinity of the Moravian towns, 5 October 1813, and a fierce battle was fought. Tecumseh's Indians were in possession of a thick wood, who, with the British regulars, had formed their line of battle, on advantageous ground. Gen. Harrison, with his aids, Com. Perry, Capt. Butler, and Gen. Cass, led the front line, while Col. Johnson, with the mounted men, was ordered to charge at full speed, and break their line. They were immediately in motion, and though the horses recoiled on receiving the fire of the British and Indians, yet, it was momentary, and their impetuosity bore down all before them. The enemy's line was broken in an instant and Johnson's mounted men were formed on their rear, and poured in a tremendous fire upon them. The British officers finding it in vain to rally again at this point, surrendered. A body of savages under Tecumseh, still disputed the ground, and Col. Johnson fell, in the thickest of the fight, almost covered with wounds. Tecumseh in person flew towards him, with his tomahawk raised, to give him the fatal blow. Johnson, though faint from loss of blood, had strength to draw his pistol, and laid Tecumseh dead at his feet.

When the mighty chief fell, the Indians all left the ground. At another point, a division attempted to make an impression upon the American infantry, but the venerable Gov. Shelby (one of the heroes of King's mountain) supported them with another regiment, and the enemy were immediately routed. The hottest of the fight was where Tecumseh and Johnson fell. Thirty Indians and six Americans lay within a few yards of the spot. Proctor fled with great precipitation, but his carriage was taken with all his papers, and even his sword. Eight pieces of artillery were taken, six of which were brass. Three of these were trophies of the revolution, which were surrendered by Hull. The Americans had not above 50 killed and wounded. Of the British 600 were taken prisoners, and 70 killed and wounded, and upwards of a hundred Indians were left on the field. Thus ended the Indian wars in the west. Their combination was now entirely broken up, and the frontier settlements, which for a long time had endured all the horrours of Indian barbarities, were, in some degree, liberated.

FINIS.

INDEX.

In the following Index, some explanations may be wanting, as it differs from works of this kind in general. All Indian names of places are given; but places having only an English name, are not given, unless they have been noted for some depredation, or having their situations described. And as every circumstance in a history may be found by an Index of proper names, it was thought needless to name them, as it only increases prolixity.

A

Acushnet 98.
Adams' Hist. Neweng. 30, 32, 49, 68.
Adams President John 151.
Adams Samuel xii.
Addington Isaac 157, 217, 251.
Agamenticus 24.
Agawom 89, 119, 144, 298.
Agincourt battle 265.
Akkompoin, Philip's uncle, killed 110.
Albemarl Duke of 207. [238.
Alden Cap. John 196, 197, 201, 228,
Alden John 297.
Alden William 226.
Alderman 47, kills Philip 126.
Alexander dies 18, 134, 148.
Allen's Biog. Dict. xii, xiv, 24, 28, 31, 38, 133, 145, 150, '2, '6, 207.
Allen Samuel 181.
Allen Thomas 181.
Allerton John 297.
Allerton Mr. Isaac 297.
Almy Cap. John 18, 40.
Andover 220.
Andros Cap. Elisha 194, 201, 204.
Androscoggin 184, 186.
Andros Sir Edmund 120, 150, 151, 152, 154, 164, 173, 250.
Annawon xiv, 106, 124, 127, 129, 131, 132, 133, 134, 136, 137, taken 138, put to death 146.
Annnawon's rock 136.
Aponaganset 50, 51, 98, 100.
Appleton Maj. Samuel 55, 57.
Aquetneck 19.
Arrowsike 163, 169, 327
Arruhawikwabemt 324.

Assawomset 27, 97.
Asuhmequin 133, 134, 135, 142.
Aubert carries off natives 287.
Augur Lieut., killed 314.
Awashonks 21 to 27, 57, 76 to 83, 85 to 92, 111.

B

Baker Thomas 190.
Baker Lieut., killed 275.
Barlow's Columbiad iv, 46, 128.
Barns —— 102.
Barrow Sam 115, 119
Baxter —— 49
Bean Cap., killed 347.
Beard ——, killed 313.
Beers Cap., killed 54.
Belcher Cap. Andrew 62, 253.
Belcher Mr., wounded 33.
Belknap's Amer. Biog. xv, 24, 32, 134, 287, '8, '9, 293, '4, 299, 300.
Belknap's Hist. N. H. xiii, 21, 152, 161, 164, 186, 187, 203, 259, 284, 289, 315, 331.
Bellomont Gov. 250.
Bennet Sergeant 57.
Benython Cap. 311.
Berry Lieut., killed 347.
Billington John 297.
Blin Cap. 327.
Bliss Mr. A. 136.
Boad —— 226.
Bomazeen 329, killed 330.
Bourne Cap. 328.
Bowen Peter 337, 338.
Bozman's Hist. 177.
Bracket Cap. 166, 191, 224, 236, '7.
Bradford Maj. 30, 55, 84, 85, 96.

INDEX.

Bradford Mr. Wm. 290, 294, 296, 297, 300, 301, 302.
Bradstreet Gov. 152, 157.
Braton Stephen 197.
Brewster Mr. William 297.
Bridgewater 25.
Bridgway Jarman 228, 229, 230.
Britterige Richard 296, 297.
Broclebank Cap., killed 70.
Brookfield 53.
Brown Cap. John 252, 281.
Brown Mr. James 27, 29, 31.
Brown Peter 297.
Bulkley Gershom 62.
Bull's garrison 57.
Bump John 144.
Butler Cap. 351, 352.

C.

Calef's Hist. witchcraft 196, 220.
Canonchet 73, taken 107, killed 108.
Canonicus, killed 104.
Canton Corporal, taken 234.
Carver Gov. John 133, 296, 297, 298, dies 301, 302.
Carver's Travels 21.
Castine Baron De St. 152, 164, 165, 176, 219, 226, 233, 261.
Caughnewaga, 318.
Cawley Robert 226, 228.
Chamberlain John 334.
Champlain Cap. 220.
Chelmsford 64.
Chesly —— 312.
Chignecto 228, 282.
Chilton James 297.
Chubb Cap. 219, killed 220.
Chubb Sergeant, killed 326.
Church Benjamin xii.
Church Deac. Benj. xii.
Church Charles xii.
Church Caleb xi, 197.   [274, 281.
Church Cap. Constant xi, 251, 257,
Church Edward xii, 252, 281.
Church Joseph xi.
Church Thomas xi.
Clark Cap. Wm. 253.
Clark Gov. 153.
Clark Lieut. 169.
Clark Richard 297.
Clark's garrison 72, 96.
Clark's island 299.
Clinton Hon. De Witt 68.
Cocheco 161, 314.
Coddington Gov. Wm. 38.
Cole Col. B. 339, 340.
Cole Cap. James 252, 264, 281.

Colman Dr. Benjamin iv.
Conestogoe massacre 342 to 345.
Conscience, taken 149.
Contoocook 317, 337.   ['7 '8
Converse Cap. James 189, 192, 194,
Cook Cap. John 252, '7, 274, 281.
Cook Elisha 160.
Cook Francis 297.
Cook John 101.
Cousins Isaac, killed 314.
Crackston John 296, 297.
Cranfield Gov. 186.
Cranston Gov. John 38, 39, 52.
Croghan Geo. 351.
Cross ——, killed 314.
Cudworth Maj. 30, 35, 36, 37.
Curwin Jonathan 221.
Cushnet 98.

D.

D'Aillebout 318.
Danforth Gov. 156, 160, 166,
Dartmouth 50, 51.
D'Aubri Nicholas 187.
Davenport Cap., killed 58.
Davies Col., killed 347.
Davis Cap. Silvanus 160, 163.
D'Caliers 320.
Deborahuel 225.
Deerfield 54, 243, 321.
Demot, 187.
Dennison Cap. 56, 64, 73, 107
Dermer Cap. Thomas 301.
D'Frontenac Count 224, 230.
Dillano —— 101 to 105.
D'Mantel 318.
D'Monts 220,
Doney 184, 185, 190.
Dorey Edward 296, 297.
Douglass' Hist. 42, 51, 52, 74, 98, 142, 145, 245, 256, 259, 271, 277, 284, 286.
Drake Sir Francis 287.
Dubois 282, 284.
Dudley Col., killed 351.   [256, 285,
Dudley Gov. Joseph 250, 251, 253,
Dudley Thomas 152, 249.
Dustan Mrs. Hannah 315 to 317.
Dwight Dr. 146, 308.
Dyer Cap. John 252, 281.
D'Young 261.

E.

Earl Ralph 51, 52.
Eaton Francis 297.
Edee Sergeant 269.
Edmunds Cap. 52, 176.

INDEX. 357

Eels, Cap. 51, 52.
Fliot, Rev. John, 21.
Eliot Cap. John 326, 327.
Eliot's Biog. Dictionary 28, 62, 145, 150, 152, 179, 181, 207, 216.
Eliot Robert 206.
Endecott Cap. 305, 306.   [21.
English, probable numbers of in 1675,
English Thomas 297.

F.

Farmer and More's Collections xii, 103, 257, 296, 331, 335, 336, 338.
Fallriver xv, 48.
Fernald William 206.
Fivenations 68.
Fletcher Moses 296, 297.
Fogland ferry 42.
Forbes William 101, 209, 215.
Forefathers' day 300.
Forefathers' rock 300.
Frontenac Gov. 224, 230.
Frost Cap. 313.
Frost Major 203, 206.
Frye Cap. James 334.
Fryer Cap. Nathaniel 203, 206.
Frye Rev. Mr. 330, wounded 334.
Fuller Cap. 36 to 39.
Fullam Sergeant, killed 334.
Fuller Edward 297.
Fuller Mr. Samuel 297.

G.

Gage Gen. 290.
Gallop Cap. killed 58.
Gallop Cap. John 304, 305.
Gardiner Cap. killed 58.
Gardiner Richard 296.
George 21, 79.   [221.
Gidney Col. Bartholomew 196, 220,
Giles Lieut. 271.
Gill Mr. 32, 33.
Goff General 54, 55.
Golding Cap. 45, 46, 120, to 123.
Gold island 43.
Goodman 297.
Gorham Cap. John 221, 247, 252, 255, 262, 270, 273, 279, 281.
Gorton Rev. Samuel 28, 104.
Gosnold Bartholomew 287.
Gourdan Mons. 260, 263, taken 265, 267, 268, 270, 283.
Green island 257.
Grenville Sir Richard 287.
Grimstone 291.

H.

Hadley 108.
Halifax fort 214.

Hall Cap. Nathaniel 156, 158, 170,
Hammond William, killed 33. [171.
Hancamagus 186.
Hanno xv.
Harman Cap. 326, 328, 329, 330
Harradon Cap. John 256, 281.
Harrison Gen. 346, 347, 350.
Harris' Hist. Dorchester 178.
Hatch Cap. 206.
Hatfield 55.
Havens Jack 86, 90.
Hawkins 186, 187, 188, 194.
Hawthorne John 161, 196, 221, 238, 239, 241, 242.
Hazelton Charles 22.
Henchman, Cap. 47, 52, 53.
Hill Cap. 284.
Hilton Maj. Winthrop, killed 257, 263, 270, 273, 274, 279, 281, 284.
Hinkley Gov. Thomas 20, 153, 155, 160, 180, 182.
Holmes' Amer. Annals xii, 21, 34, 49, 54, 55, 69, 70, 96, 108, 135, 150, 152, 153, 177, 207, 270, 276, 287, 289, 290, 294, 298.
Honeywel Lieut. 203, 236.
Hook Francis 206.
Hopkins Gen. 347.
Hopkins Mr. Stephen 94, 297.
Howland Isaac 89, 90, 91, 114.
Howland Jabez 88, 89, 114, 118, 127 131, 143.
Howland John 89, 114, 297.
Hoyt's Researches 55, 68, 354.
Hubbard's Narrative xiv, 20, 21, 22, 27, 28, 30, 32, 34, 35, 36, 37, 39, 43, 47, 49, 52, 54, 55, 56, 57, 63, 69, 73, 91, 106, 109, 110, 112, 114, 117, 118, 124, 126, 134, 139, 142, 144, 146, 148, 149, 166, 196, 201, 209, 228, 303, 309, 311, 314, 330.
Hubbard Rev. Wm. xiv.
Huckings Mrs. 187, 188.
Hudibras 24.
Hunt Cap. 288, 289, 301.
Hunter Cap. 49.
Hutchinson Maj. 201.
Hutchinson Cap. 36, 53.
Hutchinson's History iii, xiii, xiv, 20, 28, 29, 30, 31, 32, 34, 36, 37, 49, 50, 63, 68, 74, 96, 103, 120, 133 134, 135, 145, 146, 154, 163, 177 178, 220, 221, 228, 230, 238, 241, 256, 265, 277 278, 284, 285, 290, 296, 323.
Hyrcania xv, 354.

358 INDEX.

I.

Iberville 219, 220.
Ingersol Lieut. 314.
Indian bridge 336, 337.
Indians, number of in 1675, 20.
Irish Mrs. xv.
Iroquois 224.

J.

Jaques Lieut. 329.
Jarvis Cap. 271.
Jefferies 150.
Johnson Cap killed 58.
Jones Cap. 295.

K.

Keekamuit 34.
Kennebeck 171.
Keyes Solomon, wounded 333.
Kickapoos 346.
Kimball Thomas, killed 315.
King Cap. 206.
King, no such dignity among Indians
Kirk Sir David 150.

L.

Lafaure 161, 258, 264.
Lake —— 41.
Lake Cap., killed 163.
Lamb Cap. Joshua 252, 281.
Lancaster 64, 259.
Larking Cap. 236.
Lateril Mr. 236.
Lathrop Cap. Joseph 200.
Lathrop Cap., killed 54.
Lathrop John 181.
Lee Abraham, killed 163.
Lee Mrs. 163, 164.
Lee Rev. Samuel xii, 199.
Leister Edward 297.
Leverett Gov. John 52, dies 145,
Lightfoot Cap. 100, 104, '5, 111, 167.
Littleeyes 25, taken 99, 104.
Littlefield Cap. John 200, 203.
Lovewell Cap. John 330 to 336.

M.

Magnus Queen 103, 108.
Makin Thomas xvi, 148, 346.
Manhattans 303.
Mansell Sir Robert 220.
Malagash 327.
Maquas 224.
Maquoit 189, 206.
March Cap. 206, 286.
Margeson Edmund 296, 297.
Marlborough 64, 65
Marshall Cap., killed 58.
Martin Mr. Christopher 297.

Martyn Richard 206.
Mason Cap. John 306, 307, 308.
Mason Samuel 160. [301, 340.
Massassoit xiii, 18, 94, 110, 133, 134,
Mather's Magnalia xii, xiv, 20, 22,
  26, 47, 50, 65, 126, 145, 169, 170,
  171, 176, 177, 179, 184, 187, 189,
  191, 192, 202, 206, 207, 210, 213,
  220, 240, 241, 315, 317, 339, 341.
Mattapoiset 32, 105.
Mattatoag 104.
Maxfield Mr. —— 179.
Mayflower, a ship 294.
Mayr point 191.
Medfield 64.
Menis 231, taken 274.
Menival Gov. 278.
Merrymeeting bay 325.
Metacomet xiii.
Middleborough 51, 65, 93.
Miles Rev. John 31, 32.
Minot's Hist. 214.
Mogg, killed 330.
Mohawks 54, 68, 142, 224.
Mohegans 17.
Mouhogan 222.
Monogenest 233.
Mooanam 134.
Monopoide 107.
Montinicus 161, 255.
Montreal 224, 320.
Morse and Parish's Hist. Newengland 124, 339, 340.
Morse's Annals 31, 124, 126, 138.
Morton's Memorial xiii, 23, 27, 28,
  30, 89, 133, 134, 154, 249, 251,
  289, 295, 296, 298, 299, 301.
Morton Thomas 23, 24.
Mosely Cap. Samuel 56, 57.
Mossipee 184, 283.
Moulton Cap. 326, 328, 329, 330.
Mounthope 22.
Mullins Mr. William 297.
Munponset 94, 95.
Myrick Cap. Isaac 252, 264, 281.

N.

Namskeket 299. [108.
Nanunttenoo, taken 107, put to death
Narragansets xiii, 17, 18, number of
  in 1675, 20, 36, 54.
Naskeag 236, 252.
Nathaniel 129, 130, 131.
Nauset 299.
Neff Miss Mary 315, 316, 317
Nemasket 96.
Netops 67, 91.
Newengland gift 284.

INDEX. 359

Newichwannock 313.
Nicholson Col. 185, 278, 317.
Nihantick 307.
Ninigret 104, 108.
Nipmucks 53, 65, 69.
Nipnet 91.
Nomquid 85.
Norridgwock 237, 329.
Northfield 54.
Norton Cap., killed 303, 304.
Nunnaquahquat 39.
Nunnuit Peter 27, 57.

O.

Oldham Mr. John, killed 303, 304,'5.
Omens 20, 126.
Osamekin 340.
Otis James xii.
Owens Col., killed 347.

P.

Paine Lieut. John 228.
Passammaquoddy 236.
Patuxet 52.
Paugus, killed 334.
Pawcatuck river 307.
Peasfield battle 37 to 46.
Pejepscot 179, 184, 190, 206.
Pemmaquid 209, 210, 219.
Penn Gov. John 343.
Penn Gov. William 342.
Penhallow's Hist. vii, 184, 185, 203, 256, 257, 258, 259, 260, 261, 275, 277, 284, 324, 325, 330, 332, 333.
Pennacook 161, 186.
Peperel Mr. 254.
Pequots 17, war with 302.
Perpodack 192.
Peter 57, 77, 84, 88, 124.
Philip King xiii, origin of his name 18, killed 123.
Philips Gov. 326.
Phillips' garrison 311.
Phips Sir Wm. 152, 154, 163, 175, 177, 207, 208, 212, 214, 216, 234, 278, 339.
Pierce Cap. 64, killed 72.
Pigwocket 161, 331.
Pike Maj. Robert 182, 183, 184, 203.
Pitkin Wm. 160.
Plaisted Lieut. 203.
Plaisted Roger 196, killed 313.
Plumer Col. Daniel 257.
Plumer Gov. Wm. 203.
Plymouth 17, 65.
Pocasset 19, 27.
Pokanoket xiii, 18, 22, 29.
Popham Sir John 171.

Poppasquash 127, 129.
Potock 63.
Prentice Cap. Thomas 32, 56, 60.
Prince Gov. 18, 339.
Prince's Chronology vii, xiii, 24, 94, 135, 289, 294, 296.
Pring Martin 288.
Proud's Hist. xvi, 148, 342, 345.
Providence 64.
Pumham, killed 56, 63, 104.
Punkatees battle 37 to 46.
Purchase Mr. —— 300.

Q.

Quabaog 53, 118.
Quadequinah 110.
Quaucut 39.
Quebeck 177, 234.
Qunnapin 103, 104, 111.

R.

Ralegh Sir Walter 287, 293.
Ralle Sebastian 325, 329, killed 330
Ramsdel Joseph 194.
Rehoboth 36, 64.
Ridgdale John 296, 297.
Robertson's Hist. Amer. xv. 306
Robins Lieut., killed 334.
Robinson Mr. ——, killed 312.
Robinson John 326, 327.
Robinson Rev. John 290.
Rogers Cap. Geo. 256, 257, 281
Rogers Thos. 297.
Rouville 321, 322.
Rowlandson Mrs. 103.
Russel's garrison 51.

S.

Sabatis 337, killed 338.
Sabin 87.
Sachueeset 85.
Sagadahock 171, 201.
Samoset 301.
Sandford Maj. 102, 120, 121.
Sassacus, killed 308.
Sassamon 19, 21, 27.
Savage Ensign 34.
Savage Maj. 35, 36.
Scattacook 68, 320.
Schenactada 318.
Schuyler Maj. 319, 321.
Scituate 65.
Sconticut 104.
Scottaway Cap. 172, 173, 175.
Shanelere, killed 235.
Sharkee Mons. 260, '7, '9, 282.
Sharp Lieut., killed 70.
Shawomet 56.

INDEX

Sherburn Cap. 205.
Siely Cap., killed 58.
Siene, a ship 271.
Signecto 228, 282.
Sippican 89, 106, 143.
Sixnations 68, 320.
Skakit 299.
Smallpox 178, 195.
Smith Cap. John 222, 288, 301.
Smith Cap. Thos. 256, '7, 281.
Smith Maj. 56, 62. [224, 319.
Smith's Hist. Newyork xiii, 68, 180,
Smithson Cap. 228.
Snow's Hist. Boston 145, 178.
Sogkonate ix, 19.
Sogkonesset 74.
Soule George 297. [281, 327.
Southack Cap. Cyprian 238, 255.
Southworth Nath. 89, 170, 192, 193.
Speedwell, a ship 294.
Squakeag 54.
Squando 309.
Squannaconk 124, 132, 136.
Squanto 301.
Standish Cap. 134, 297.
Stone Cap. 303, 304.
Stoughton Gov. Wm. 216.
Subercase Gov. 276.
Sudbury 65, 69, 70.
Sullivan's Hist. Maine 160, 163, 164,
 '6, '9, 171, '6, '9, 180, '7, '9, 190,
 '1, '2, 214, 222, '3, '6, 236,'7, 311.

T.

Taconnet 214, 328.
Talcot Maj. 108, 117, '8.
Tecumseh 346, 350, '1, killed 352.
Tilley Edward 296, 297.
Tilley John 296, 297.
Tinker Thomas 297.
Tippecanoe battle 347. [death 146.
Tispaquin 96, 115, 142, '4, put to
Tockamona 111.
Totoson 115, '16, '18, '19.
Treat Maj. Robert 54, 64.
Trumbull's Hist. U. S. xiii, 20, 29,
 50, 68, 141, 319, 320, 330.
Trumbull's Hist. Con. 29, 37, 38, 50,
 '6, 62, 63, 73, 103, '8, 126, 200,
Tuisset 339. [303,'7.
Turner Cap. 68, '9, 305.
Turner John 297.
Tyasks 106, 124.

U.

Umpame 23.
Uncas, killed 306.
Underhill Cap. 305, 307.

V.

Vaughan Maj. 203, 206.
Vaudreuil Gov. 259, 285, 321, 323.
Villeau Cap. 239.
Villebon 192, 231, '4, '5, 241.
Virginia, ancient limits of 293, 294.

W.

Wachuset 69, 80.
Wadsworth Cap., killed 70.
Waldron Maj. 161, killed 162.
Wallaston Cap. 24.
Walley John 160, 177, 207, 215.
Walton Cap. 184, '5, 203, '6, '24.
Wamesit 64.
Wampanoags xiii, 48.
Wampom, value of 141, '2.
Wamsutta 134.
Warren Mr. Richard 297.
Warwick 56, 63, 64.
Weetamore 27, 32, 47,'8, 50, '7, 103.
Wepoiset 87.
Wequash 307.
Wessagusset 24.
Weymouth 64.
Wheelwright Esq. John 200, '3.
White Mr. Wm. 297.
Wilcox Daniel 17.
Willard Cap. Simon 156, 158.
Willard Maj. 54.
Williams Cap. 122.
Williams' Hist. Vermont 321, '3.
Williamson Cap. Caleb 252, 281.
Williamson's Hist. N. Car. 68.
Williams Rev. John 284, 321, '3.
Williams Rev. Roger 28, 68.
Williams Thomas 297.
Wincol John 206, 314.
Winepang 326.
Winnipissaukee 325.
Winslow Gilbert 297.
Winslow Hon. Josiah 26, 30, 52,
 55, 56, 64, 93, 147.
Winslow Josiah 328.
Winslow Mr. Edward 26, 94, 133,
 134, 147, 297, 302, 340.
Winthrop Gov. John 52.
Winthrop's Hist. Neweng. 24, 91,
 96, 104, 145, 203, 303, 341.
Wisememet, killed 330.
Witchcraft 156, 196, 216, 238, 241,
Woosamequin 133, 134.
Worumbos 186, 187, '9 '94
Wyman Seth 332, '4.

Y.

York Joseph 223, 226.

www.ingramcontent.com/pod-product-compliance
Lightning Source LLC
Chambersburg PA
CBHW071151300426
44113CB00009B/1160